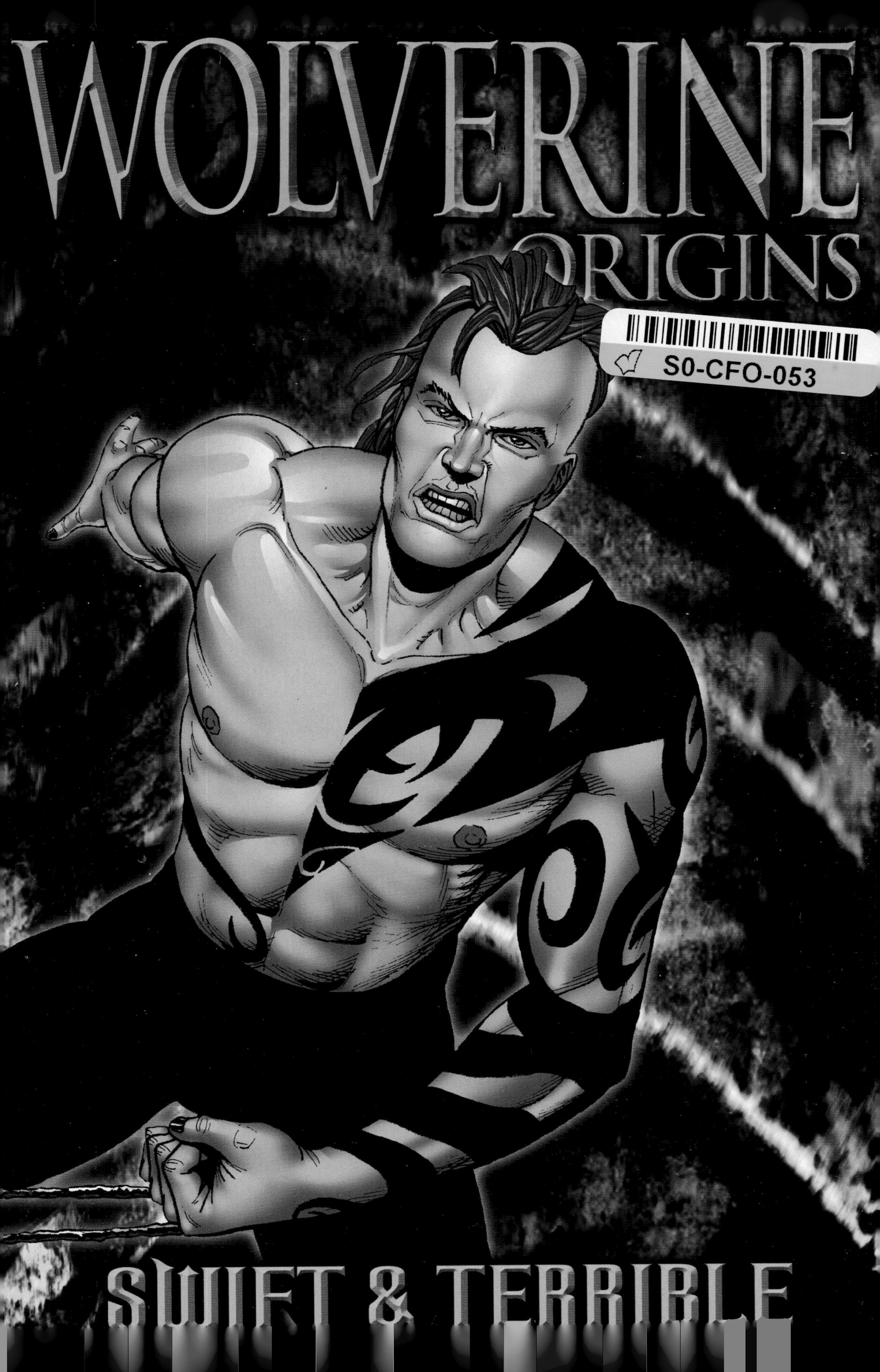
WOLVERINE
ORIGINS
SWIFT & TERRIBLE

WOLVERINE ORIGINS

SWIFT & TERRIBLE

Writer: **Daniel Way**
Artist: **Steve Dillon**
Colors: **Matt Milla with Avalon Studios**
Letters: **Virtual Calligraphy's Cory Petit with Randy Gentile**
Cover Art: **Joe Quesada, Danny Miki & Richard Isanove (Issues #11-13)**
and Marko Djurdjevic (Issues #14-15)
Assistant Editors: **Michael O'Connor & Aubrey Sitterson**
Editor: **Axel Alonso**

Collection Editor: **Jennifer Grünwald**
Assistant Editors: **Cory Levine & Michael Short**
Associate Editor: **Mark D. Beazley**
Senior Editor, Special Projects: **Jeff Youngquist**
Senior Vice President of Sales: **David Gabriel**
Production: **Jerron Quality Color & Jerry Kalinowski**
Vice President of Creative: **Tom Marvelli**

Editor in Chief: **Joe Quesada**
Publisher: **Dan Buckley**

WOLVERINE: ORIGINS VOL. 3 — SWIFT AND TERRIBLE. Contains material originally published in magazine form as WOLVERINE: ORIGINS #11-15. First printing 2007. Hardcover ISBN# 0-7851-2637-6. Softcover ISBN# 978-0-7851-2613-3. Published by MARVEL PUBLISHING, INC., a subsidiary of MARVEL ENTERTAINMENT, INC. OFFICE OF PUBLICATION: 417 5th Avenue, New York, NY 10016. Copyright © 2007 Marvel Characters, Inc. All rights reserved. Hardcover: $19.99 per copy in the U.S. and $32.00 in Canada (GST #R127032852). Softcover: $13.99 per copy in the U.S. and $22.50 in Canada (GST #R127032852). Canadian Agreement #40668537. All characters featured in this issue and the distinctive names and likenesses thereof, and all related indicia are trademarks of Marvel Characters, Inc. No similarity between any of the names, characters, persons, and/or institutions in this magazine with those of any living or dead person or institution is intended, and any such similarity which may exist is purely coincidental. **Printed in the U.S.A.** ALAN FINE, CEO Marvel Toys & Publishing Divisions and CMO Marvel Entertainment, Inc.; DAVID GABRIEL, Senior VP of Publishing Sales & Circulation; DAVID BOGART, VP of Business Affairs & Editorial Operations; MICHAEL PASCIULLO, VP Merchandising & Communications; JIM BOYLE, VP of Publishing Operations; DAN CARR, Executive Director of Publishing Technology; JUSTIN F. GABRIE, Managing Editor; SUSAN CRESPI, Production Manager; STAN LEE, Chairman Emeritus. For information regarding advertising in Marvel Comics or on Marvel.com, please

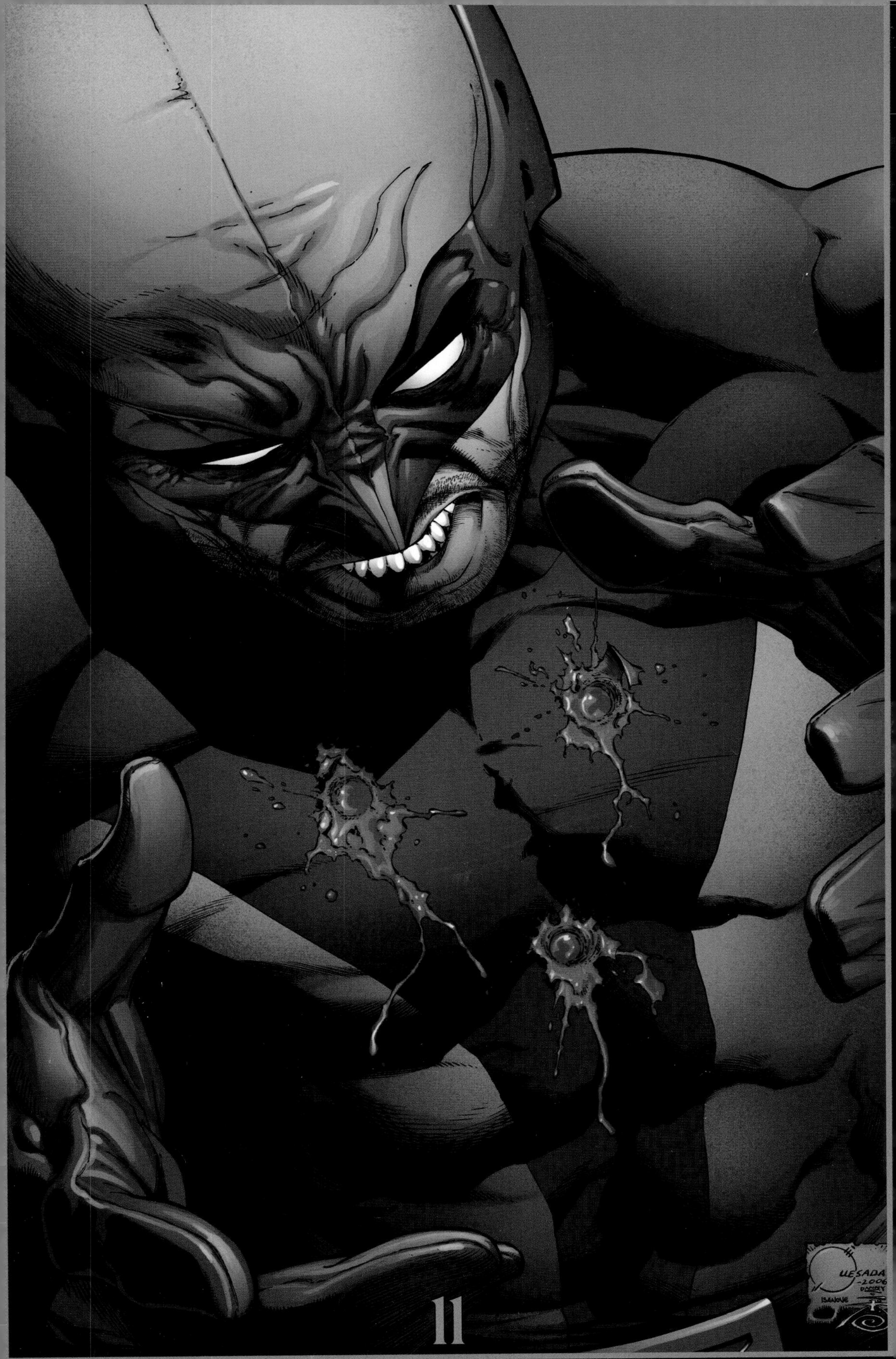
11

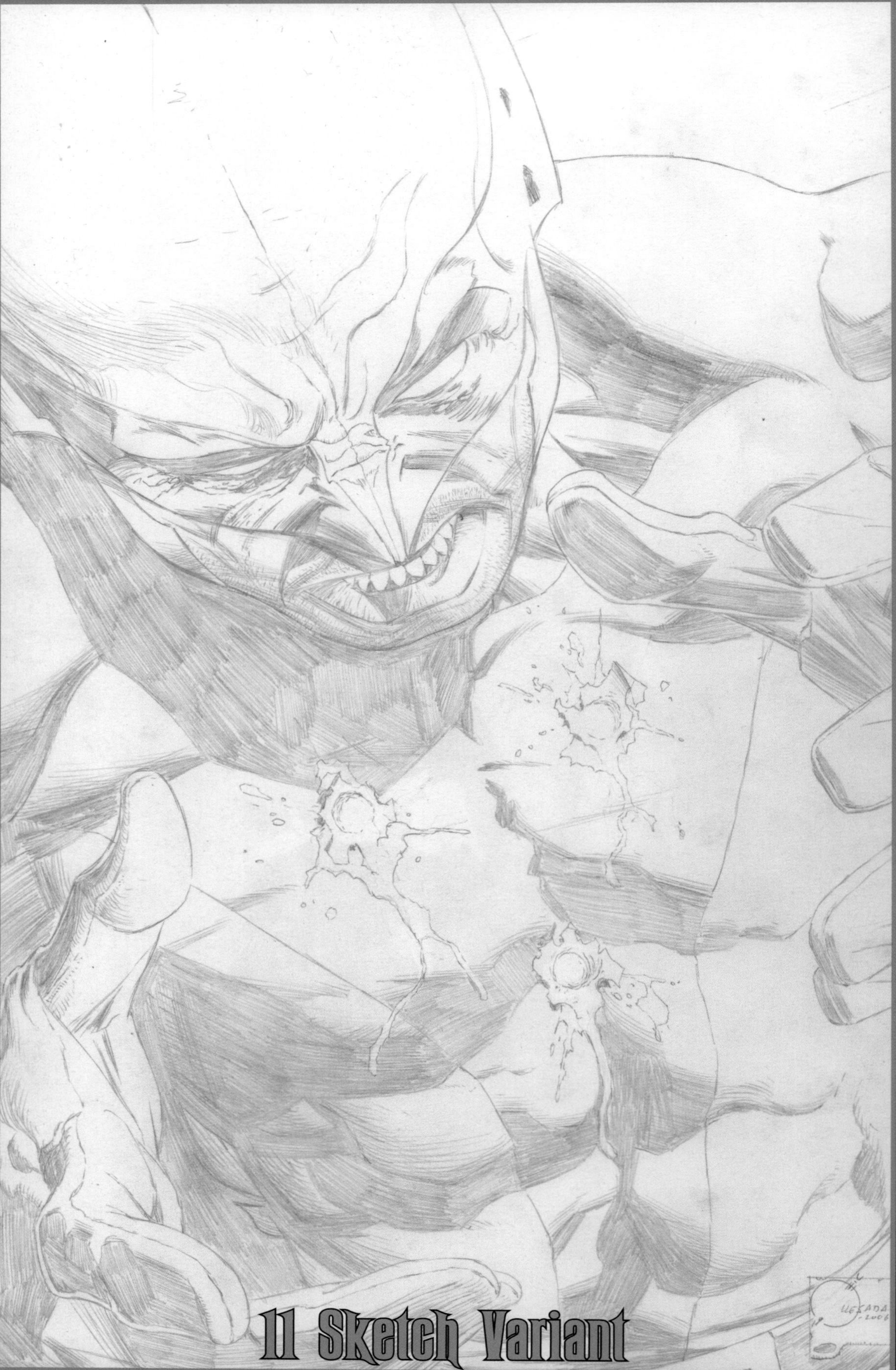

11 Sketch Variant

WOLVERINE ORIGINS

PREVIOUSLY:

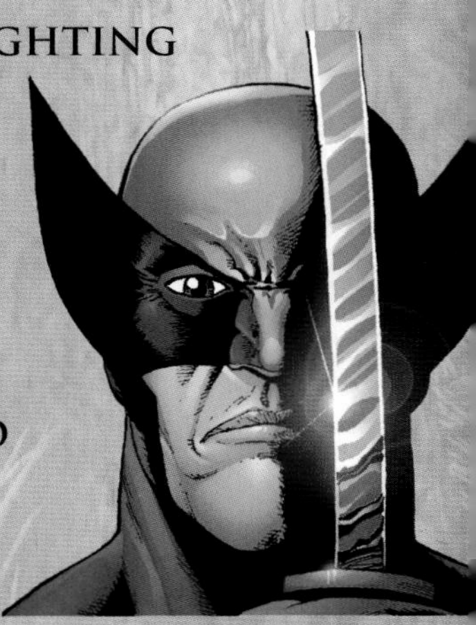

THE MUTANT WOLVERINE HAS SPENT A CENTURY FIGHTING THOSE WHO WOULD MANIPULATE HIM FOR HIS UNIQUE POWERS—SAVAGE CLAWS, HEIGHTENED SENSES, AND A HEALING FACTOR CAPABLE OF MIRACLES. AFTER REPEATED BRAINWASHING, TORTURE, AND REPROGRAMMING, WOLVERINE'S PAST WAS AS MUCH A MYSTERY TO HIM AS ANYONE.

WHEN THOSE LONG LOST MEMORIES FINALLY RETURNED TO HIM, WOLVERINE SET OUT ON A MISSION TO PUNISH THE CONSPIRATORS WHO HAD WRONGED HIM.

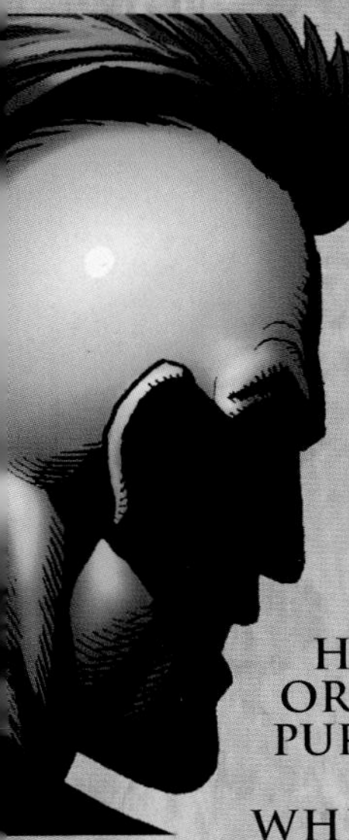

BUT IN THE MIDST OF THAT MISSION, HE DISCOVERED THAT HE HAS A SON UNDER THE CONTROL OF THE SAME SHADOWY FORCES HE WAS TRACKING.

TO AID HIM IN THE INEVITABLE CONFRONTATION, WOLVERINE SOUGHT THE ONE WEAPON THAT COULD NEGATE HIS SON'S HEALING FACTOR WITHOUT KILLING HIM—THE CARBONADIUM SYNTHESIZER. THANKS TO HIS ALLY, THE BLACK WIDOW, THE DEVICE WAS SECURED IN A SAFE-DEPOSIT BOX IN BRUSSELS.

HOWEVER, THERE WAS A PRICE TO BE PAID. WOLVERINE'S FRIEND, JUBILEE, WAS DRAWN INTO THE CONFLICT AND INJURED. TO SAVE HER LIFE, WOLVERINE SURRENDERED HIMSELF TO S.H.I.E.L.D., THE COUNTER-TERRORISM ORGANIZATION THAT HAD BEEN PURSUING HIM.

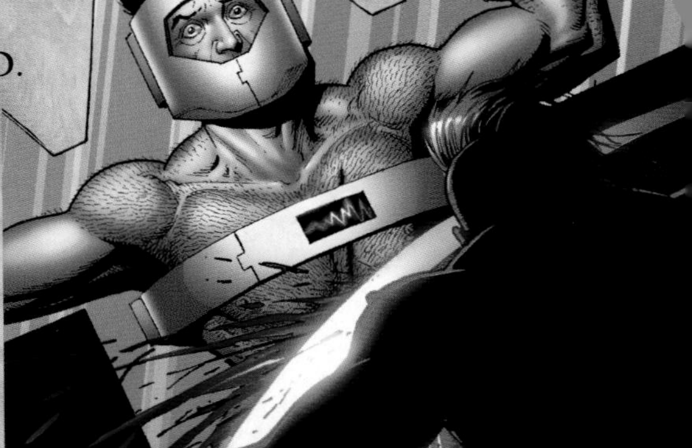

WHEN HE REGAINED CONSCIOUSNESS IN A S.H.I.E.L.D. FACILITY IN BERLIN, A SHADOWY FIGURE APPROACHED, INTRODUCED HIMSELF AS WOLVERINE'S LONG LOST SON...

...AND THEN DISEMBOWELED HIS FATHER.

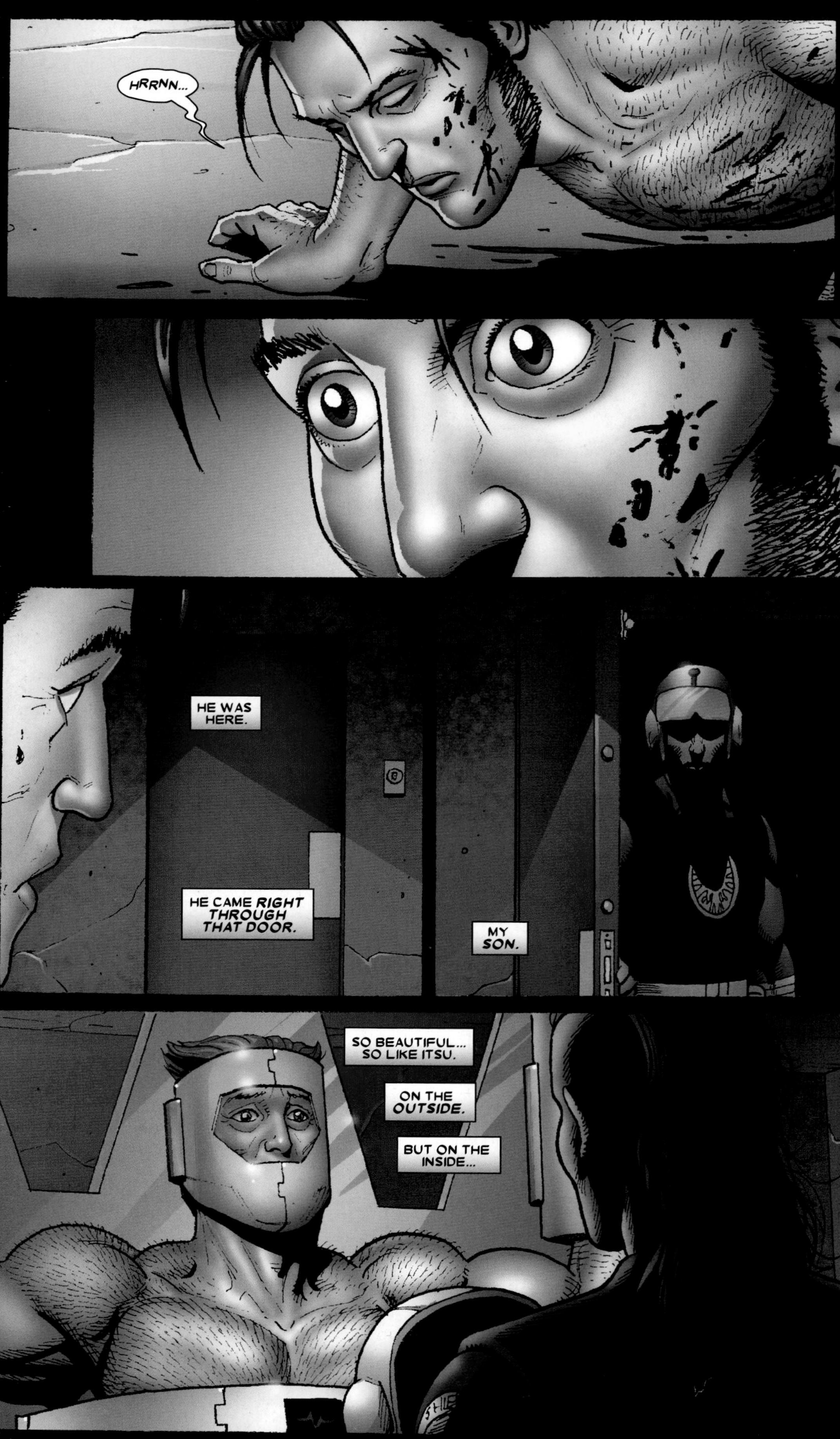
HRRNN...
HE WAS HERE.
HE CAME RIGHT THROUGH THAT DOOR.
MY SON.
SO BEAUTIFUL... SO LIKE ITSU.
ON THE OUTSIDE.
BUT ON THE INSIDE...

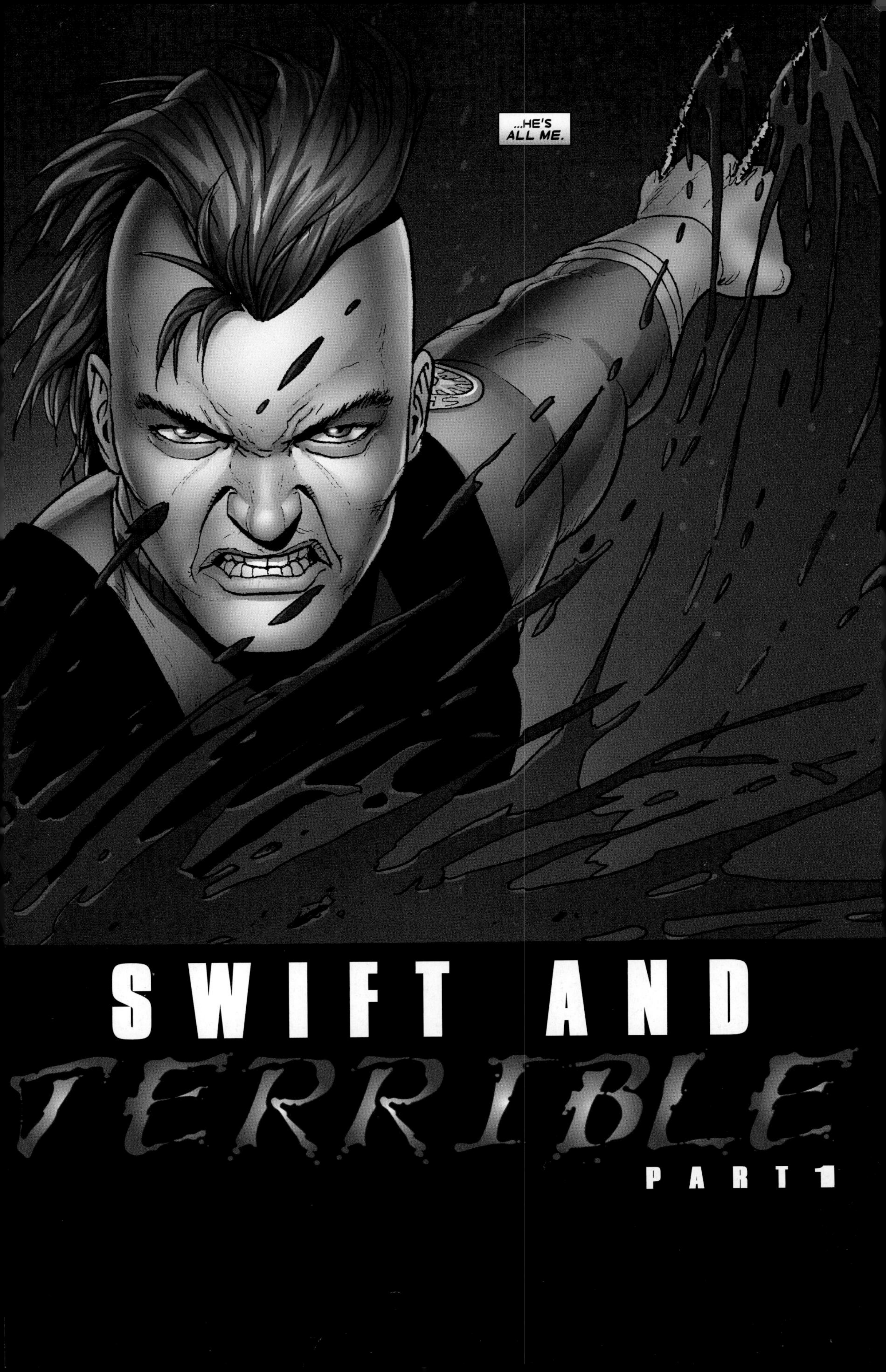
...HE'S ALL ME.
SWIFT AND
TERRIBLE
PART 1

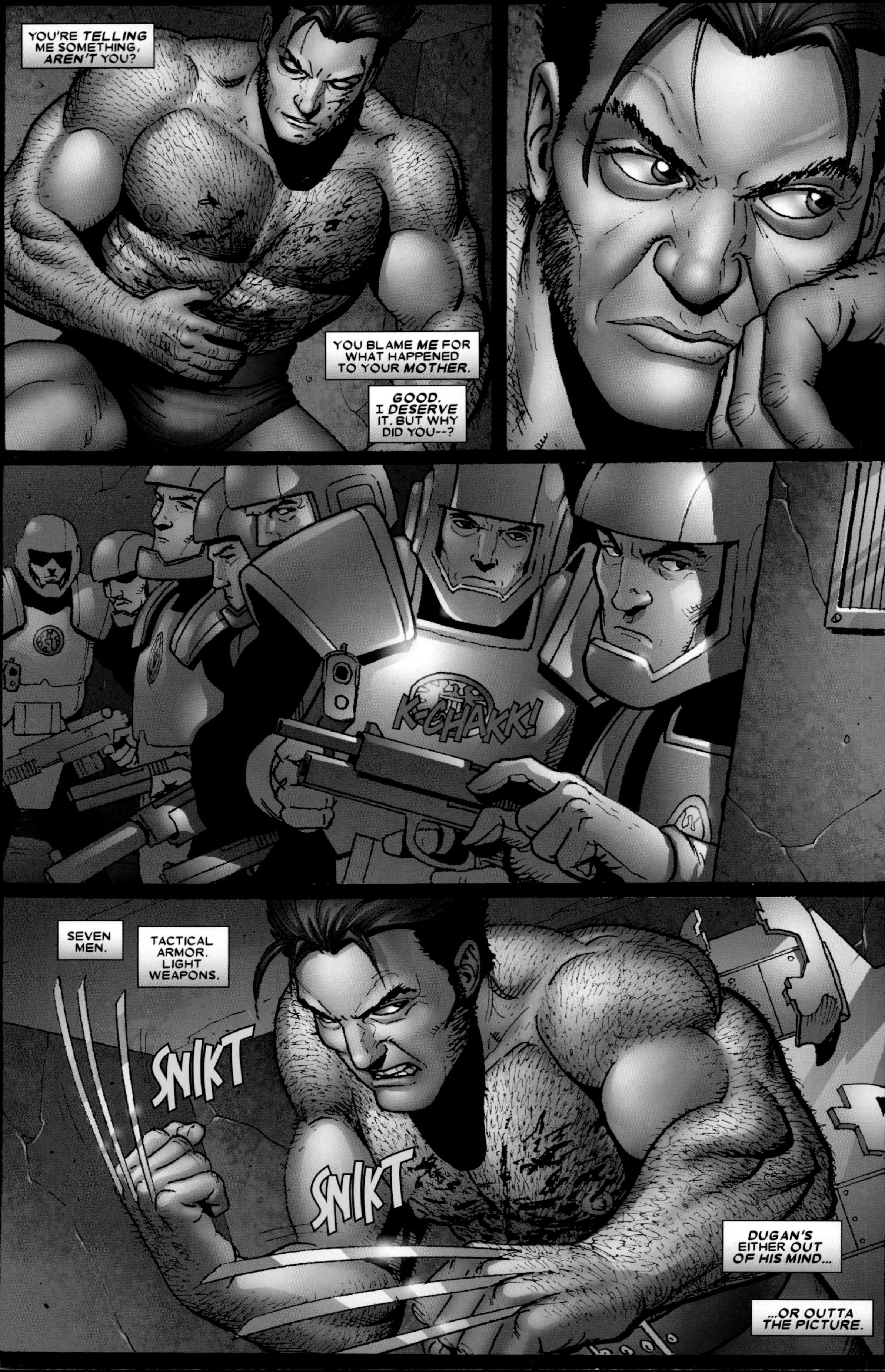
YOU'RE TELLING ME SOMETHING, AREN'T YOU?
YOU BLAME ME FOR WHAT HAPPENED TO YOUR MOTHER.
GOOD. I DESERVE IT. BUT WHY DID YOU--?
K-CHAKK!
SEVEN MEN.
TACTICAL ARMOR. LIGHT WEAPONS.
SNIKT
SNIKT
DUGAN'S EITHER OUT OF HIS MIND...
...OR OUTTA THE PICTURE.

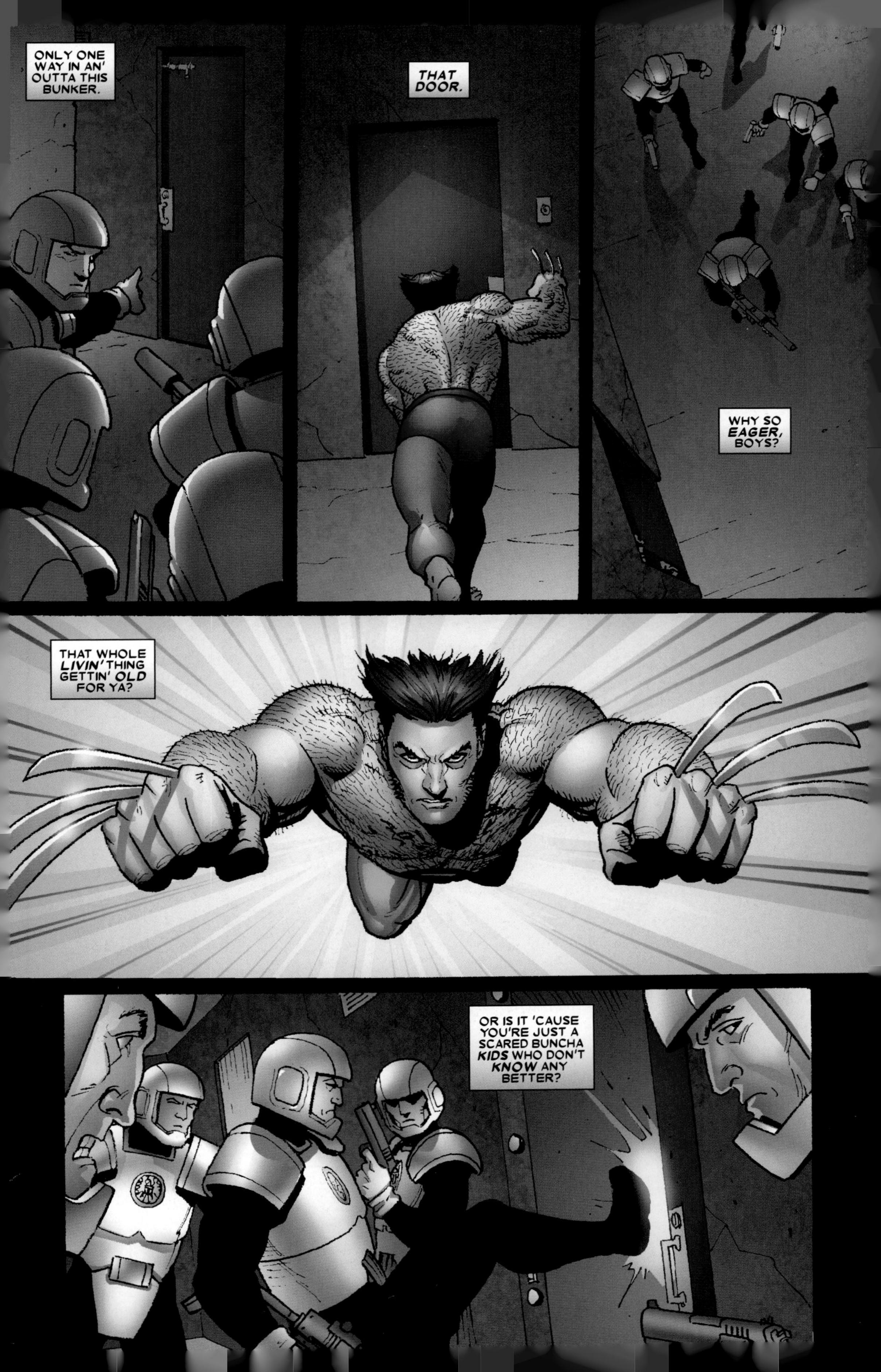
ONLY ONE WAY IN AN' OUTTA THIS BUNKER.
THAT DOOR.
WHY SO EAGER, BOYS?
THAT WHOLE LIVIN' THING GETTIN' OLD FOR YA?
OR IS IT 'CAUSE YOU'RE JUST A SCARED BUNCHA KIDS WHO DON'T KNOW ANY BETTER?

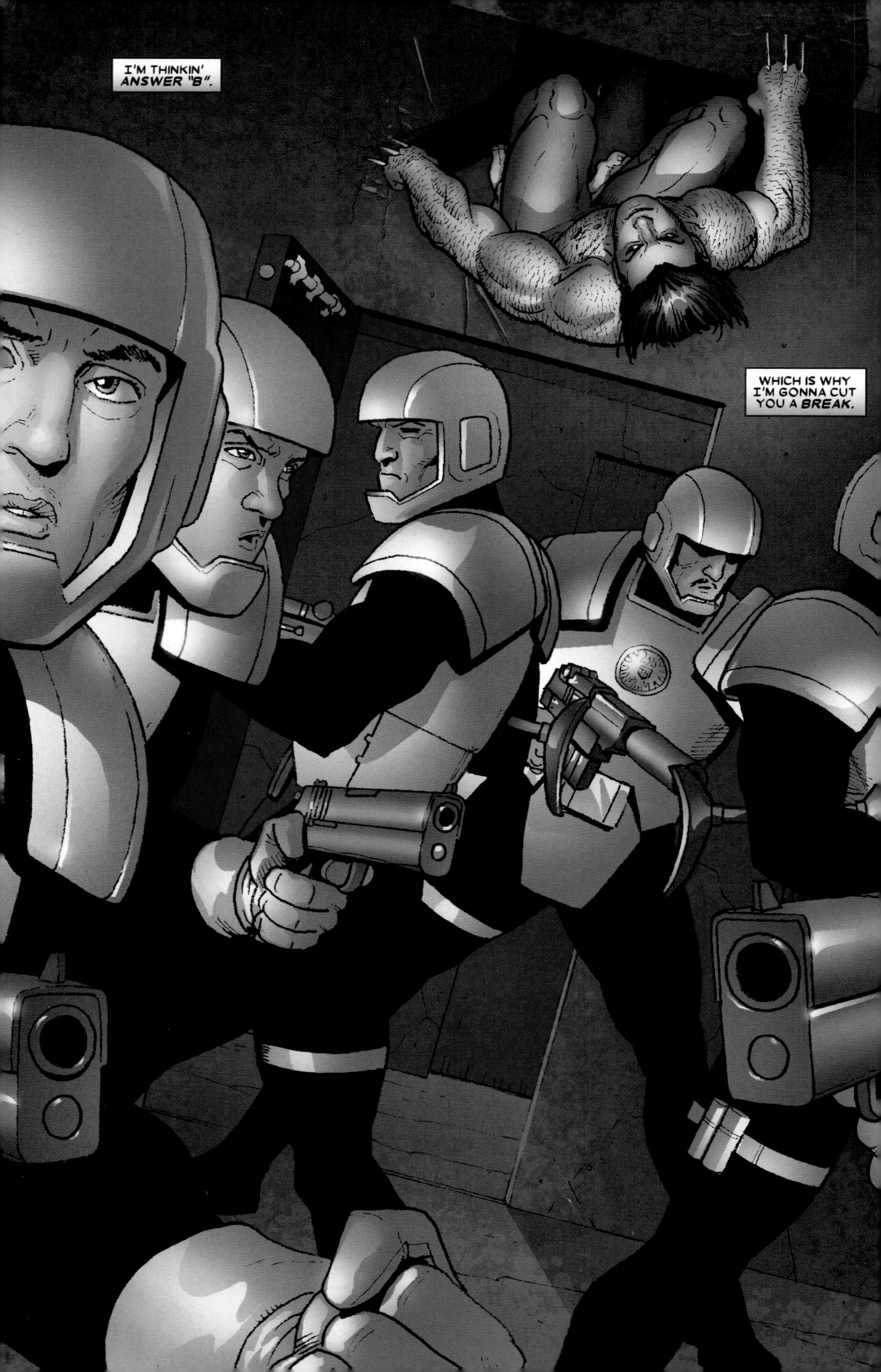
I'M THINKIN' ANSWER "B".
WHICH IS WHY I'M GONNA CUT YOU A BREAK.

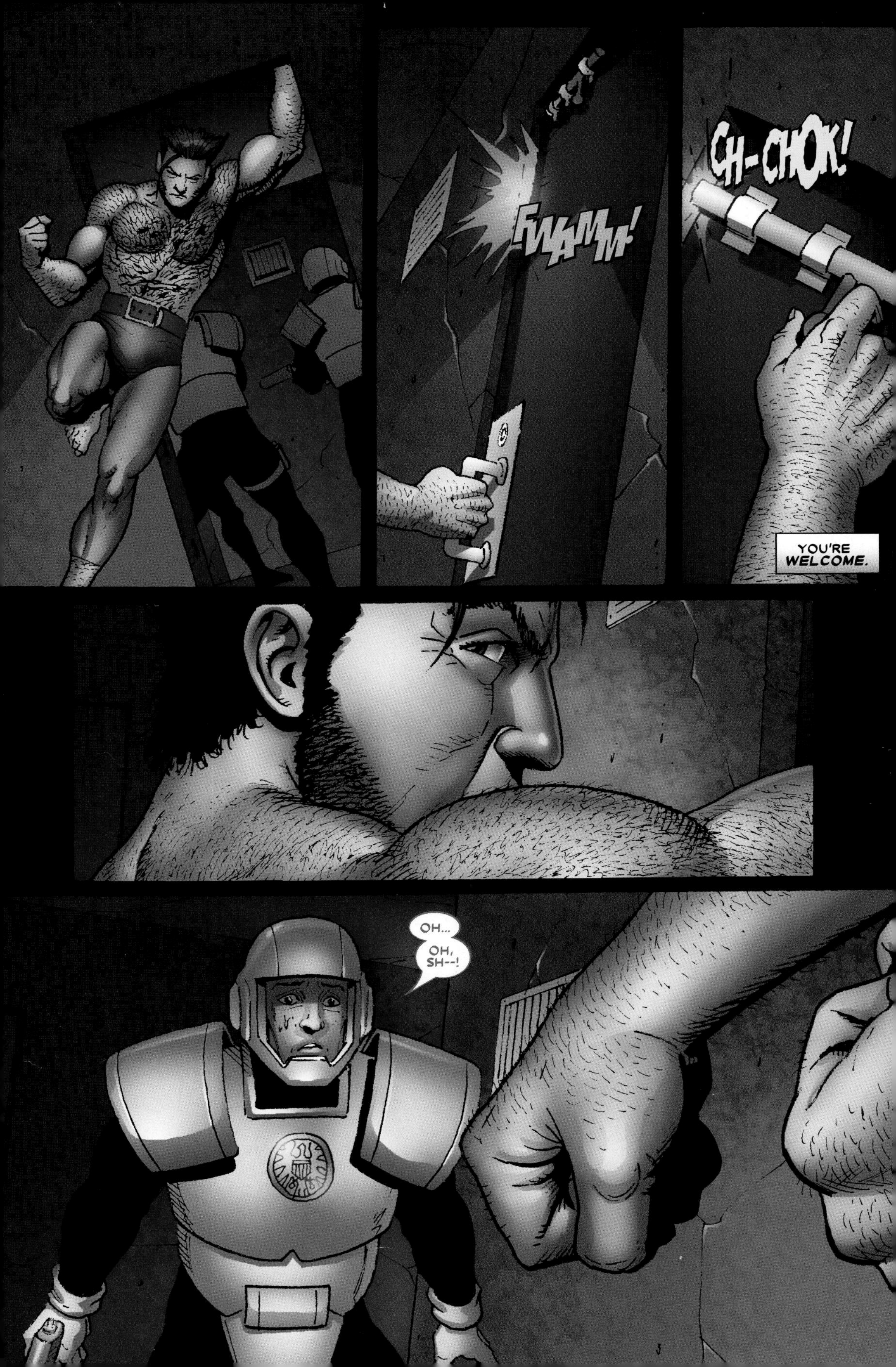
FWAMM!
CH-CHOK!
YOU'RE WELCOME.
OH...
OH, SH--!

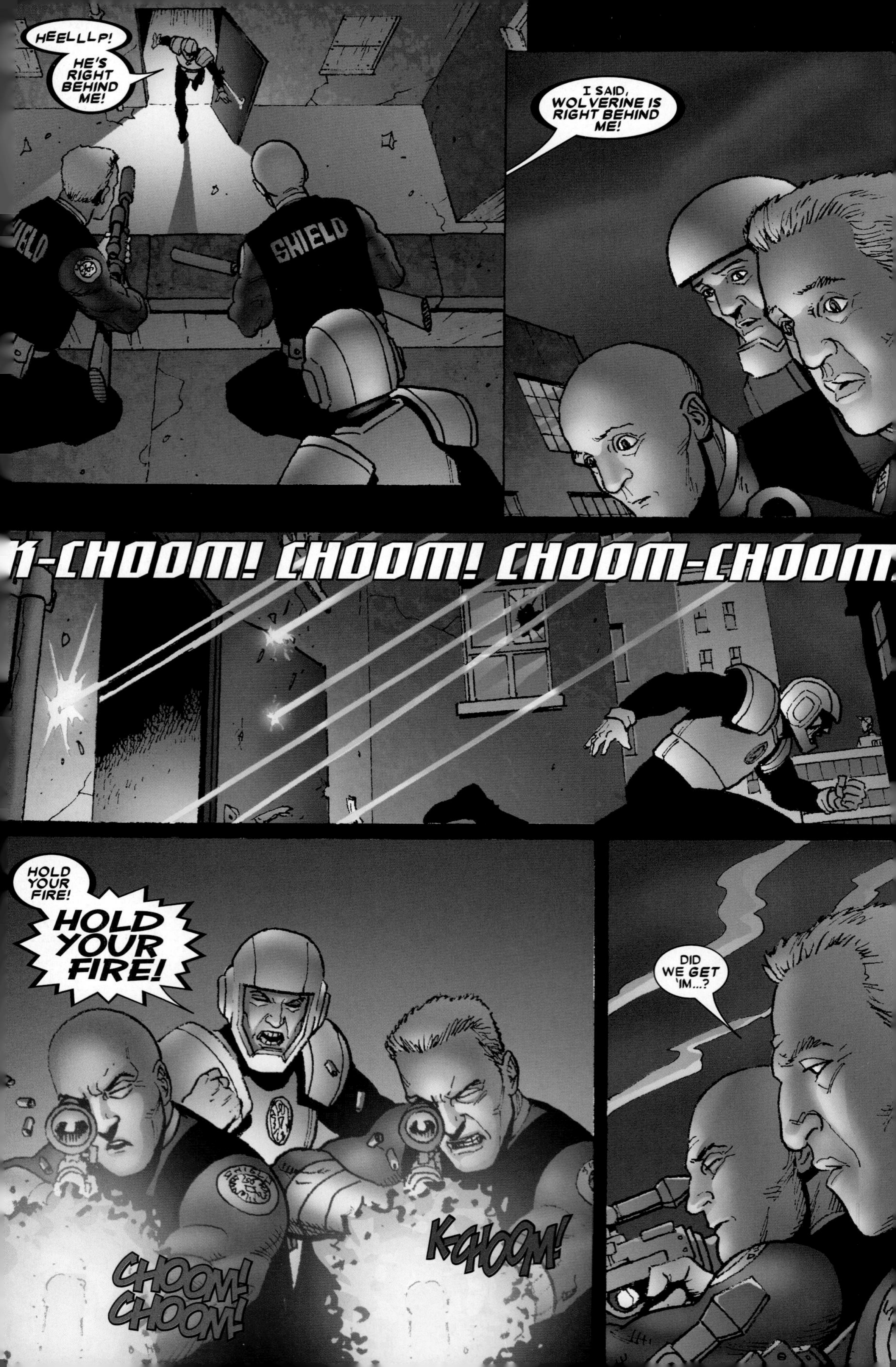
HEELLLP!
HE'S RIGHT BEHIND ME!
SHIELD
SHIELD
I SAID, WOLVERINE IS RIGHT BEHIND ME!
K-CHOOM! CHOOM! CHOOM-CHOOM!
HOLD YOUR FIRE!
HOLD YOUR FIRE!
CHOOM! CHOOM!
K-CHOOM!
DID WE GET 'IM...?

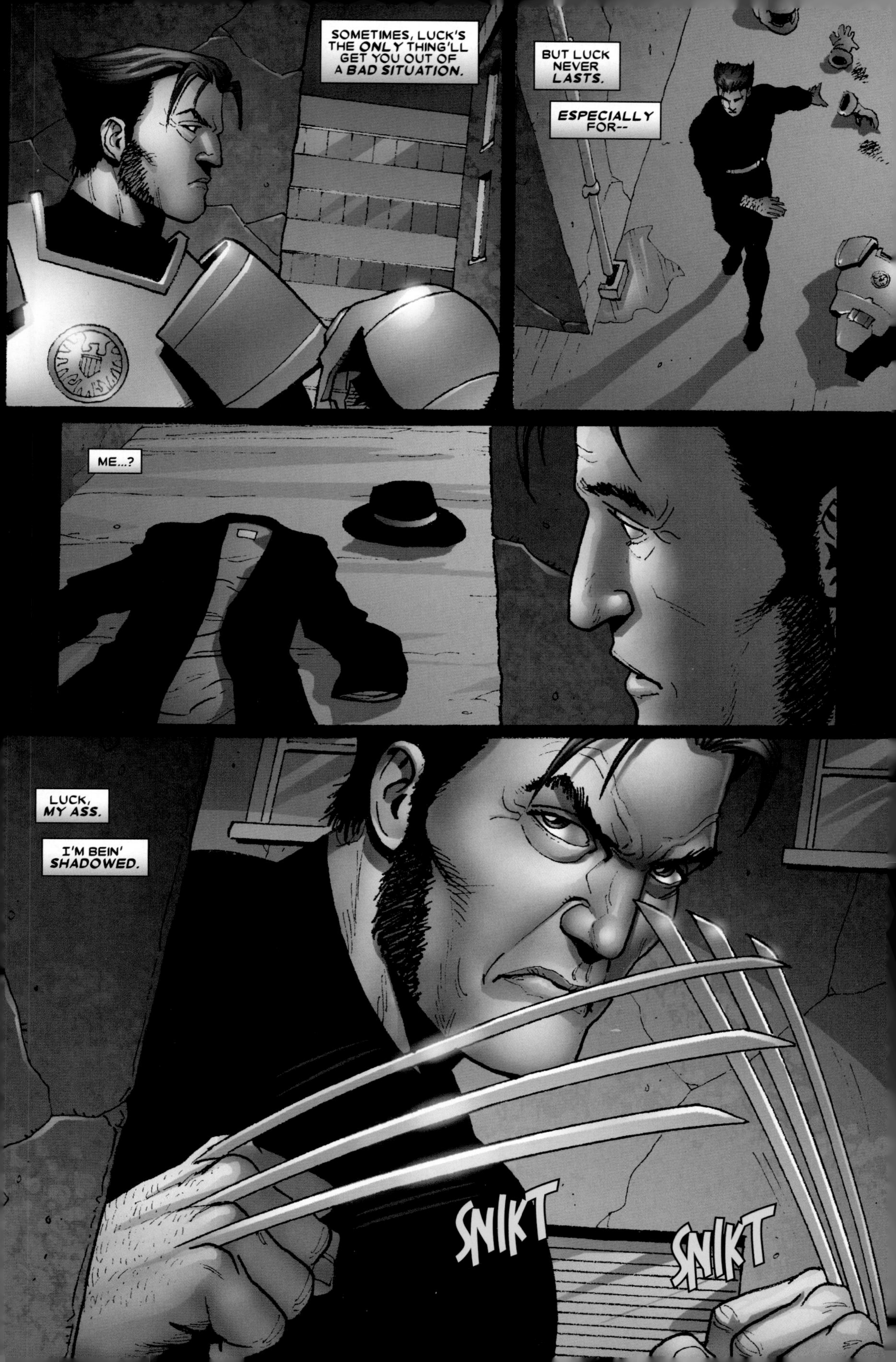
SOMETIMES, LUCK'S THE ONLY THING'LL GET YOU OUT OF A BAD SITUATION.
BUT LUCK NEVER LASTS.
ESPECIALLY FOR--
ME...?
LUCK, MY ASS.
I'M BEIN' SHADOWED.
SNIKT
SNIKT

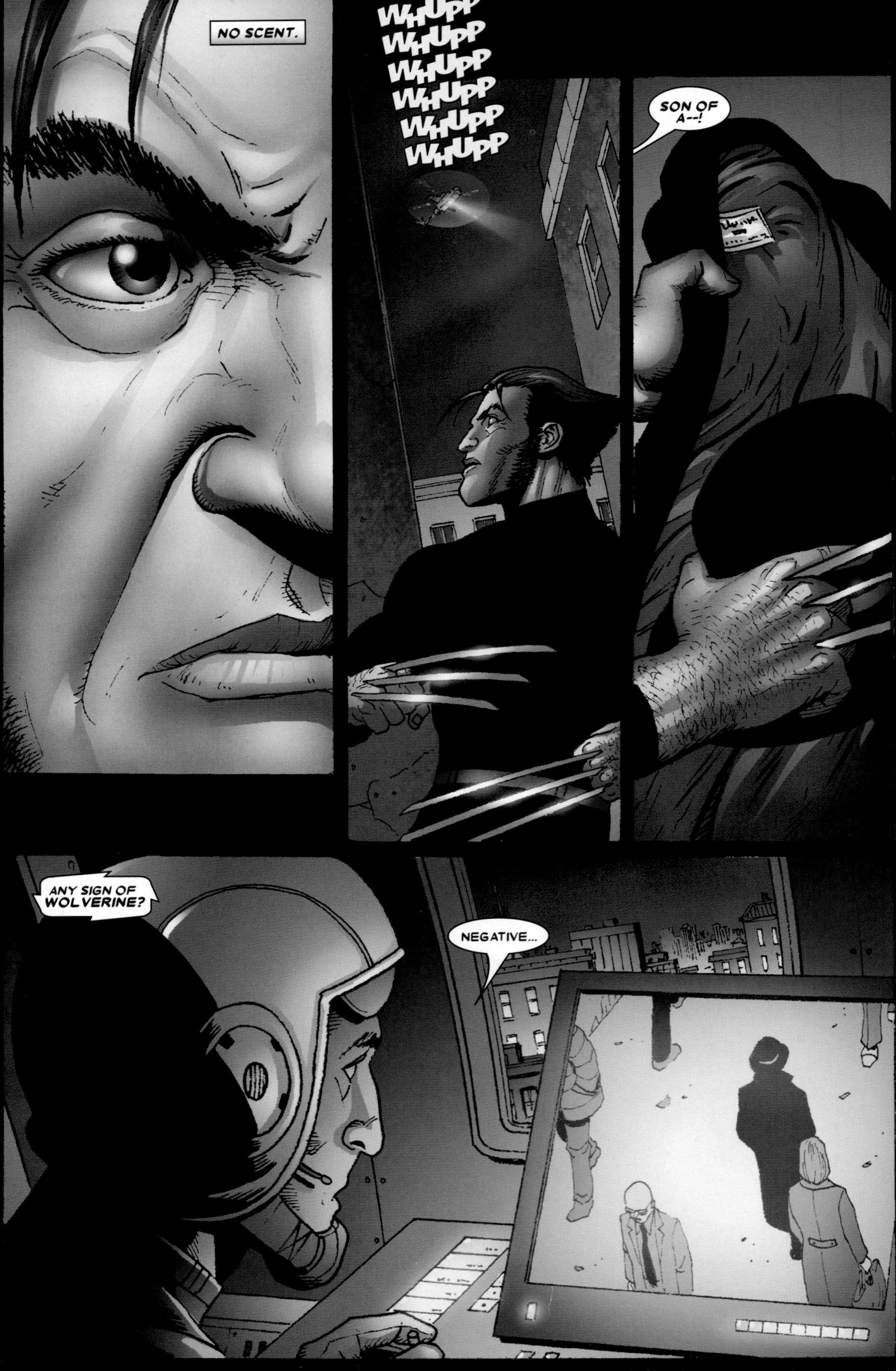
NO SCENT.
WHUPP WHUPP WHUPP WHUPP WHUPP WHUPP
SON OF A--!
ANY SIGN OF WOLVERINE?
NEGATIVE...

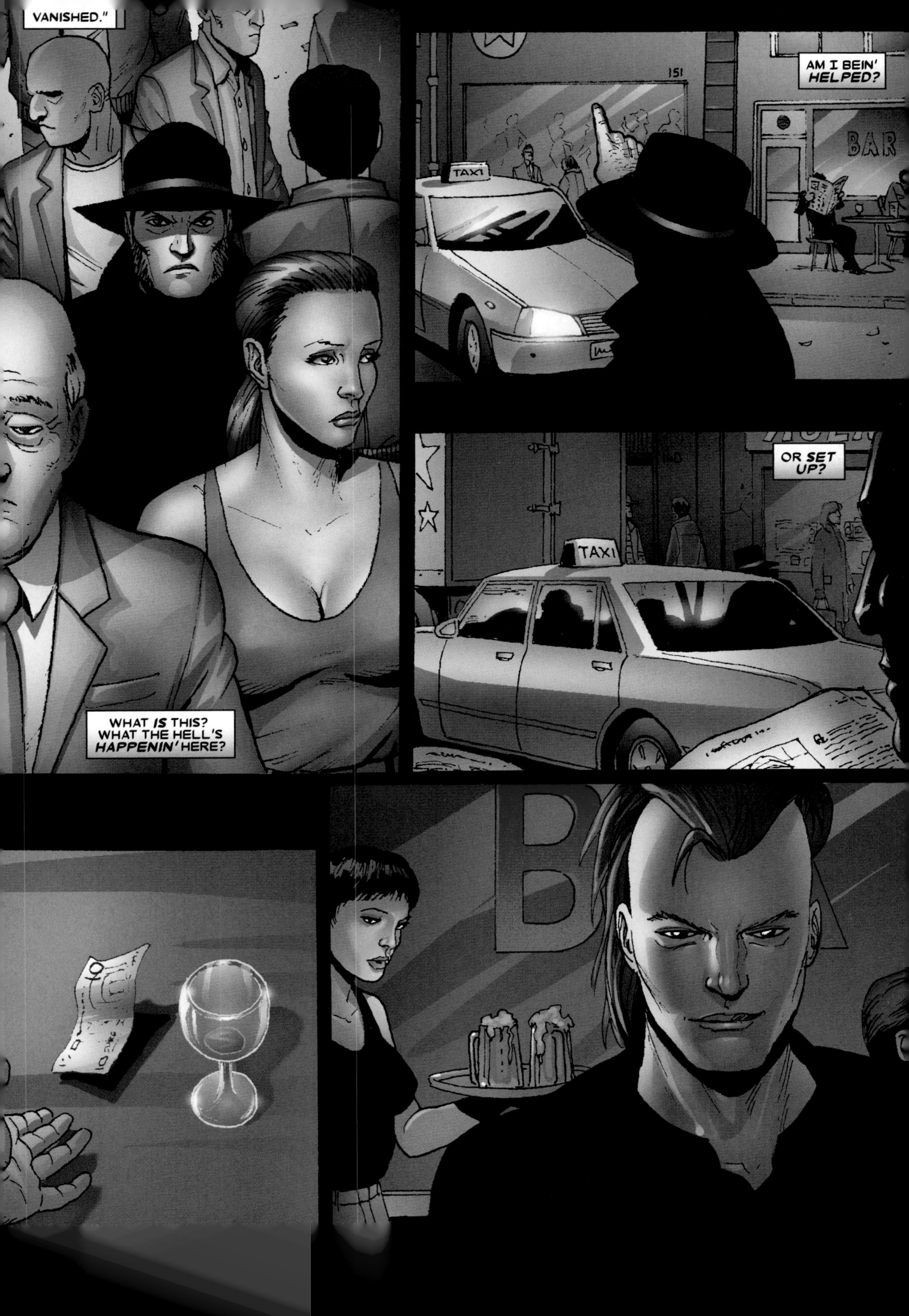
VANISHED."
WHAT *IS* THIS? WHAT THE HELL'S *HAPPENIN'* HERE?
151
TAXI
AM I BEIN' *HELPED?*
BAR
TAXI
OR *SET UP?*

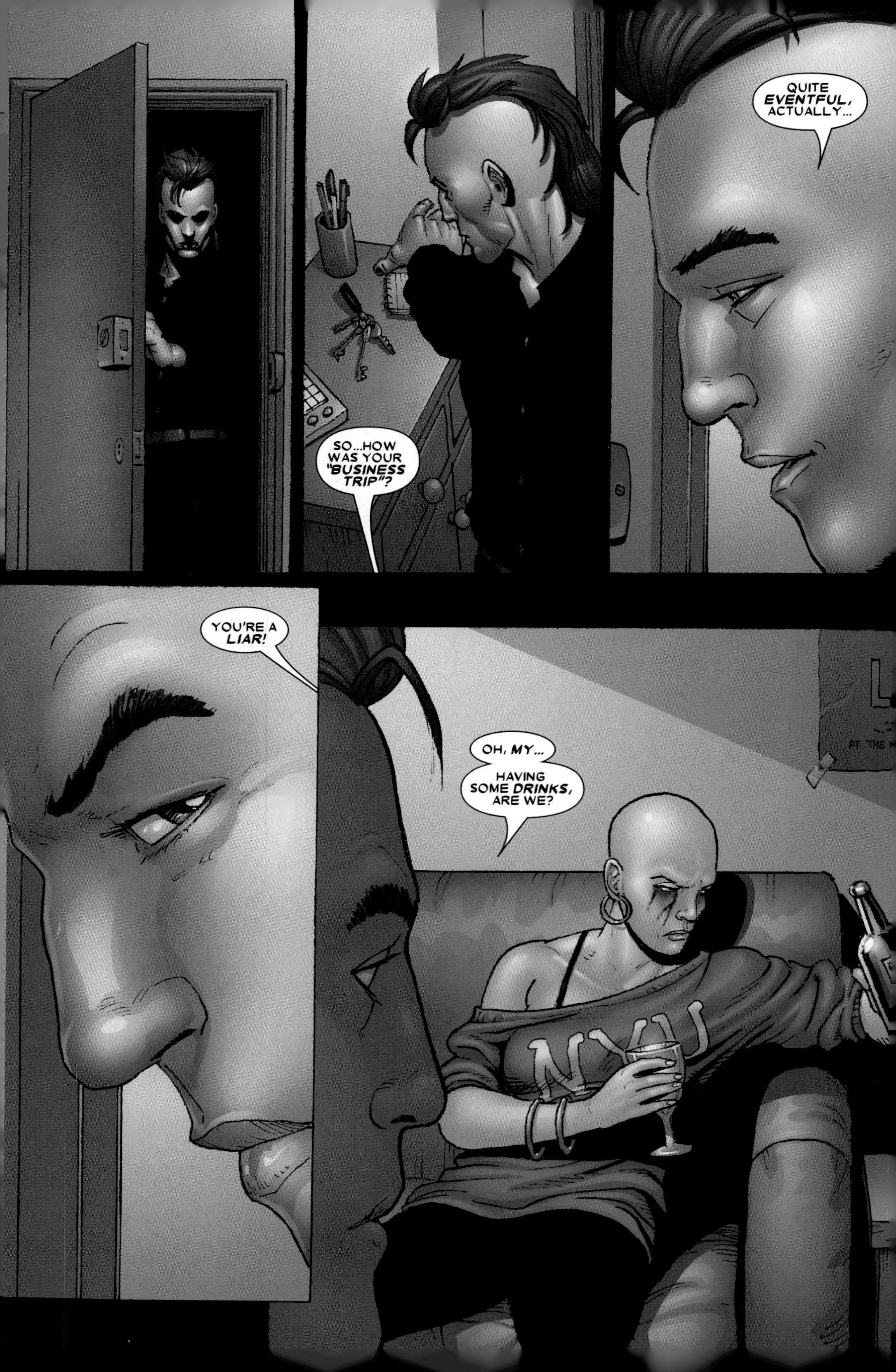
SO...HOW WAS YOUR "BUSINESS TRIP"?
QUITE EVENTFUL, ACTUALLY...
YOU'RE A LIAR!
OH, MY...
HAVING SOME DRINKS, ARE WE?
NYU

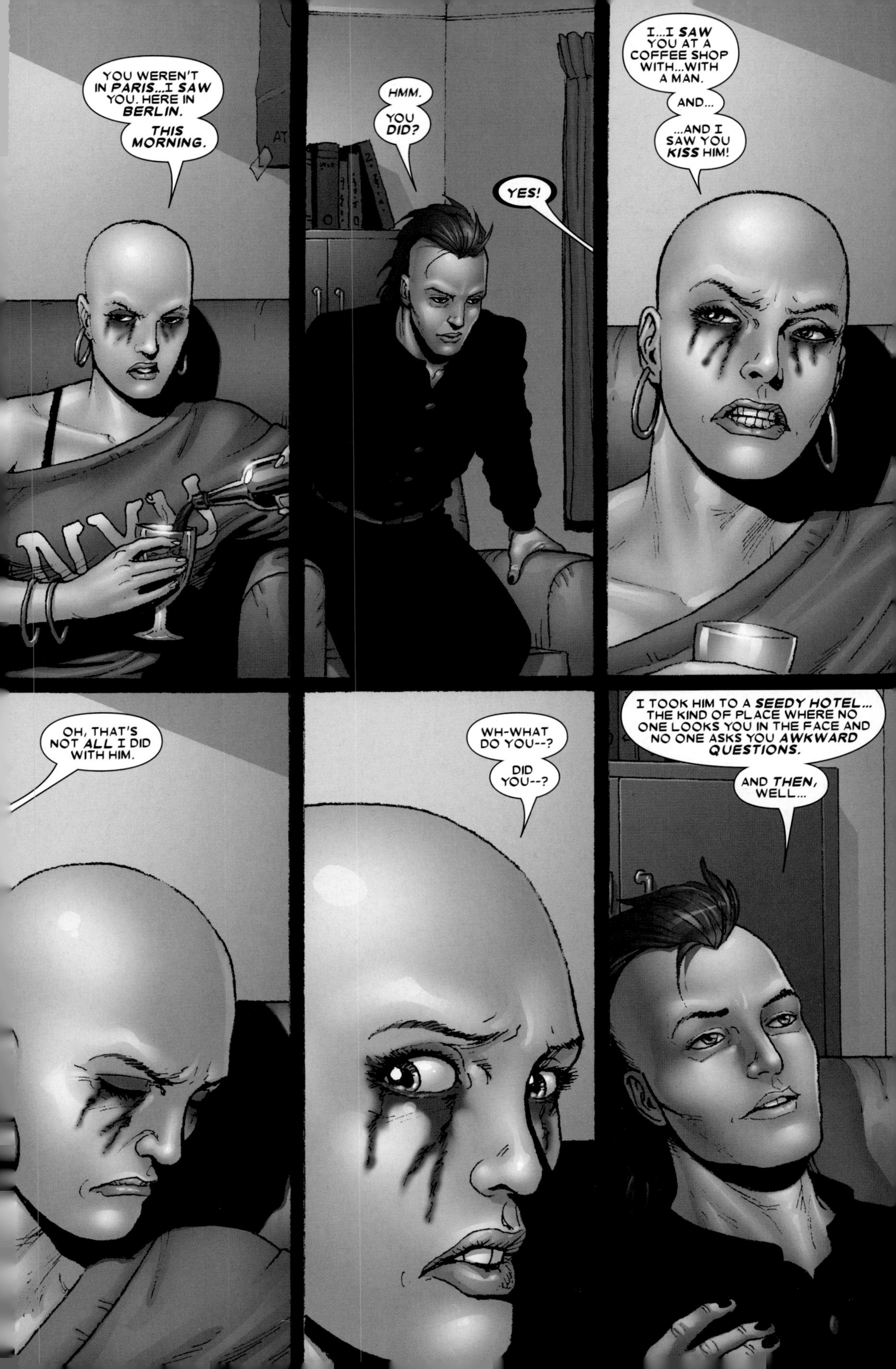
YOU WEREN'T IN PARIS...I SAW YOU. HERE IN BERLIN.
THIS MORNING.
HMM.
YOU DID?
YES!
I...I SAW YOU AT A COFFEE SHOP WITH...WITH A MAN.
AND...
...AND I SAW YOU KISS HIM!
OH, THAT'S NOT ALL I DID WITH HIM.
WH-WHAT DO YOU--?
DID YOU--?
I TOOK HIM TO A SEEDY HOTEL... THE KIND OF PLACE WHERE NO ONE LOOKS YOU IN THE FACE AND NO ONE ASKS YOU AWKWARD QUESTIONS.
AND THEN, WELL...

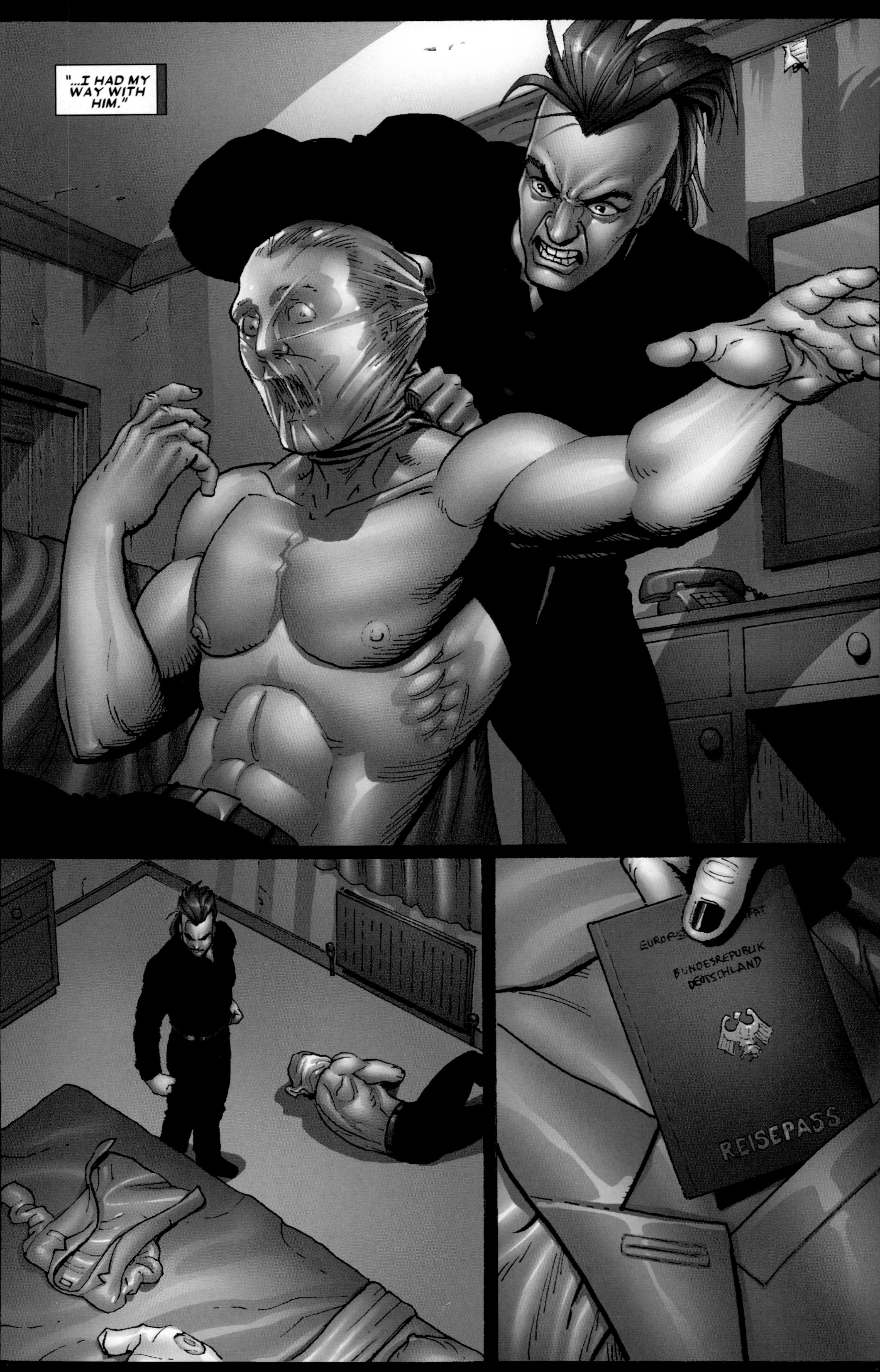
"...I HAD MY WAY WITH HIM."
BUNDESREPUBLIK DEUTSCHLAND
REISEPASS

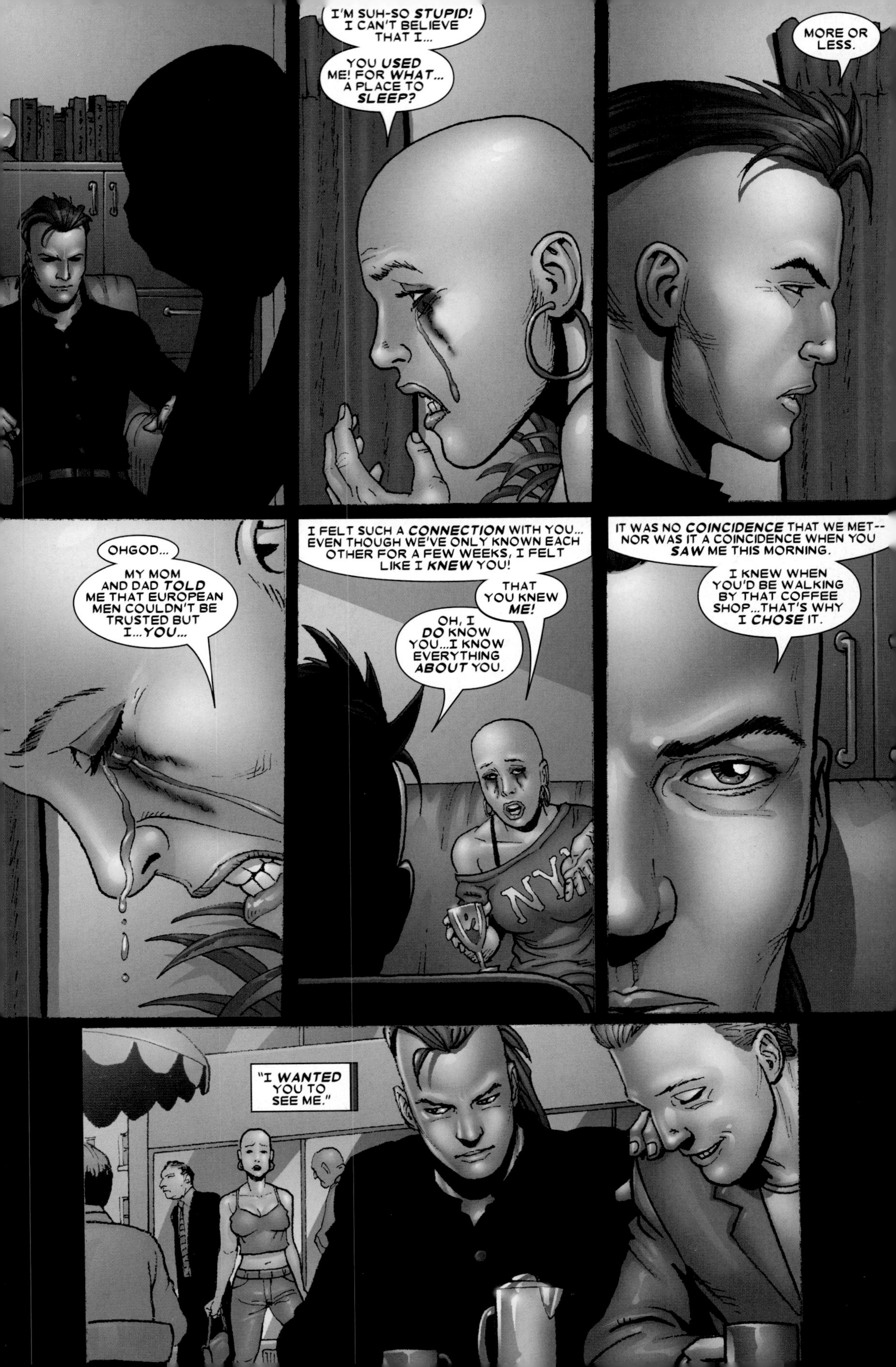

I'M SUH-SO STUPID! I CAN'T BELIEVE THAT I...
YOU USED ME! FOR WHAT... A PLACE TO SLEEP?
MORE OR LESS.
OHGOD...
MY MOM AND DAD TOLD ME THAT EUROPEAN MEN COULDN'T BE TRUSTED BUT I...YOU...
I FELT SUCH A CONNECTION WITH YOU... EVEN THOUGH WE'VE ONLY KNOWN EACH OTHER FOR A FEW WEEKS, I FELT LIKE I KNEW YOU!
THAT YOU KNEW ME!
OH, I DO KNOW YOU...I KNOW EVERYTHING ABOUT YOU.
IT WAS NO COINCIDENCE THAT WE MET-- NOR WAS IT A COINCIDENCE WHEN YOU SAW ME THIS MORNING.
I KNEW WHEN YOU'D BE WALKING BY THAT COFFEE SHOP...THAT'S WHY I CHOSE IT.
"I WANTED YOU TO SEE ME."

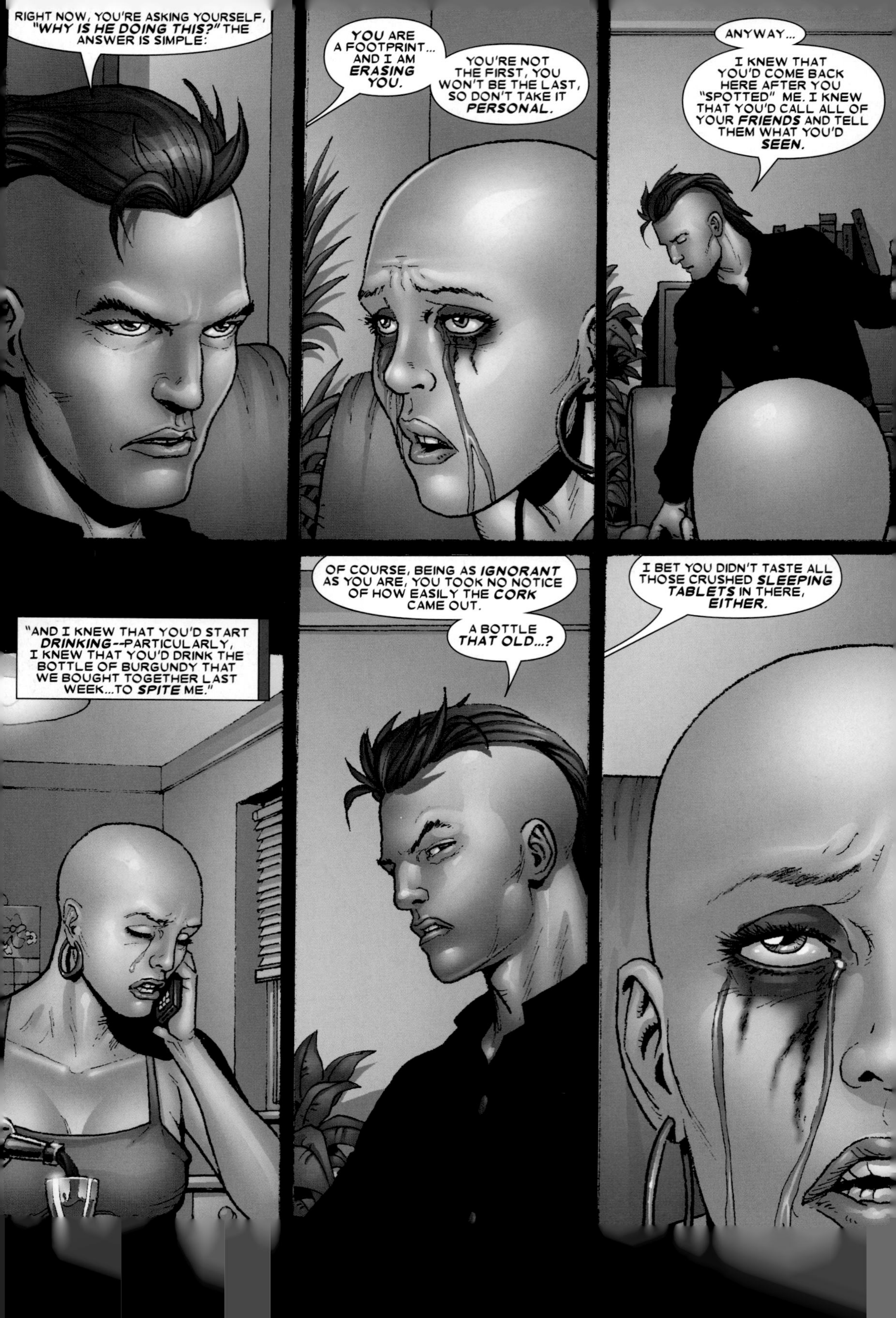
RIGHT NOW, YOU'RE ASKING YOURSELF, "WHY IS HE DOING THIS?" THE ANSWER IS SIMPLE:
YOU ARE A FOOTPRINT... AND I AM ERASING YOU.
YOU'RE NOT THE FIRST, YOU WON'T BE THE LAST, SO DON'T TAKE IT PERSONAL.
ANYWAY...
I KNEW THAT YOU'D COME BACK HERE AFTER YOU "SPOTTED" ME. I KNEW THAT YOU'D CALL ALL OF YOUR FRIENDS AND TELL THEM WHAT YOU'D SEEN.
"AND I KNEW THAT YOU'D START DRINKING--PARTICULARLY, I KNEW THAT YOU'D DRINK THE BOTTLE OF BURGUNDY THAT WE BOUGHT TOGETHER LAST WEEK...TO SPITE ME."
OF COURSE, BEING AS IGNORANT AS YOU ARE, YOU TOOK NO NOTICE OF HOW EASILY THE CORK CAME OUT.
A BOTTLE THAT OLD...?
I BET YOU DIDN'T TASTE ALL THOSE CRUSHED SLEEPING TABLETS IN THERE, EITHER.

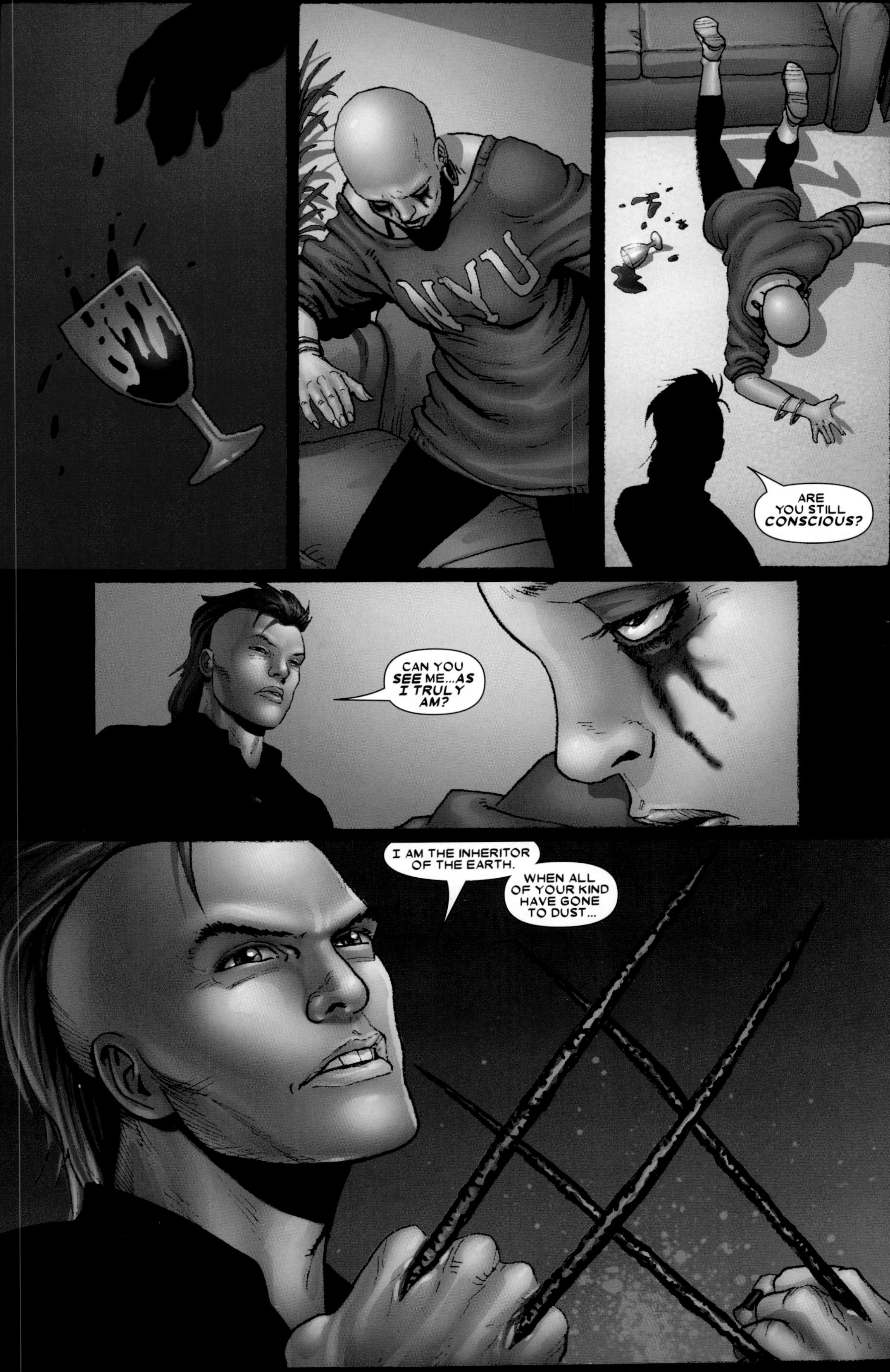
ARE YOU STILL CONSCIOUS?
CAN YOU SEE ME...AS I TRULY AM?
I AM THE INHERITOR OF THE EARTH.
WHEN ALL OF YOUR KIND HAVE GONE TO DUST...

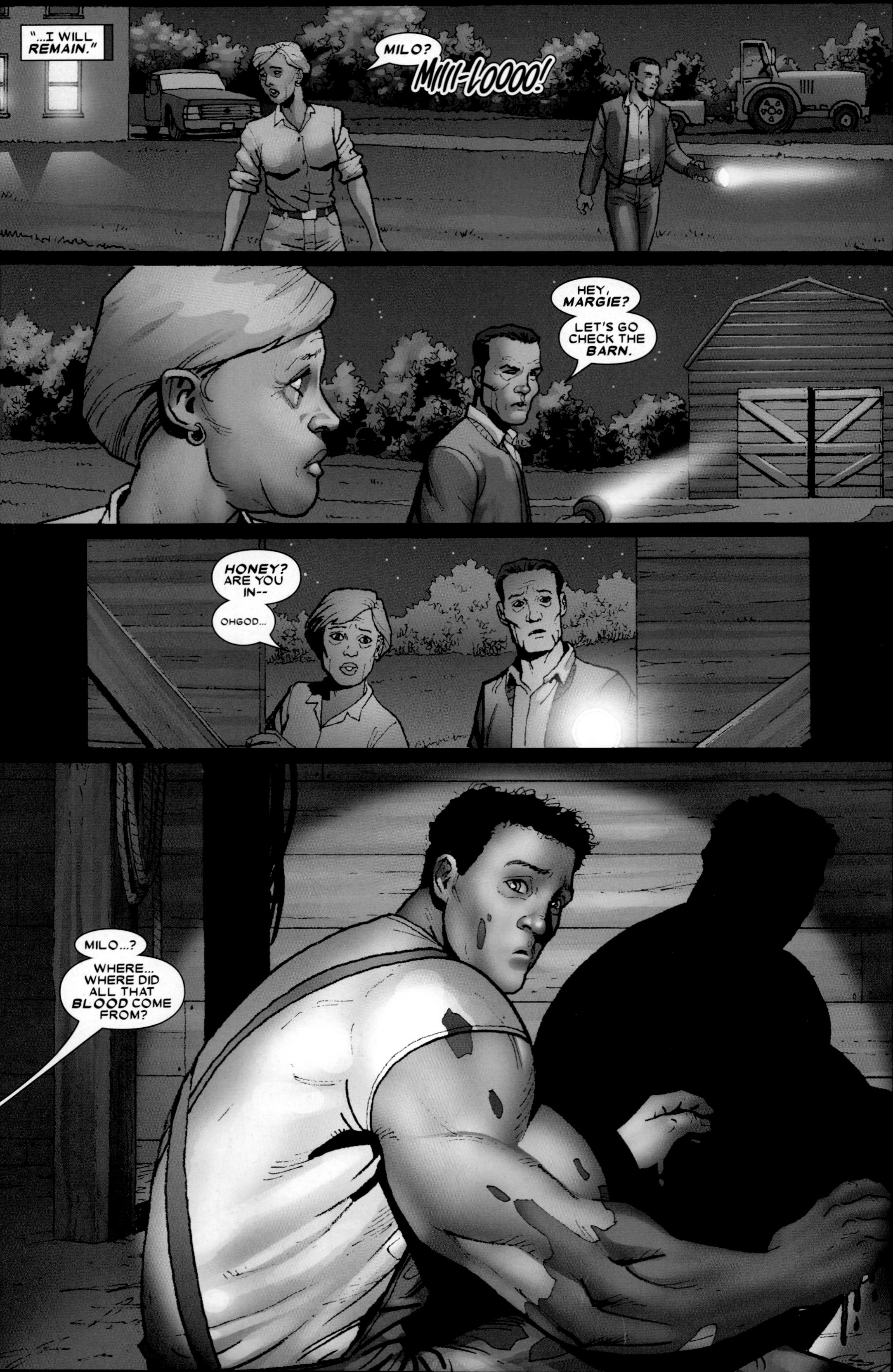
"...I WILL REMAIN."
MILO?
MIII-LOOOO!
HEY, MARGIE?
LET'S GO CHECK THE BARN.
HONEY? ARE YOU IN--
OHGOD...
MILO...?
WHERE... WHERE DID ALL THAT BLOOD COME FROM?

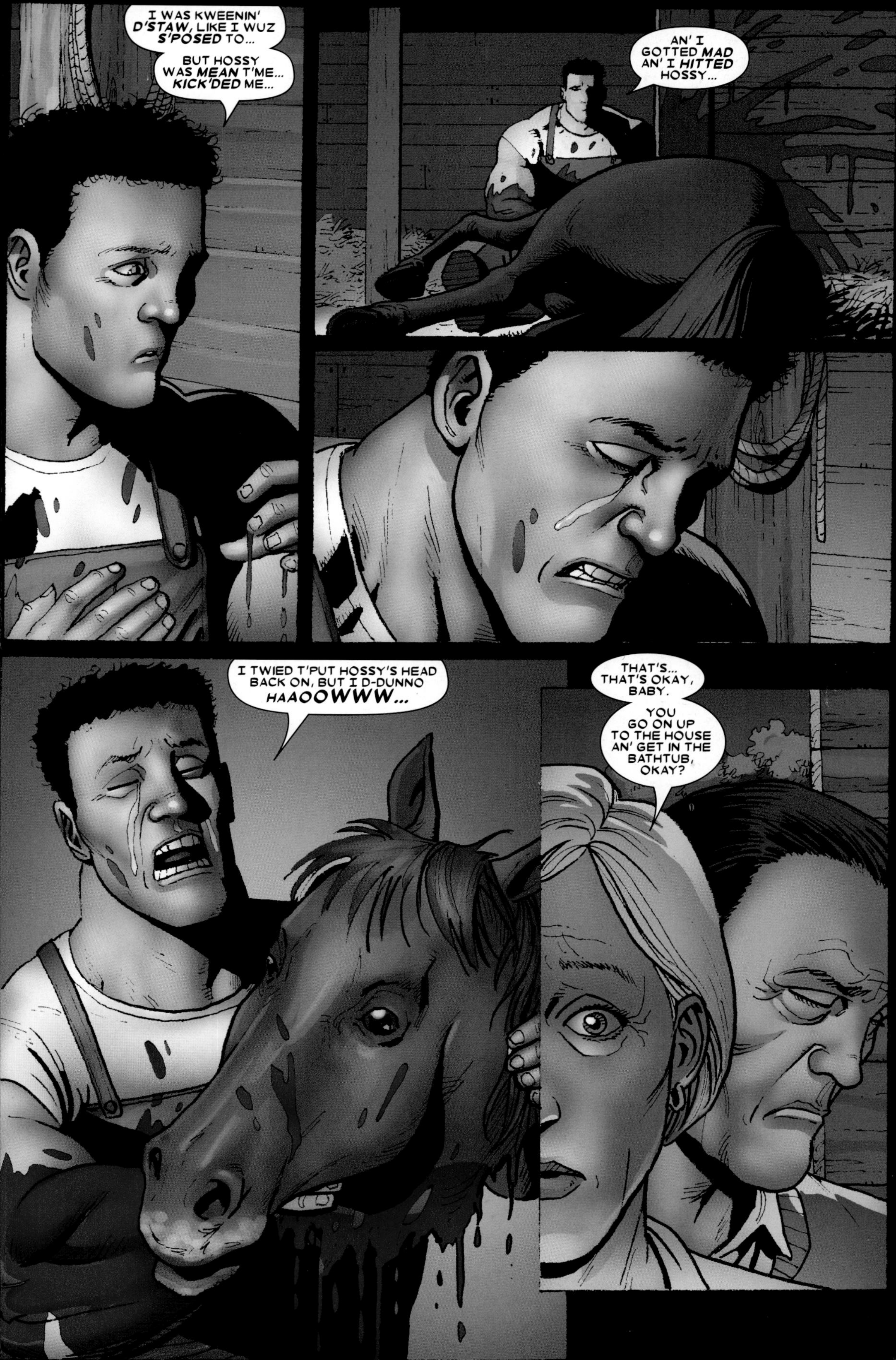

I WAS KWEENIN' D'STAW, LIKE I WUZ S'POSED TO...
BUT HOSSY WAS MEAN T'ME... KICK'DED ME...
AN' I GOTTED MAD AN' I HITTED HOSSY...
I TWIED T'PUT HOSSY'S HEAD BACK ON, BUT I D-DUNNO HAAOOWWW...
THAT'S... THAT'S OKAY, BABY.
YOU GO ON UP TO THE HOUSE AN' GET IN THE BATHTUB, OKAY?

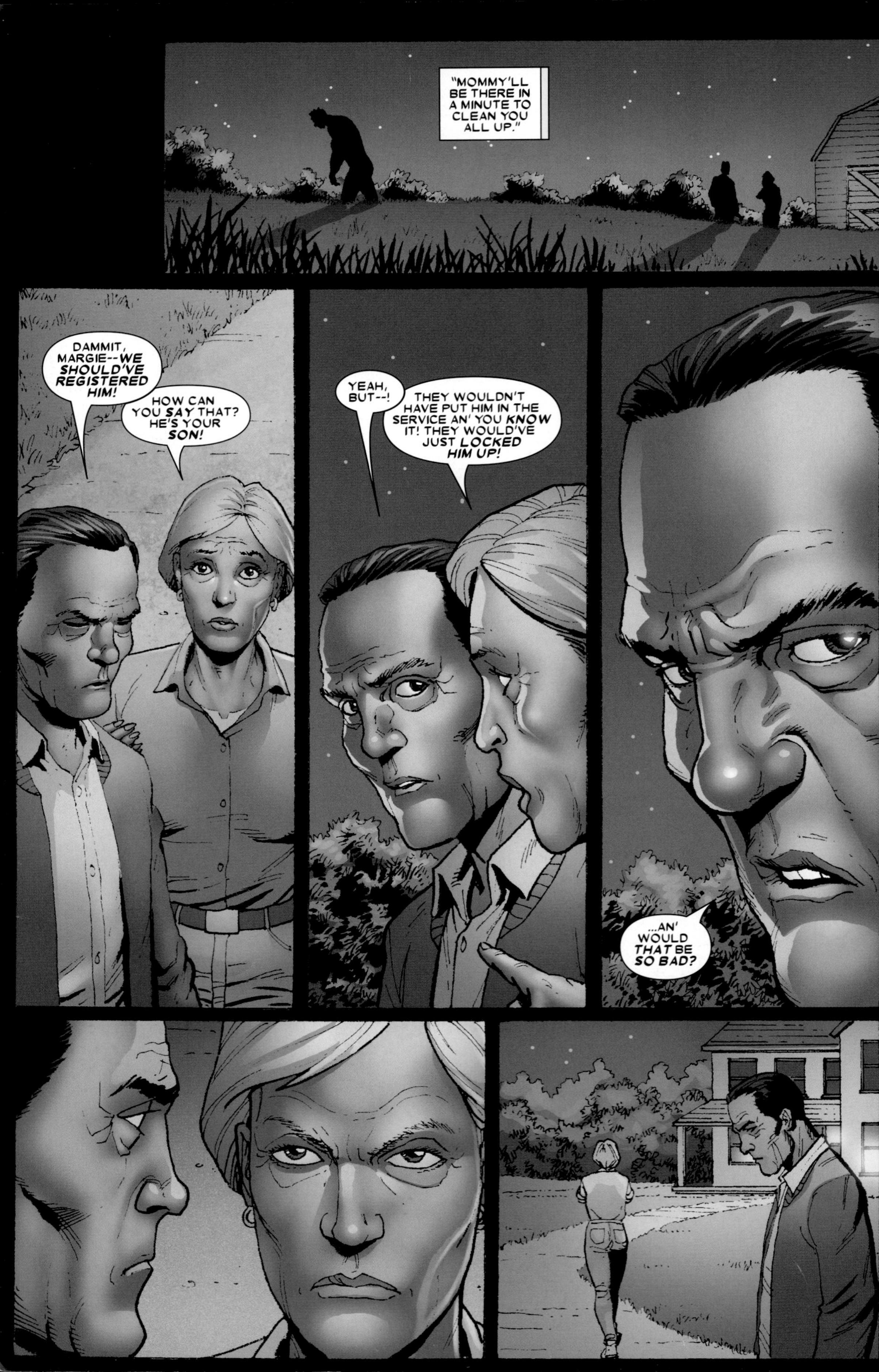
"MOMMY'LL BE THERE IN A MINUTE TO CLEAN YOU ALL UP."
DAMMIT, MARGIE--*WE SHOULD'VE REGISTERED HIM!*
HOW CAN YOU *SAY* THAT? HE'S YOUR *SON!*
YEAH, BUT--!
THEY WOULDN'T HAVE PUT HIM IN THE SERVICE AN' YOU *KNOW* IT! THEY WOULD'VE JUST *LOCKED HIM UP!*
...AN' WOULD *THAT* BE *SO BAD?*

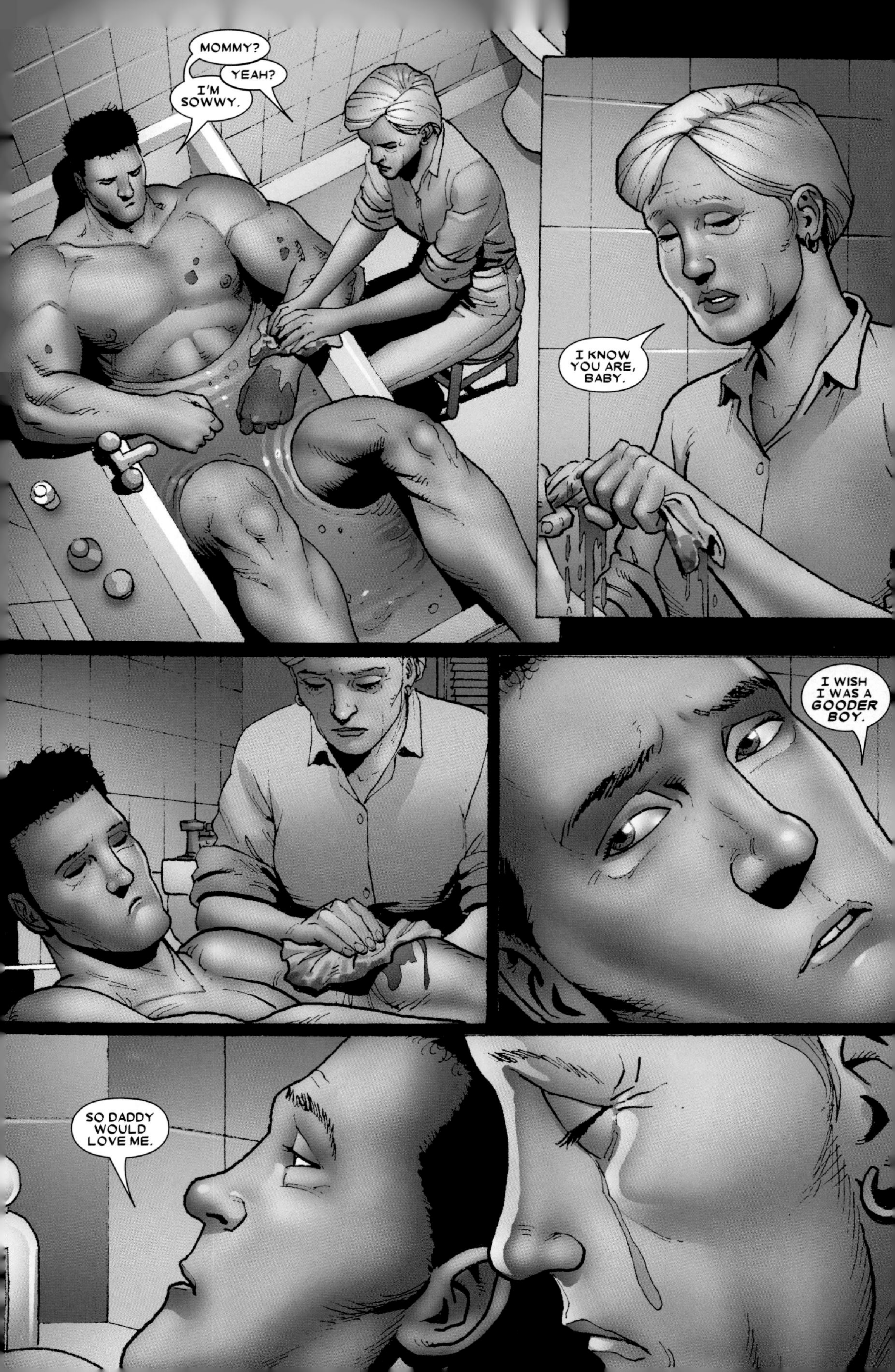
MOMMY?
YEAH?
I'M SOWWY.
I KNOW YOU ARE, BABY.
I WISH I WAS A GOODER BOY.
SO DADDY WOULD LOVE ME.

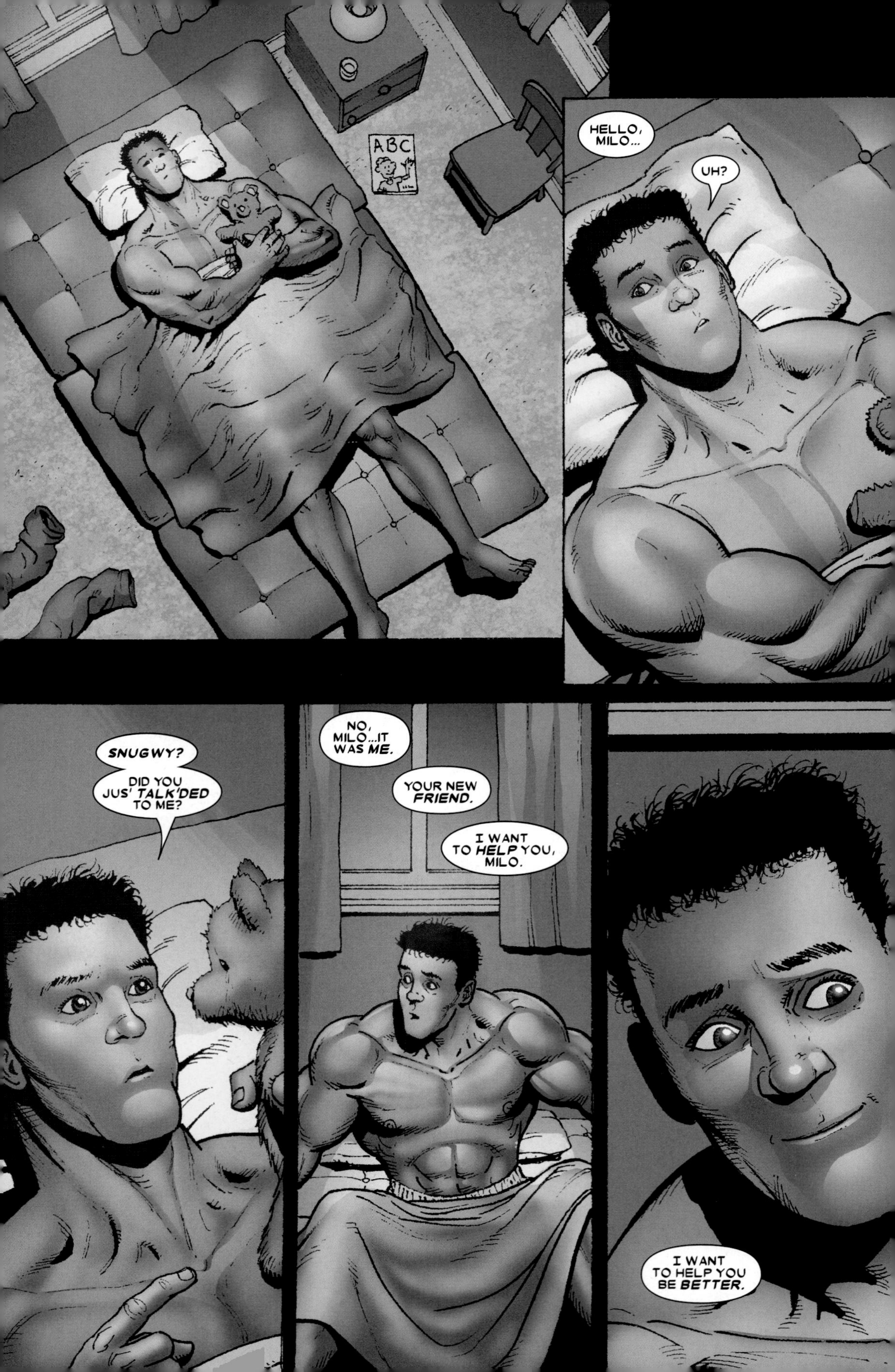
ABC
HELLO, MILO...
UH?
SNUGWY?
DID YOU JUS' TALK'DED TO ME?
NO, MILO...IT WAS ME.
YOUR NEW FRIEND.
I WANT TO HELP YOU, MILO.
I WANT TO HELP YOU BE BETTER.

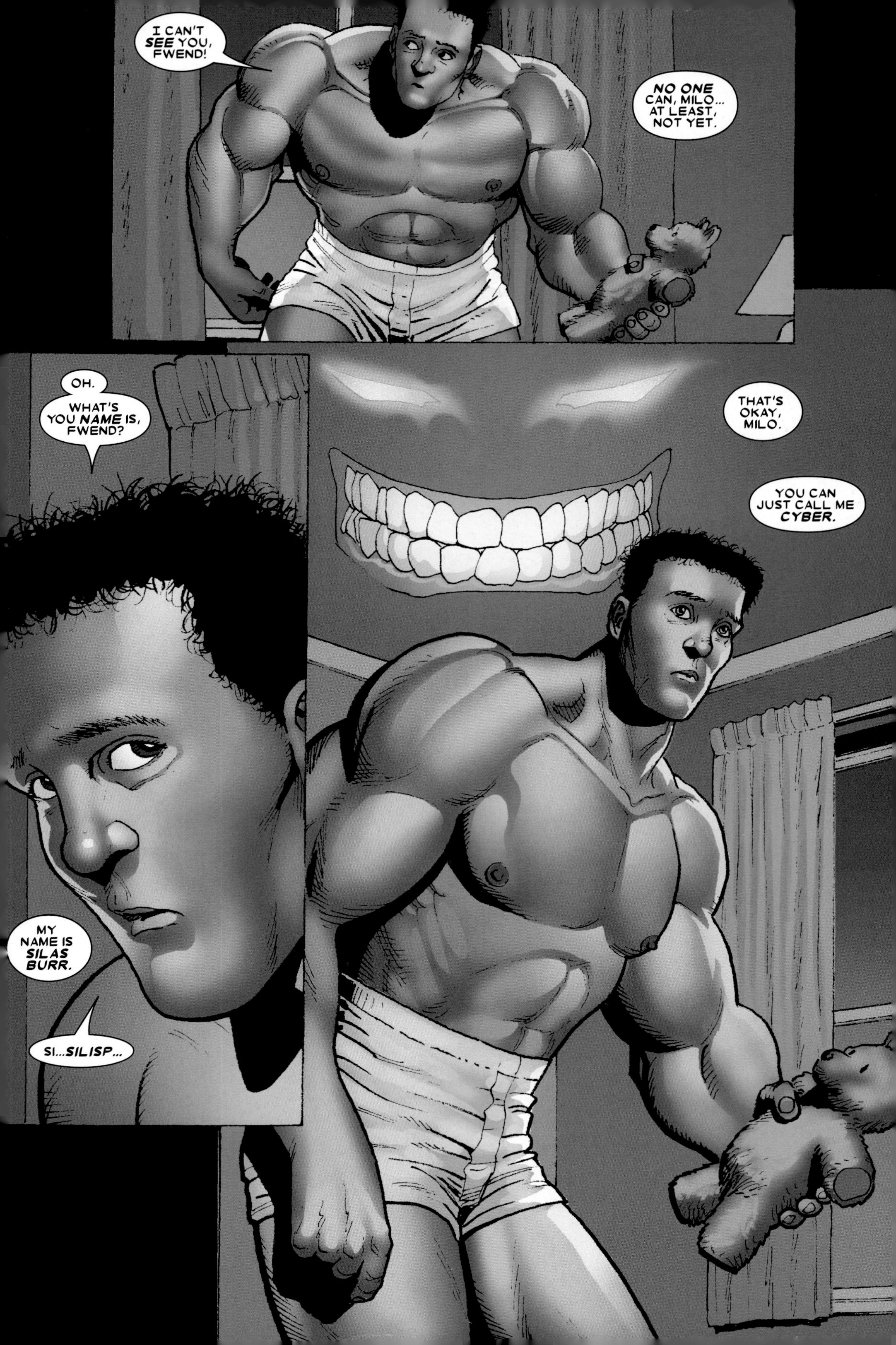
I CAN'T SEE YOU, FWEND!
NO ONE CAN, MILO... AT LEAST, NOT YET.
OH.
WHAT'S YOU NAME IS, FWEND?
THAT'S OKAY, MILO.
YOU CAN JUST CALL ME CYBER.
MY NAME IS SILAS BURR.
SI...SILISP...

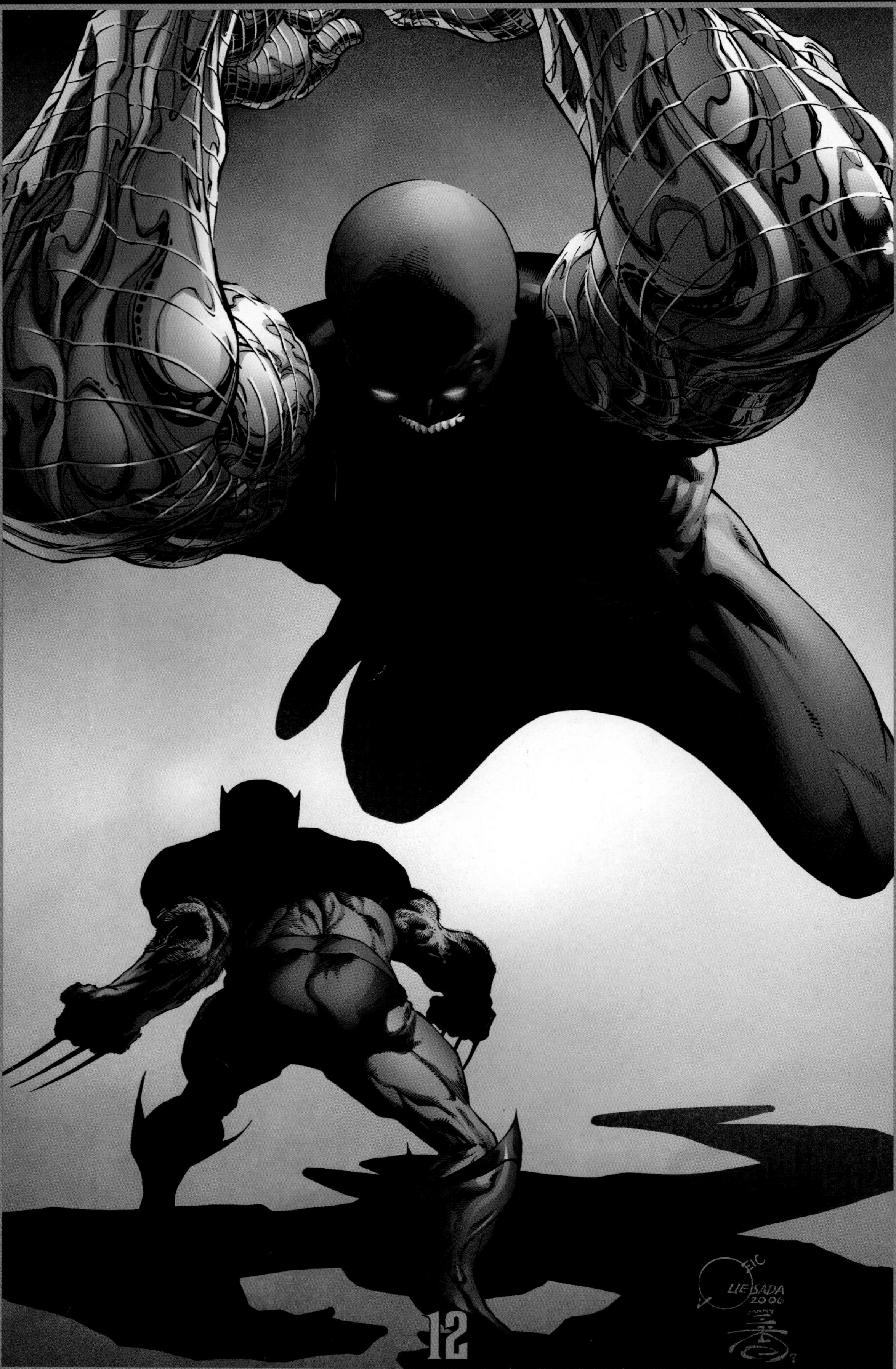
12

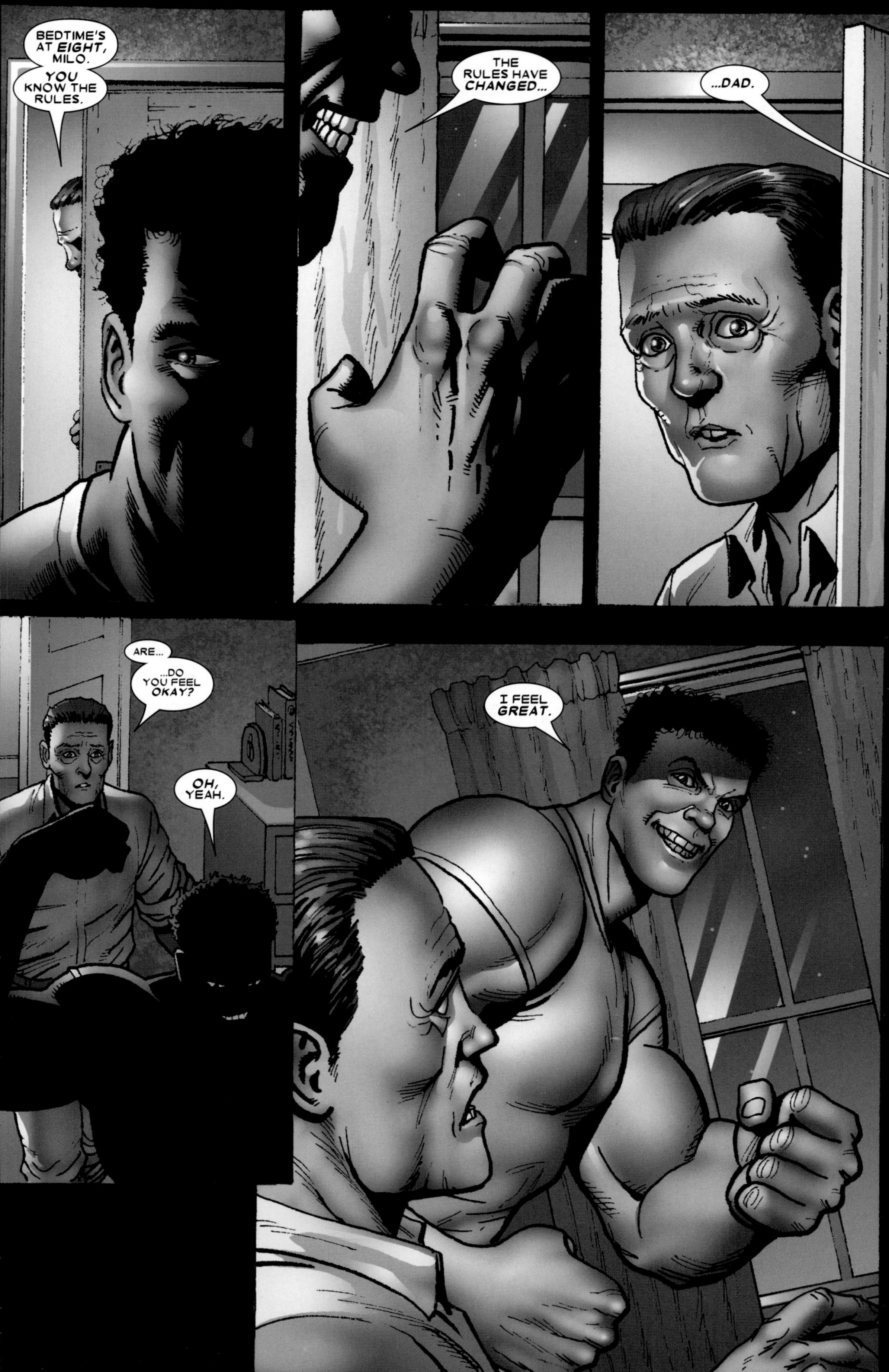
BEDTIME'S AT EIGHT, MILO.
YOU KNOW THE RULES.
THE RULES HAVE CHANGED...
...DAD.
ARE...
...DO YOU FEEL OKAY?
OH, YEAH.
I FEEL GREAT.

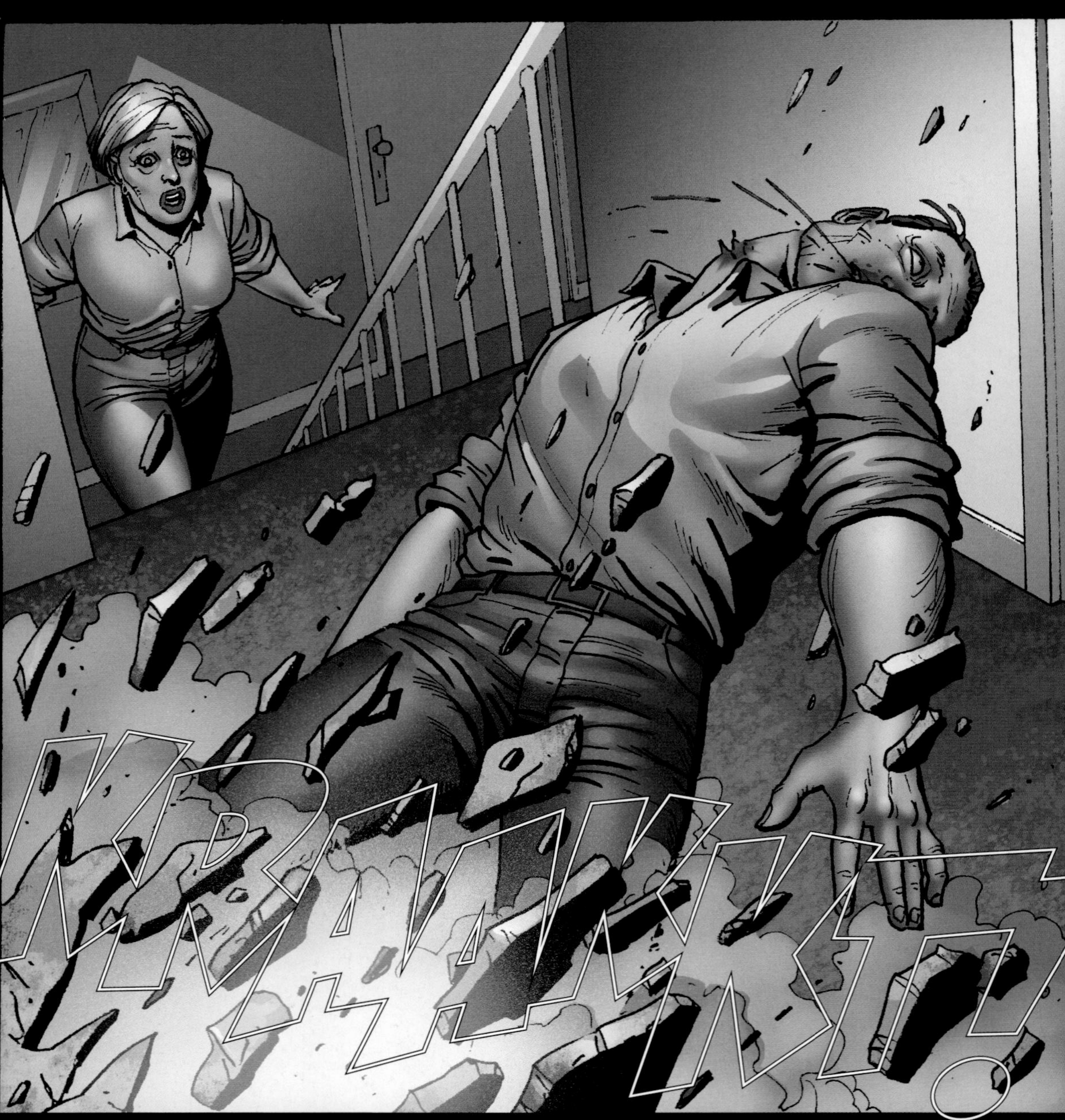

SWIFT AND TERRIBLE

PART 2

MILO--
NO!

WHAT'VE YOU DONE?!

MILO DIDN'T DO ANYTHING... I DID.

PLEASED TO MEET YOU, MADAM.

MY NAME IS SILAS BURR.

THE SHY TYPE, EH? HOW ADORABLE.

YOU SHOULD KNOW, MADAM, THAT I WILL BE... "BORROWING" YOUR SON'S BODY.

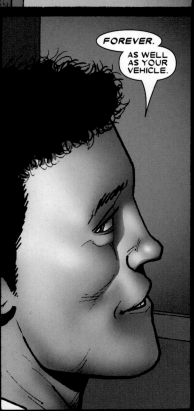

FOREVER.

AS WELL AS YOUR VEHICLE.

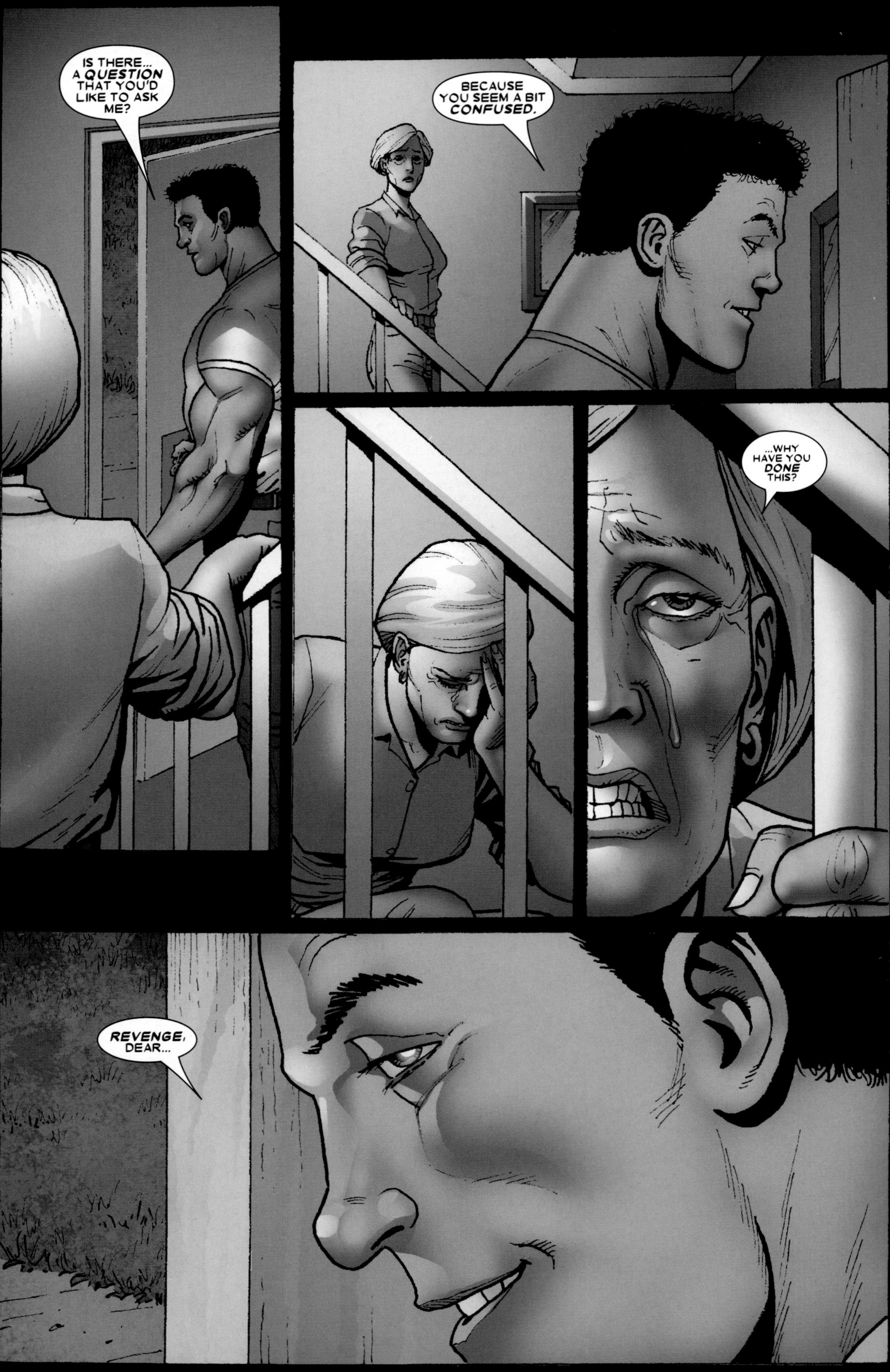
IS THERE... A QUESTION THAT YOU'D LIKE TO ASK ME?
BECAUSE YOU SEEM A BIT CONFUSED.
...WHY HAVE YOU DONE THIS?
REVENGE, DEAR...

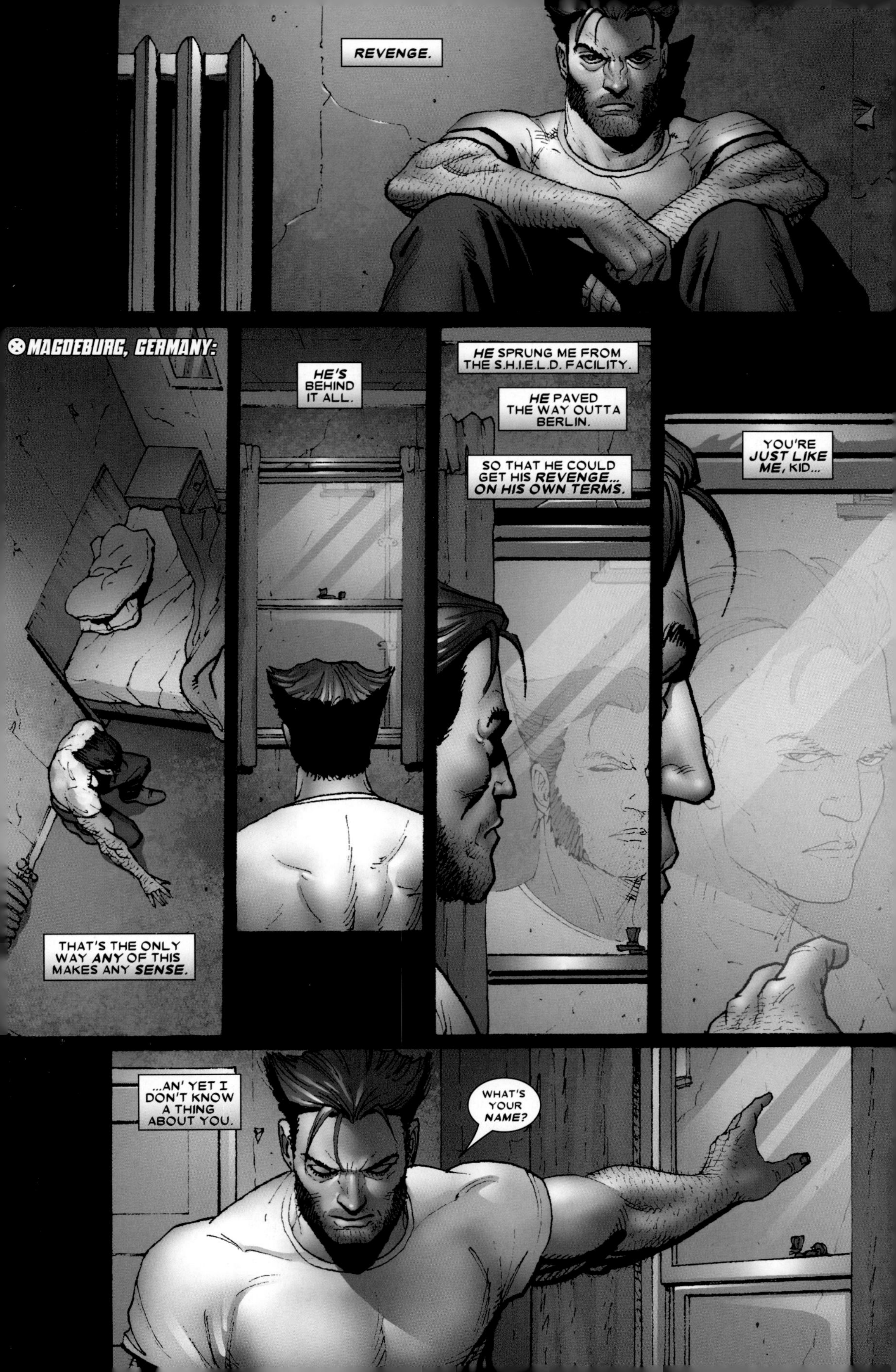
REVENGE.
MAGDEBURG, GERMANY:
THAT'S THE ONLY WAY ANY OF THIS MAKES ANY SENSE.
HE'S BEHIND IT ALL.
HE SPRUNG ME FROM THE S.H.I.E.L.D. FACILITY.
HE PAVED THE WAY OUTTA BERLIN.
SO THAT HE COULD GET HIS REVENGE... ON HIS OWN TERMS.
YOU'RE JUST LIKE ME, KID...
...AN' YET I DON'T KNOW A THING ABOUT YOU.
WHAT'S YOUR NAME?

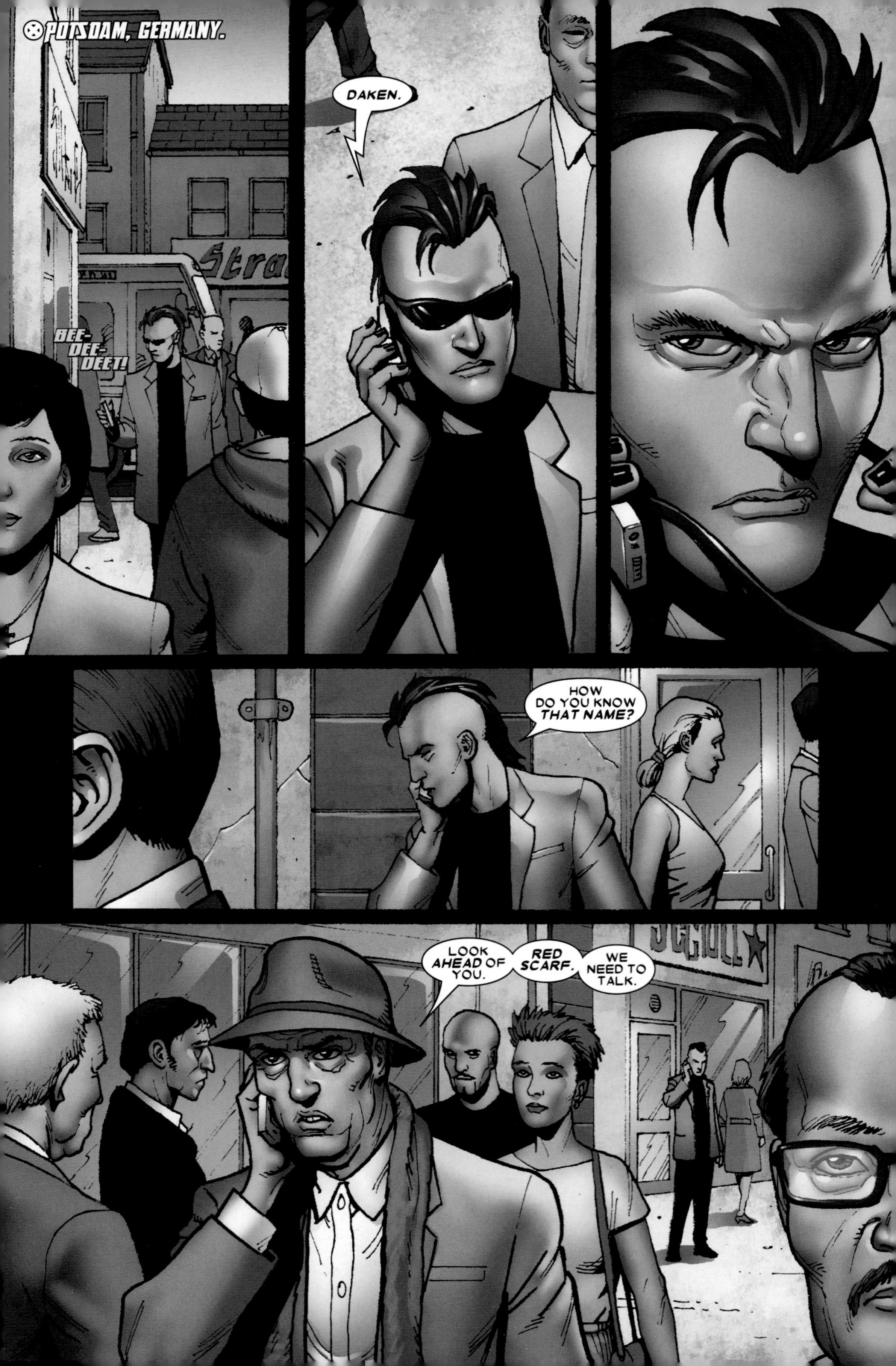
POTSDAM, GERMANY.
BEE-DEE-DEET!
DAKEN.
HOW DO YOU KNOW THAT NAME?
LOOK AHEAD OF YOU.
RED SCARF.
WE NEED TO TALK.

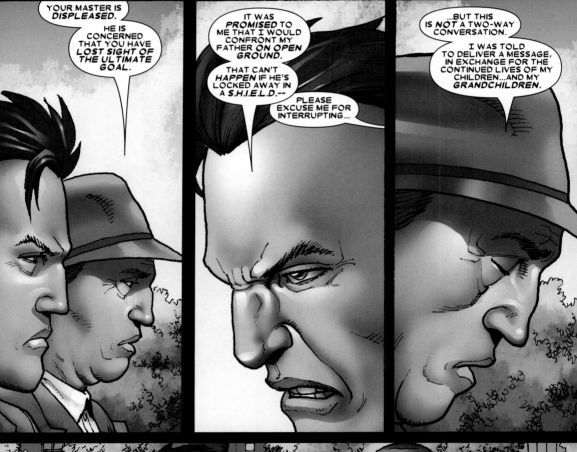

YOUR MASTER IS *DISPLEASED.*

HE IS CONCERNED THAT YOU HAVE *LOST SIGHT OF THE ULTIMATE GOAL.*

IT WAS *PROMISED* TO ME THAT I WOULD CONFRONT MY FATHER ON *OPEN GROUND.*

THAT CAN'T *HAPPEN* IF HE'S LOCKED AWAY IN A *S.H.I.E.L.D.*--

PLEASE EXCUSE ME FOR INTERRUPTING...

...BUT THIS IS *NOT* A TWO-WAY CONVERSATION.

I WAS TOLD TO DELIVER A MESSAGE, IN EXCHANGE FOR THE CONTINUED LIVES OF MY CHILDREN...AND MY *GRANDCHILDREN.*

WELL, NOW YOU'RE GOING TO DELIVER *ANOTHER* MESSAGE...

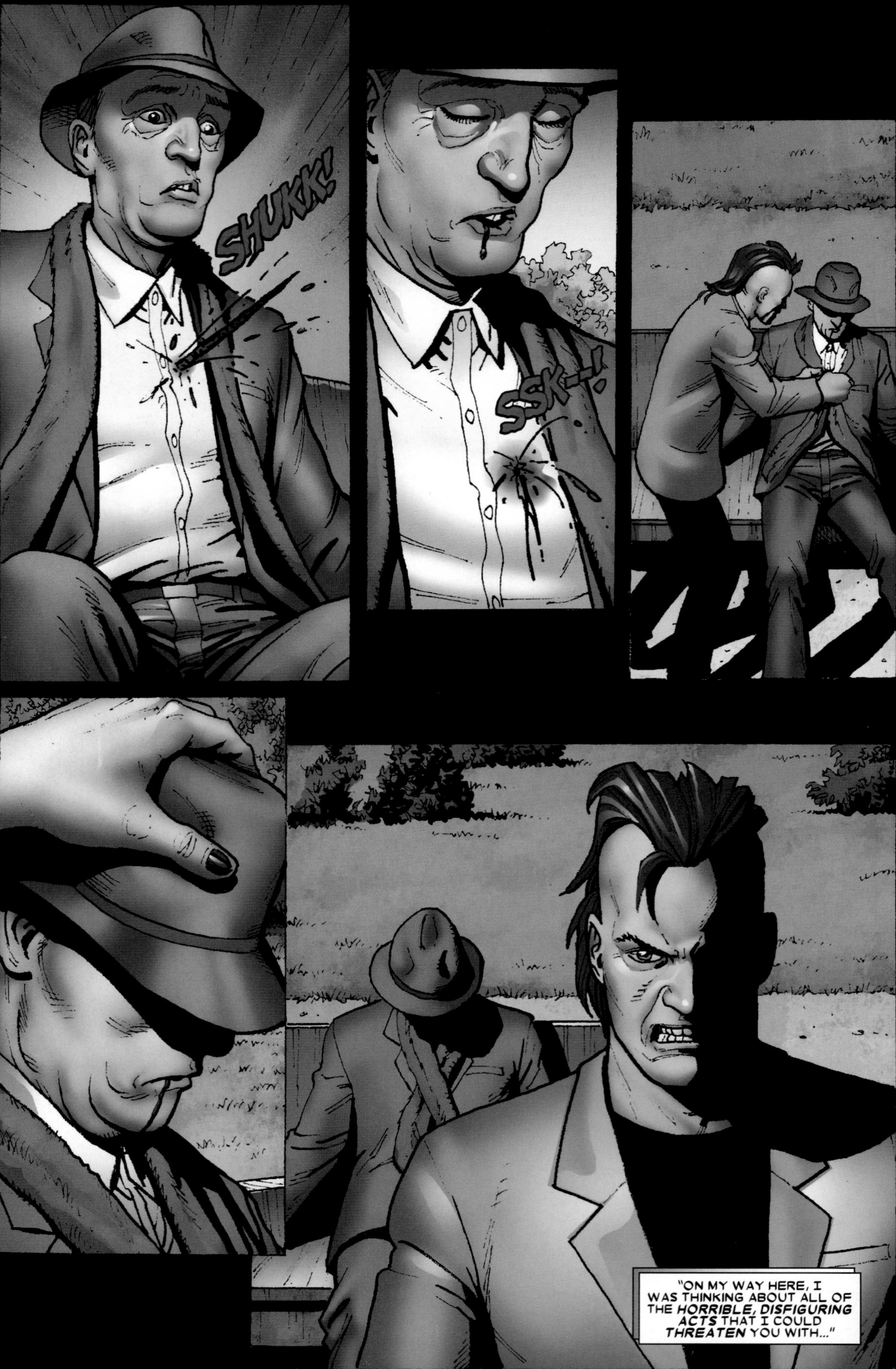
SHUKK!
SSK--!
"ON MY WAY HERE, I WAS THINKING ABOUT ALL OF THE HORRIBLE, DISFIGURING ACTS THAT I COULD THREATEN YOU WITH..."

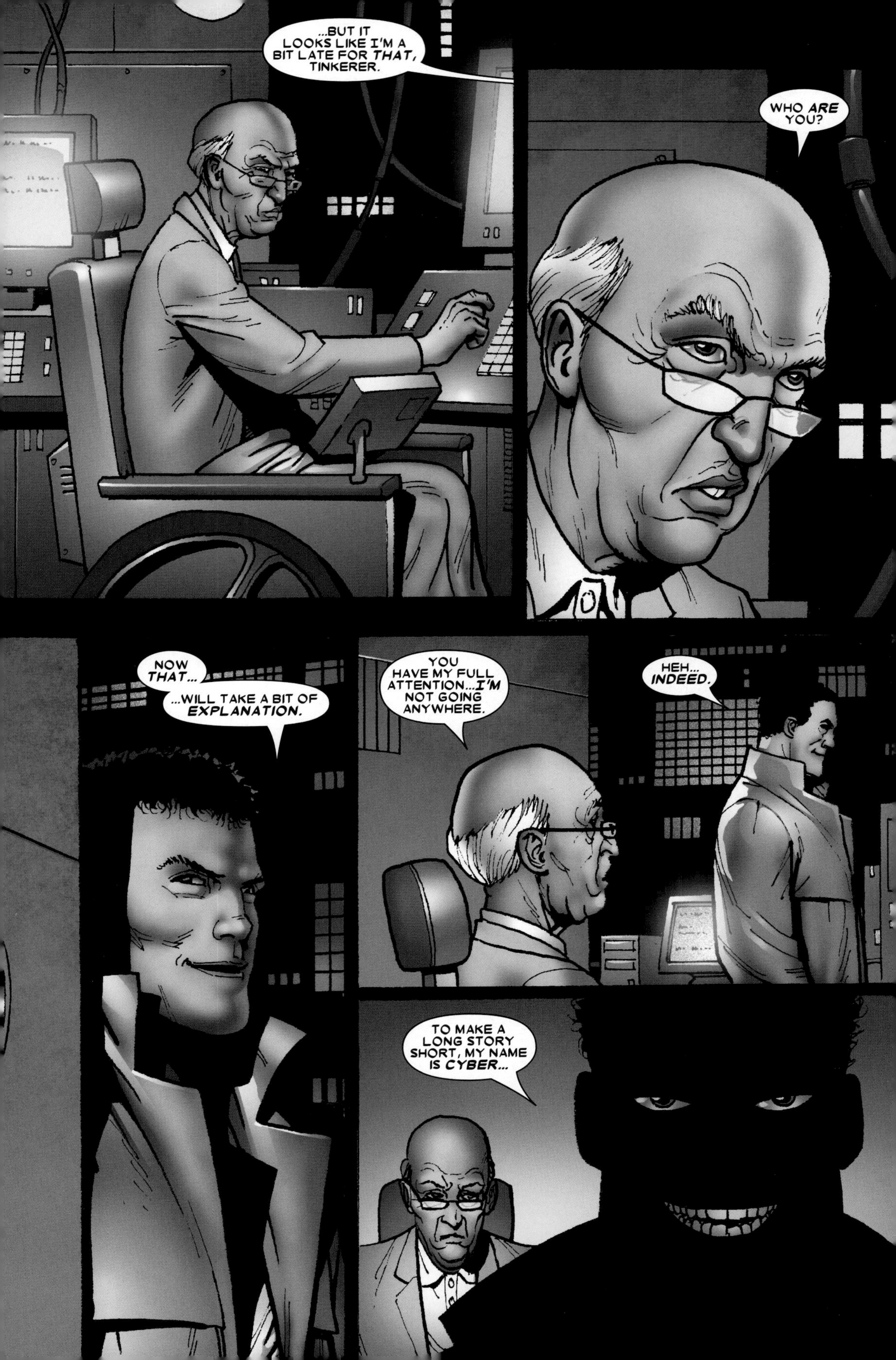
...BUT IT LOOKS LIKE I'M A BIT LATE FOR THAT, TINKERER.
WHO ARE YOU?
NOW THAT...
...WILL TAKE A BIT OF EXPLANATION.
YOU HAVE MY FULL ATTENTION...I'M NOT GOING ANYWHERE.
HEH... INDEED.
TO MAKE A LONG STORY SHORT, MY NAME IS CYBER...

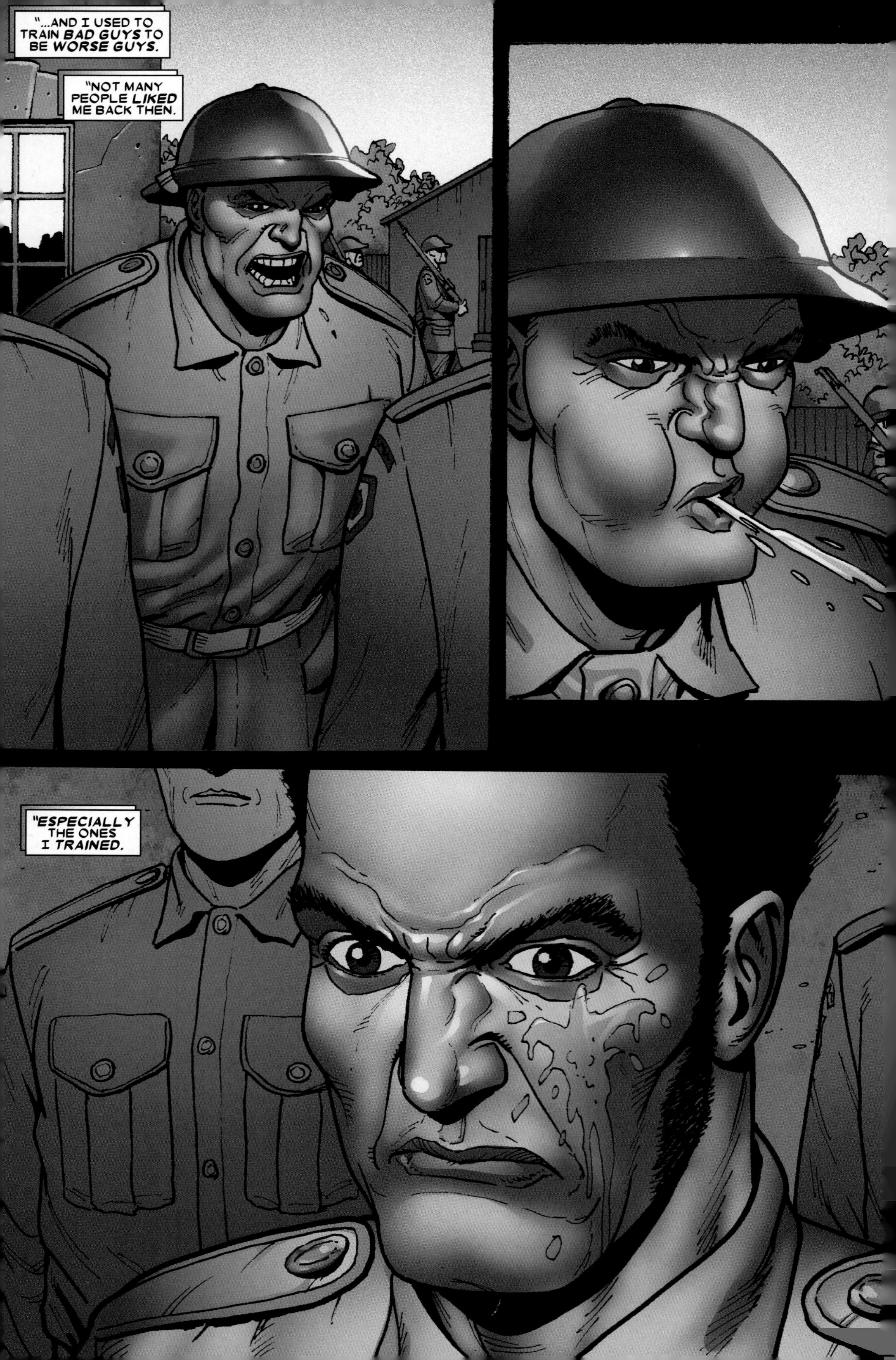
"...AND I USED TO TRAIN BAD GUYS TO BE WORSE GUYS.
"NOT MANY PEOPLE LIKED ME BACK THEN.
"ESPECIALLY THE ONES I TRAINED.

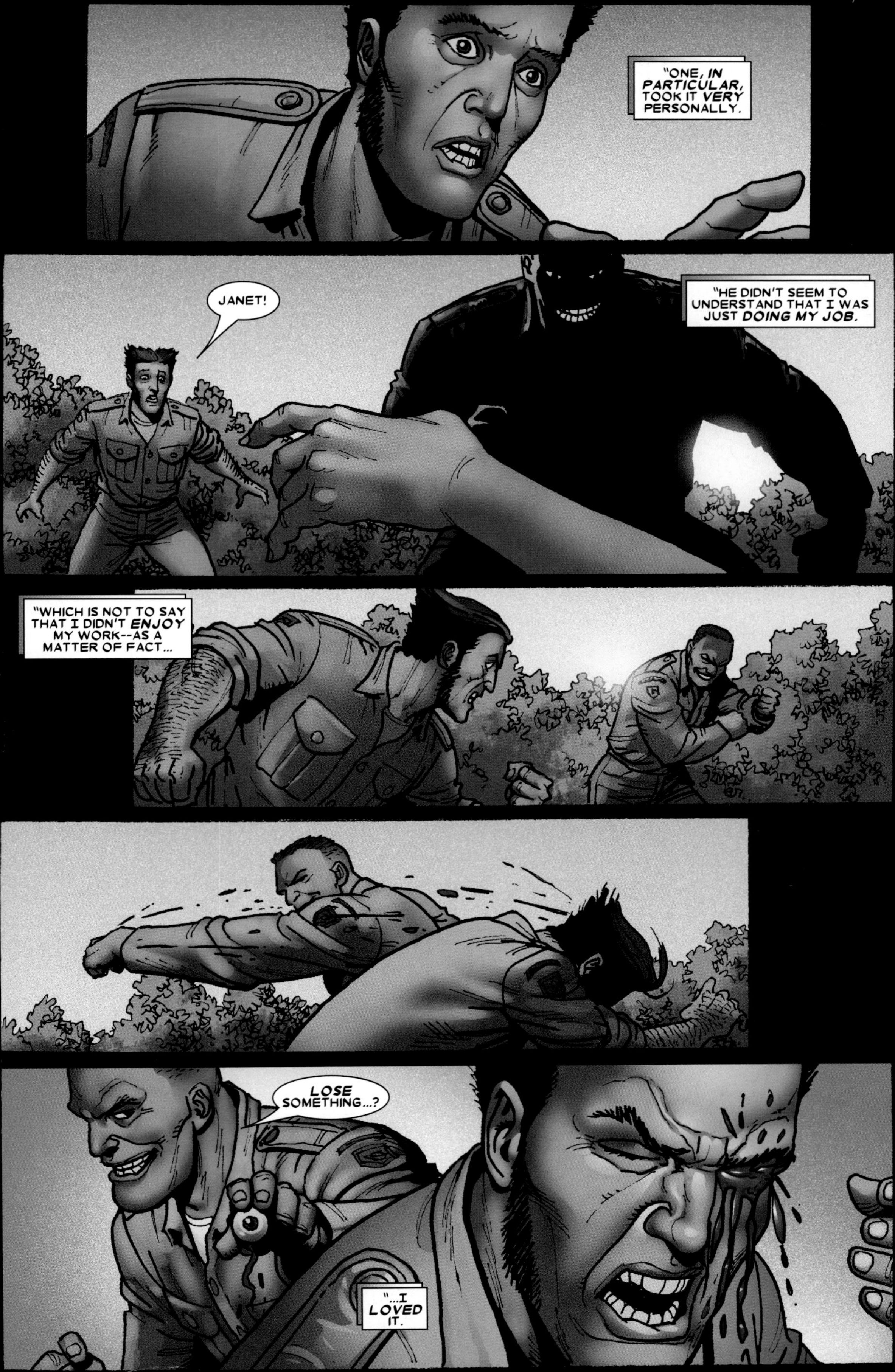
"ONE, IN PARTICULAR, TOOK IT VERY PERSONALLY.
JANET!
"HE DIDN'T SEEM TO UNDERSTAND THAT I WAS JUST DOING MY JOB.
"WHICH IS NOT TO SAY THAT I DIDN'T ENJOY MY WORK--AS A MATTER OF FACT...
LOSE SOMETHING...?
"...I LOVED IT.

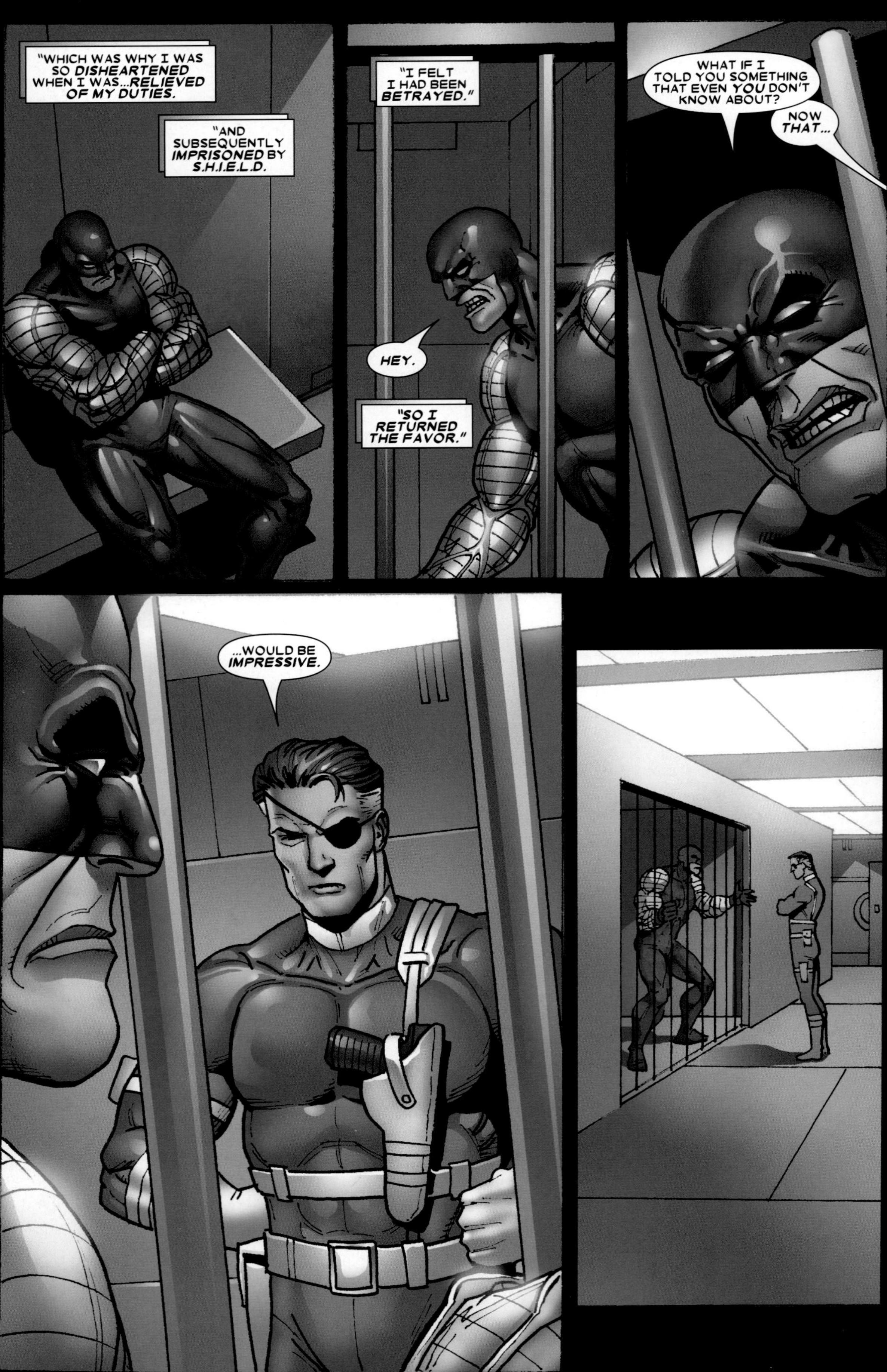
"WHICH WAS WHY I WAS SO DISHEARTENED WHEN I WAS...RELIEVED OF MY DUTIES.
"AND SUBSEQUENTLY IMPRISONED BY S.H.I.E.L.D.
"I FELT I HAD BEEN BETRAYED."
HEY.
"SO I RETURNED THE FAVOR."
WHAT IF I TOLD YOU SOMETHING THAT EVEN YOU DON'T KNOW ABOUT?
NOW THAT...
...WOULD BE IMPRESSIVE.

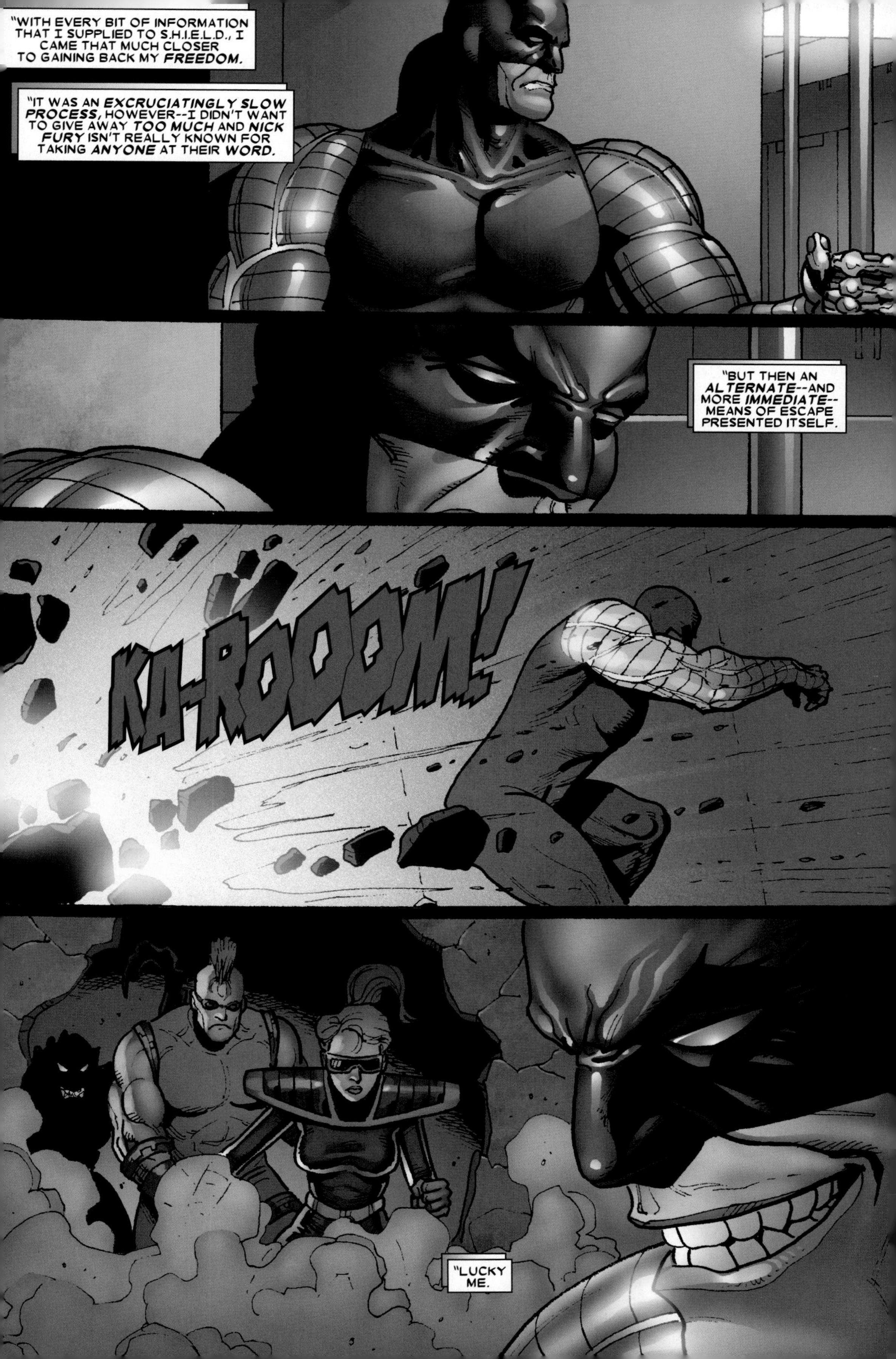
"WITH EVERY BIT OF INFORMATION THAT I SUPPLIED TO S.H.I.E.L.D., I CAME THAT MUCH CLOSER TO GAINING BACK MY FREEDOM.
"IT WAS AN EXCRUCIATINGLY SLOW PROCESS, HOWEVER--I DIDN'T WANT TO GIVE AWAY TOO MUCH AND NICK FURY ISN'T REALLY KNOWN FOR TAKING ANYONE AT THEIR WORD.
"BUT THEN AN ALTERNATE--AND MORE IMMEDIATE--MEANS OF ESCAPE PRESENTED ITSELF.
KA-ROOOM!
"LUCKY ME.

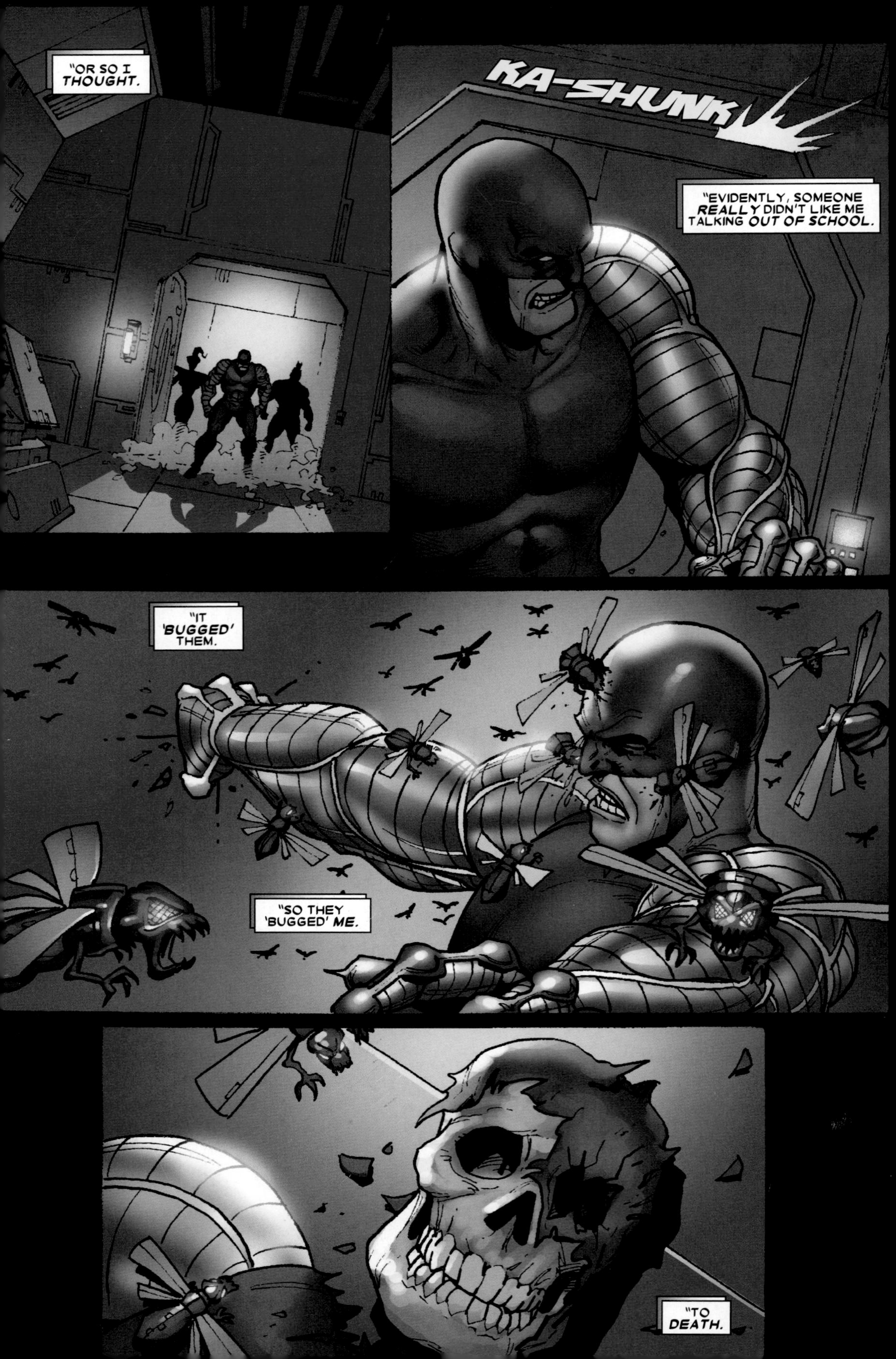
"OR SO I THOUGHT.
KA-SHUNK
"EVIDENTLY, SOMEONE REALLY DIDN'T LIKE ME TALKING OUT OF SCHOOL.
"IT 'BUGGED' THEM.
"SO THEY 'BUGGED' ME.
"TO DEATH.

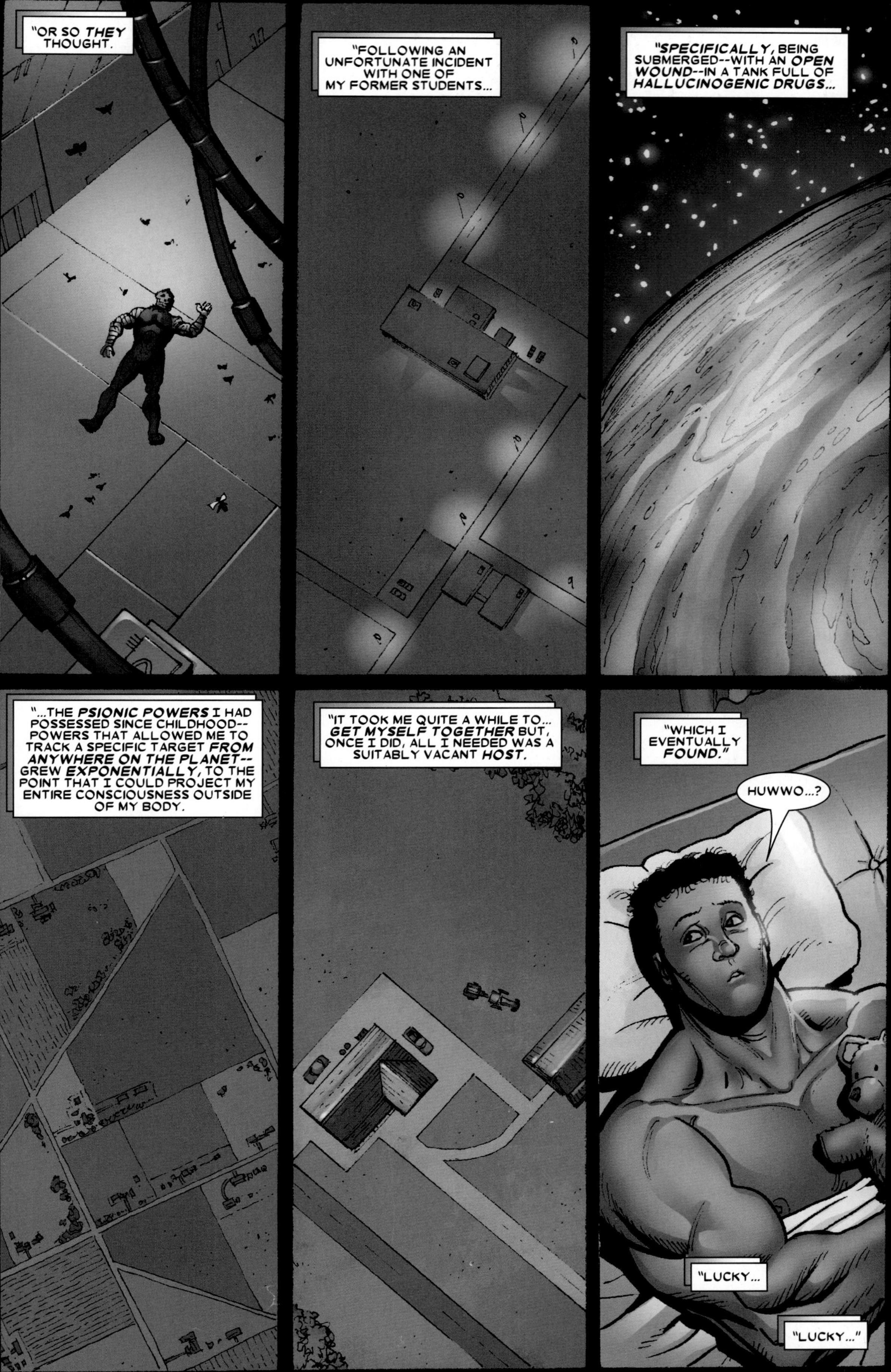
"OR SO *THEY* THOUGHT.
"FOLLOWING AN UNFORTUNATE INCIDENT WITH ONE OF MY FORMER STUDENTS...
"*SPECIFICALLY*, BEING SUBMERGED--WITH AN *OPEN WOUND*--IN A TANK FULL OF *HALLUCINOGENIC DRUGS*...
"...THE *PSIONIC POWERS* I HAD POSSESSED SINCE CHILDHOOD--POWERS THAT ALLOWED ME TO TRACK A SPECIFIC TARGET *FROM ANYWHERE ON THE PLANET*--GREW *EXPONENTIALLY*, TO THE POINT THAT I COULD PROJECT MY ENTIRE CONSCIOUSNESS OUTSIDE OF MY BODY.
"IT TOOK ME QUITE A WHILE TO... *GET MYSELF TOGETHER* BUT, ONCE I DID, ALL I NEEDED WAS A SUITABLY VACANT *HOST*.
"WHICH I EVENTUALLY *FOUND*."
HUWWO...?
"LUCKY...
"LUCKY..."

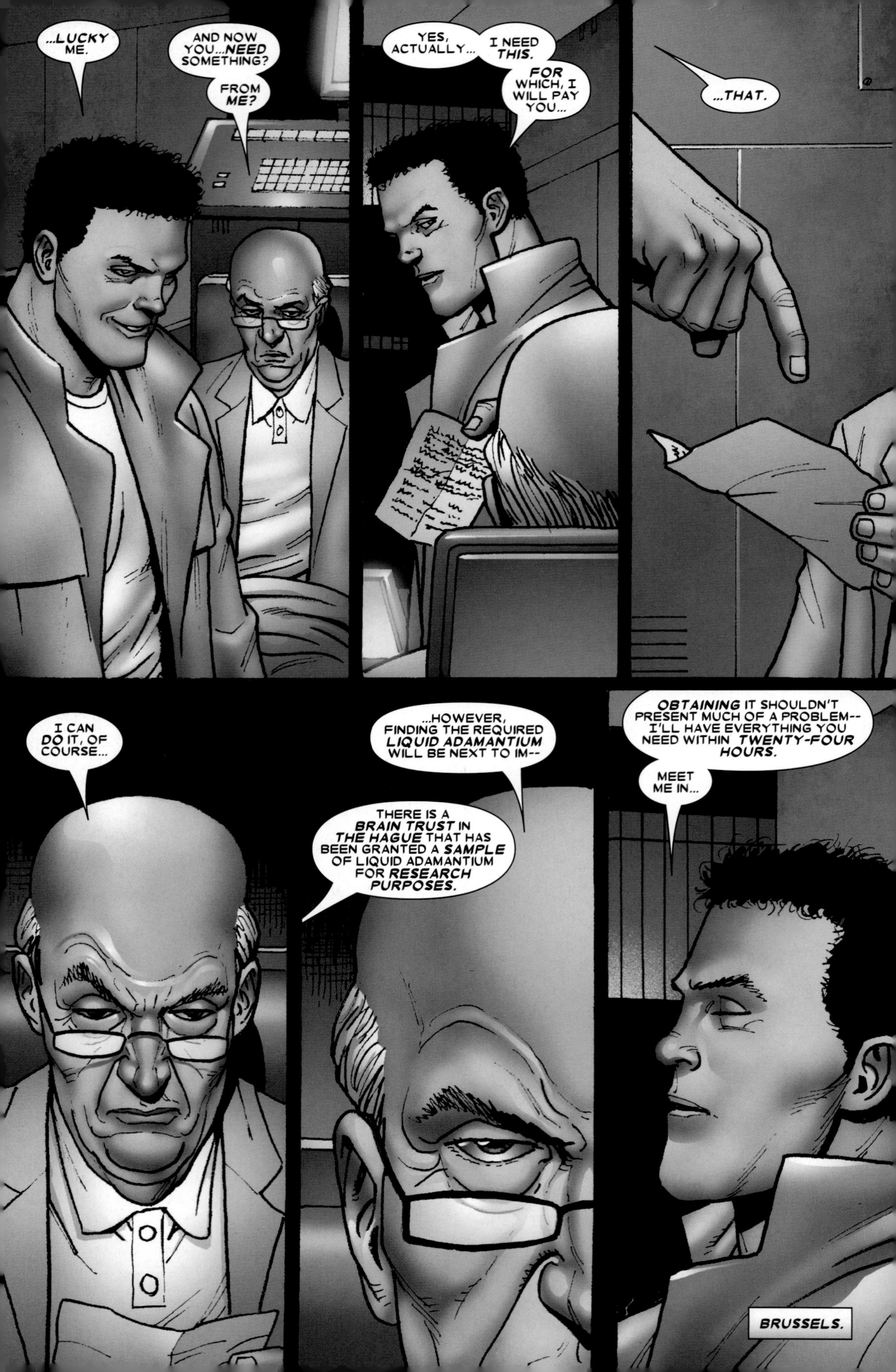
...LUCKY ME.
AND NOW YOU...NEED SOMETHING?
FROM ME?
YES, ACTUALLY...
I NEED THIS.
FOR WHICH, I WILL PAY YOU...
...THAT.
I CAN DO IT, OF COURSE...
...HOWEVER, FINDING THE REQUIRED LIQUID ADAMANTIUM WILL BE NEXT TO IM--
THERE IS A BRAIN TRUST IN THE HAGUE THAT HAS BEEN GRANTED A SAMPLE OF LIQUID ADAMANTIUM FOR RESEARCH PURPOSES.
OBTAINING IT SHOULDN'T PRESENT MUCH OF A PROBLEM-- I'LL HAVE EVERYTHING YOU NEED WITHIN TWENTY-FOUR HOURS.
MEET ME IN...
BRUSSELS.

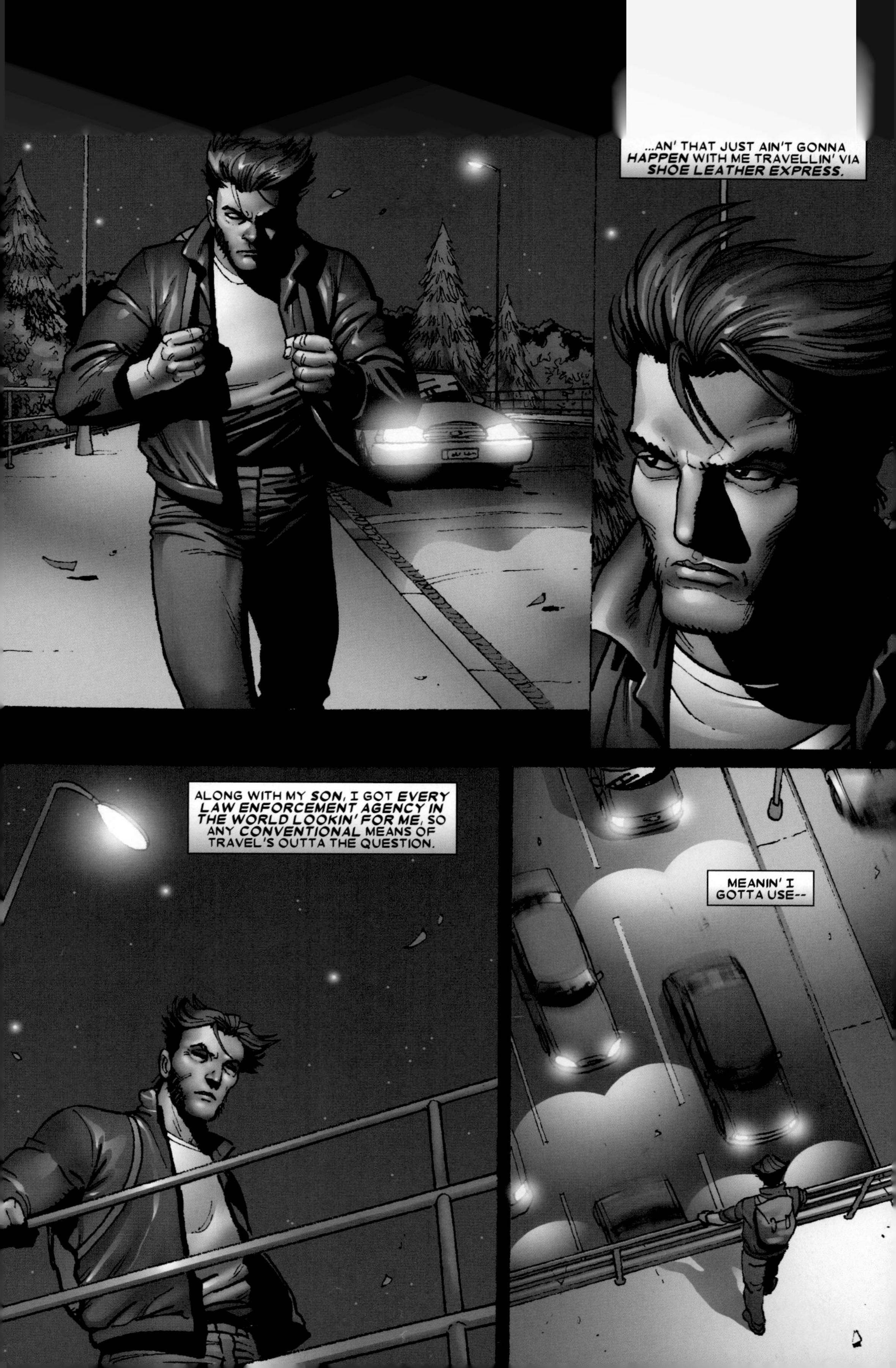
...AN' THAT JUST AIN'T GONNA HAPPEN WITH ME TRAVELLIN' VIA SHOE LEATHER EXPRESS.
ALONG WITH MY SON, I GOT EVERY LAW ENFORCEMENT AGENCY IN THE WORLD LOOKIN' FOR ME, SO ANY CONVENTIONAL MEANS OF TRAVEL'S OUTTA THE QUESTION.
MEANIN' I GOTTA USE--

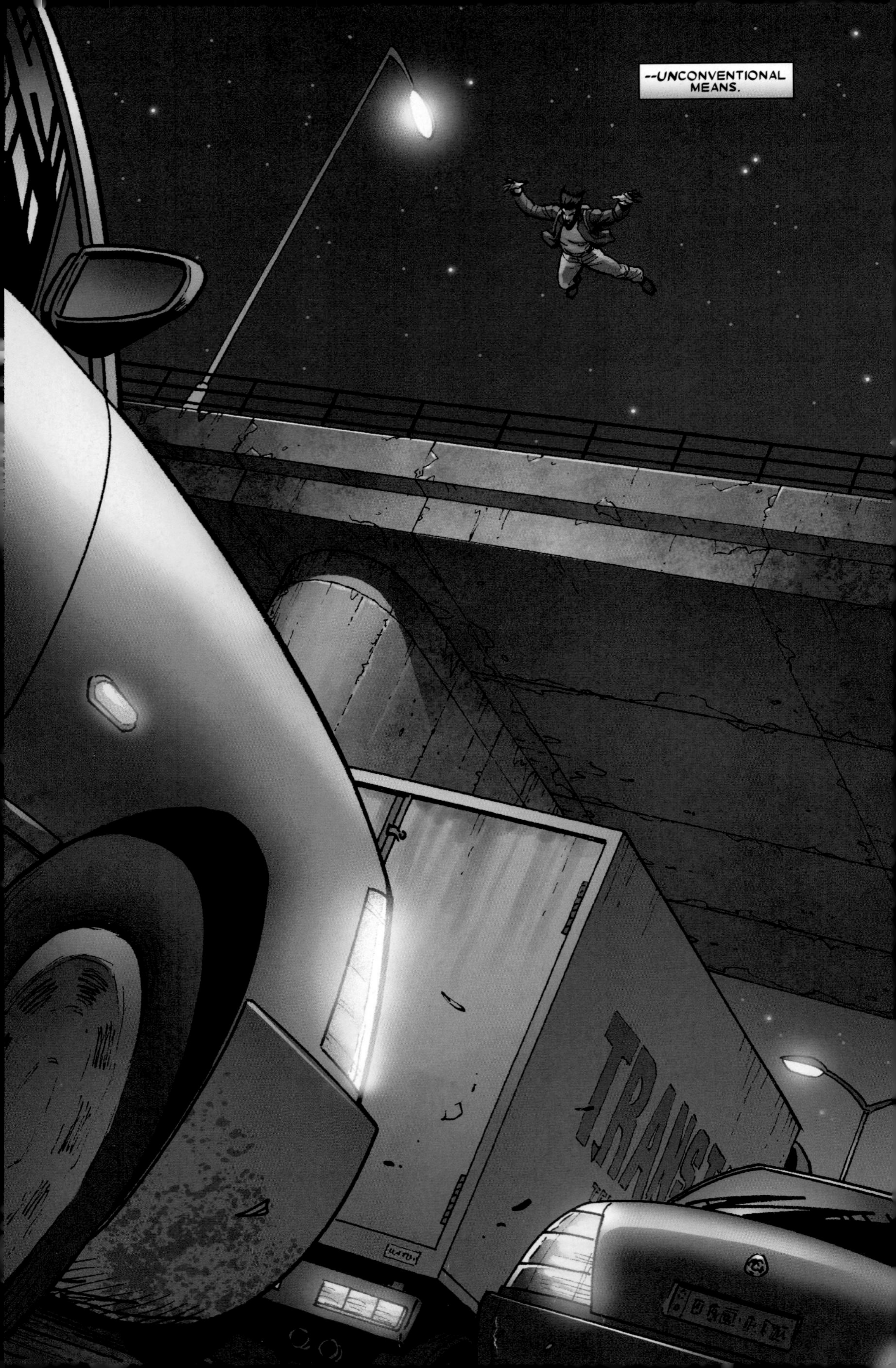
--UNCONVENTIONAL MEANS.

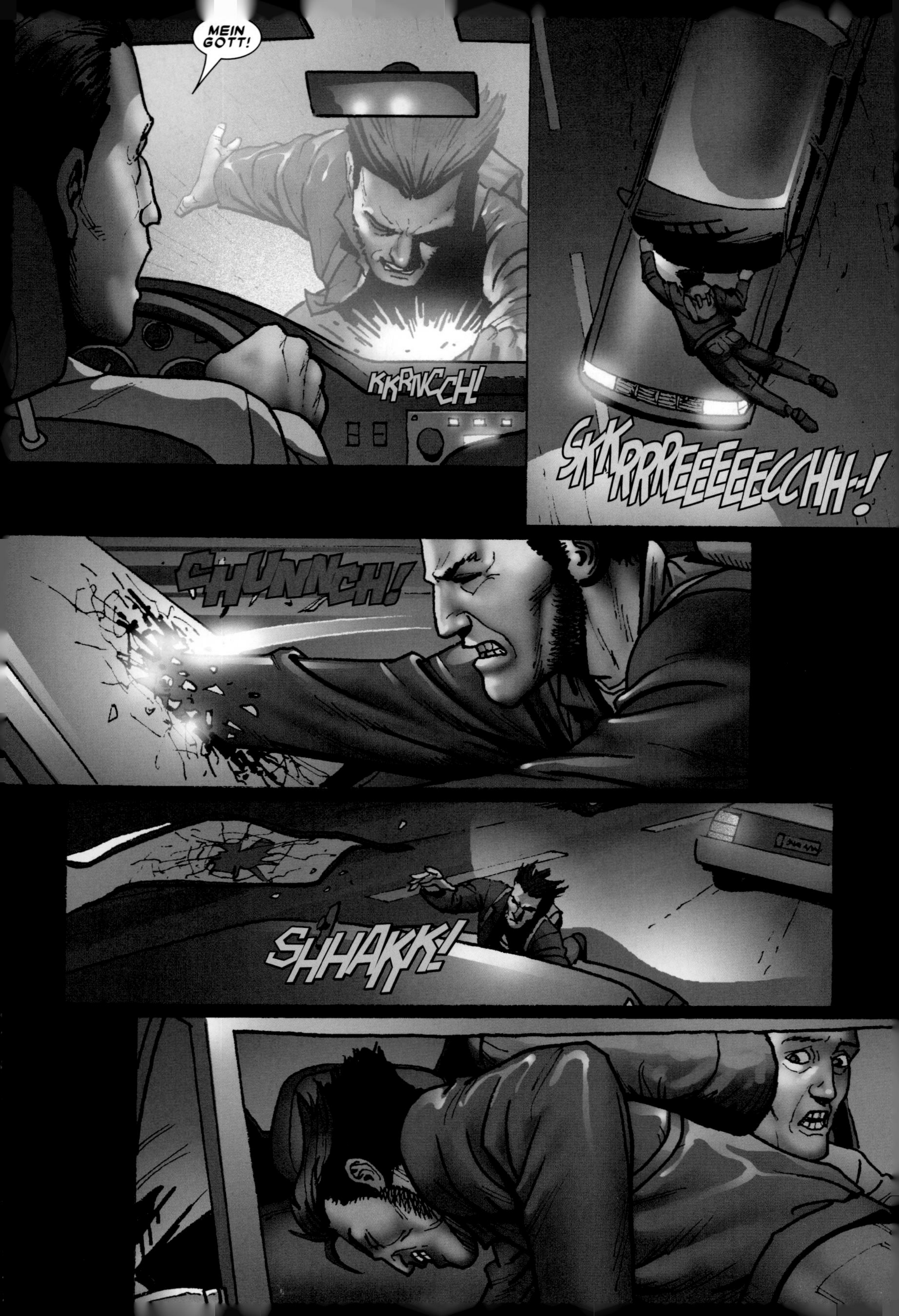
MEIN GOTT!
KKRNCCH!
SKKRRREEEEEECCHH--!
CHUNNCH!
SHHAKK!

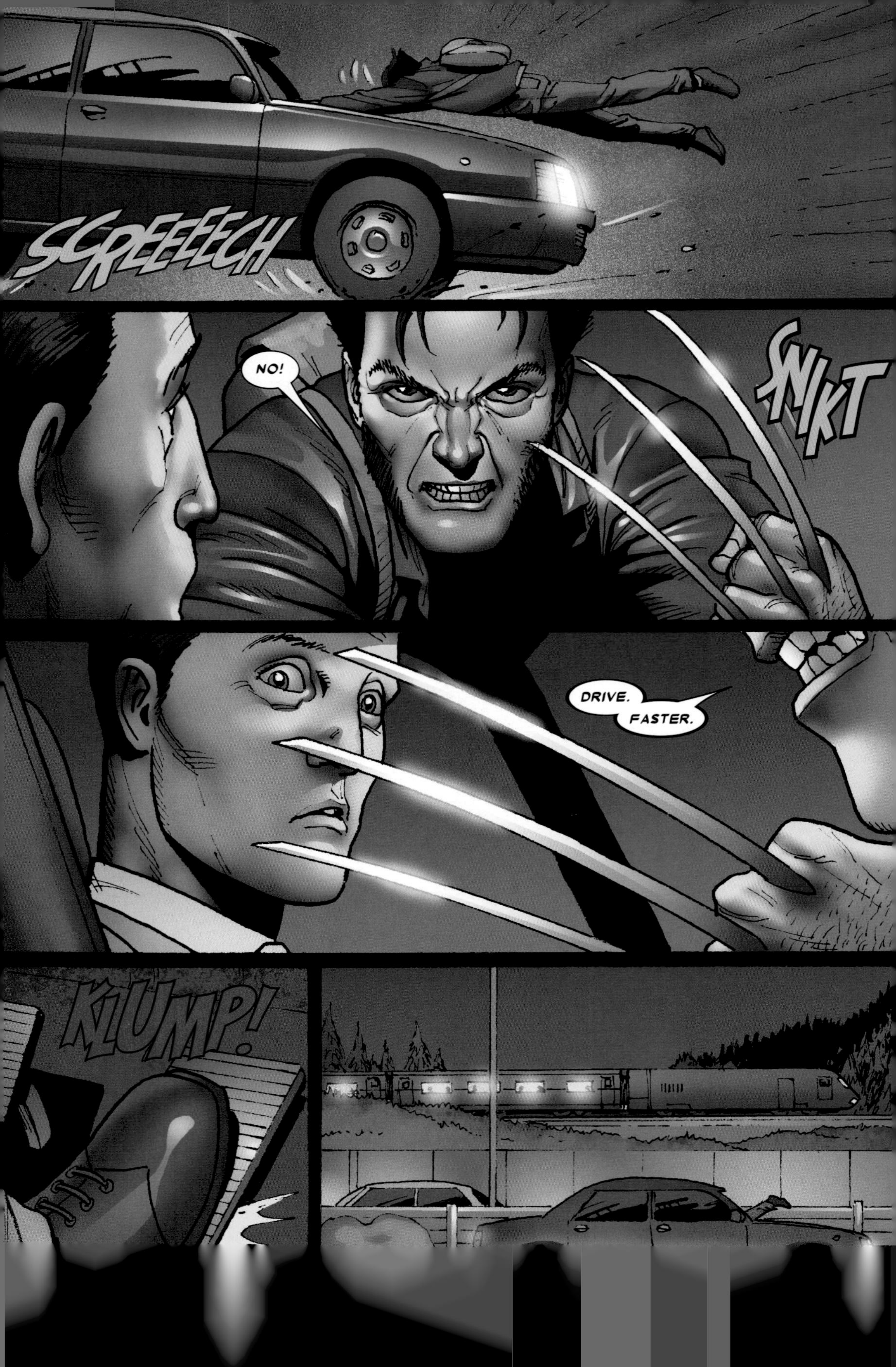
SCREEEEECH
NO!
SNIKT
DRIVE. FASTER.
KLUMP!

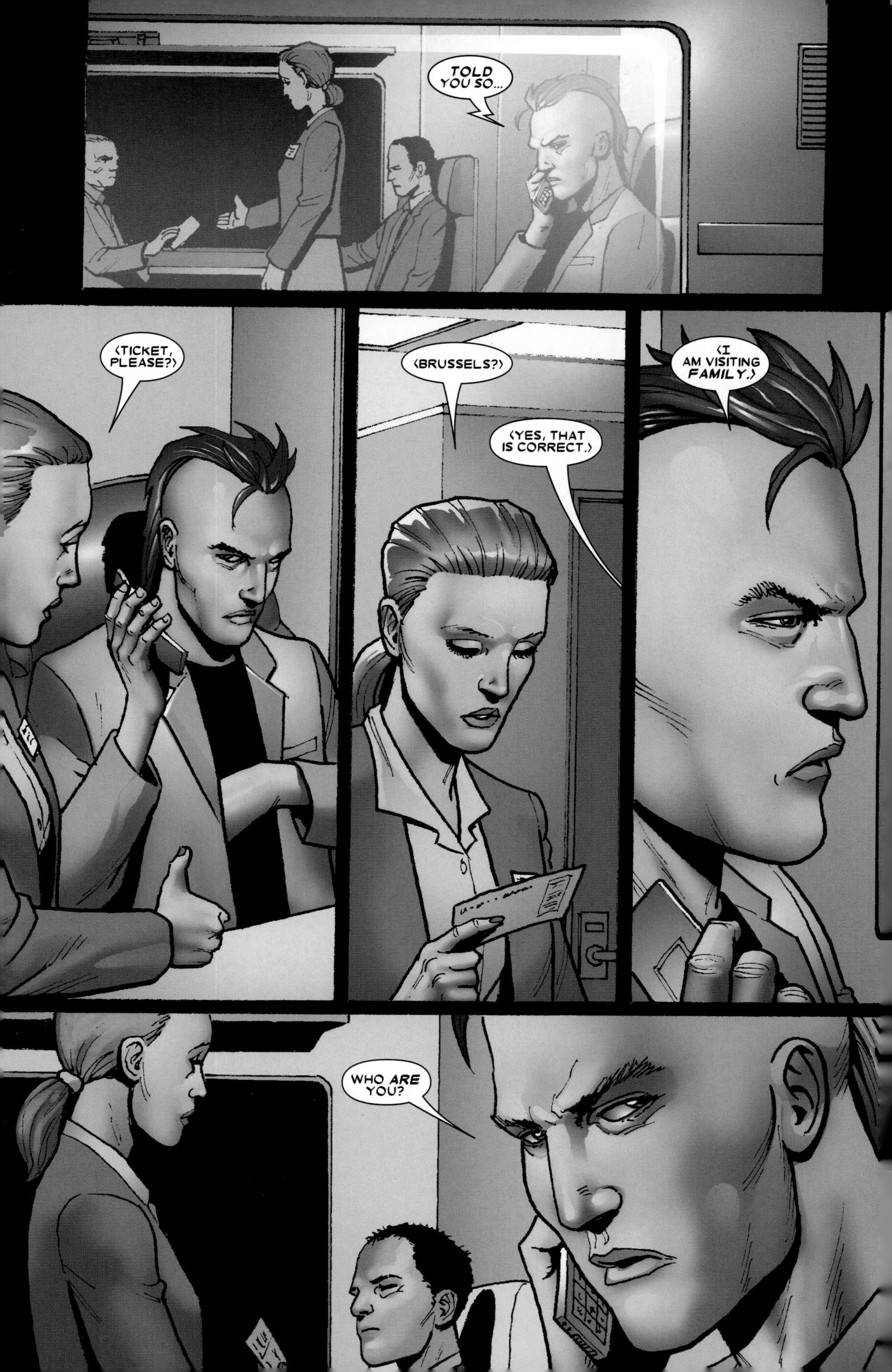
TOLD YOU SO...
‹TICKET, PLEASE?›
‹BRUSSELS?›
‹YES, THAT IS CORRECT.›
‹I AM VISITING FAMILY.›
WHO ARE YOU?

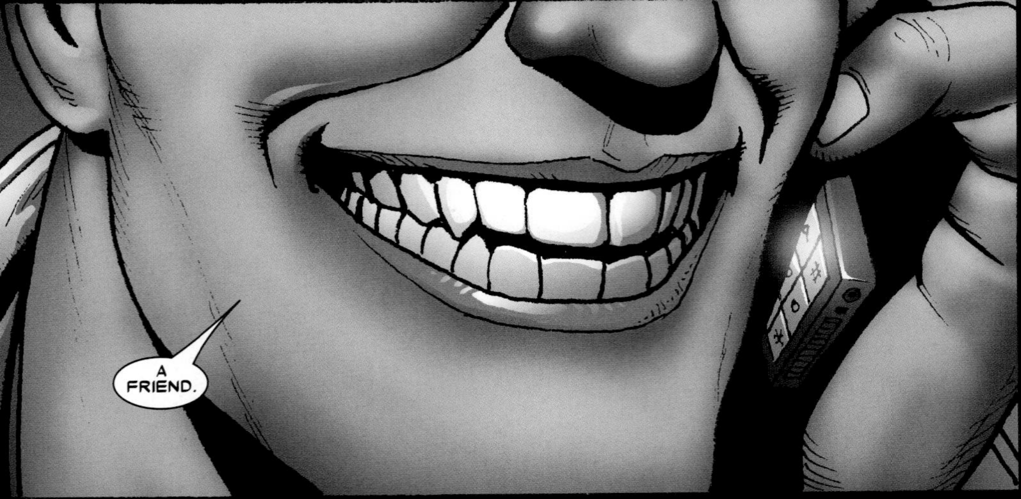
A FRIEND.

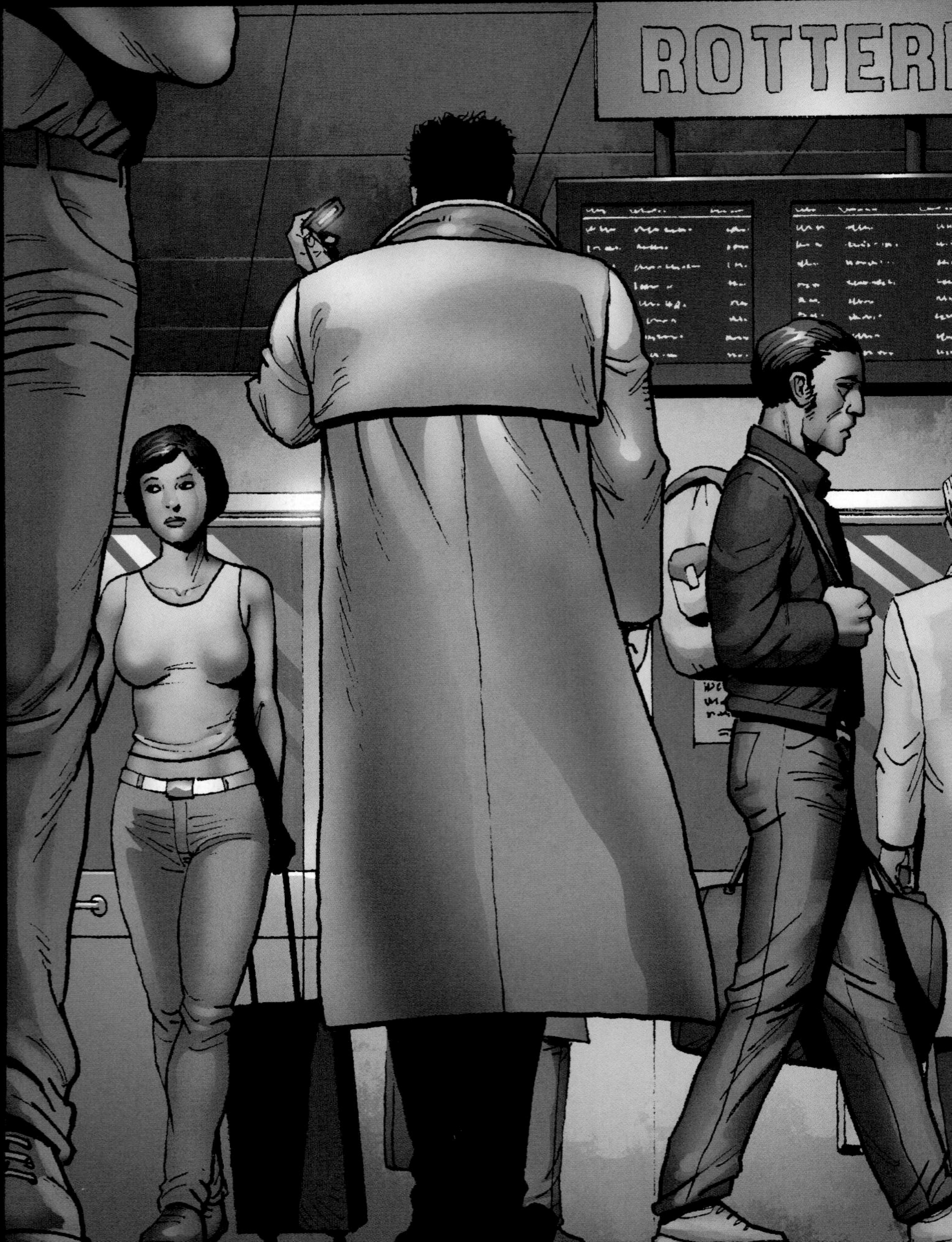
ROTTER

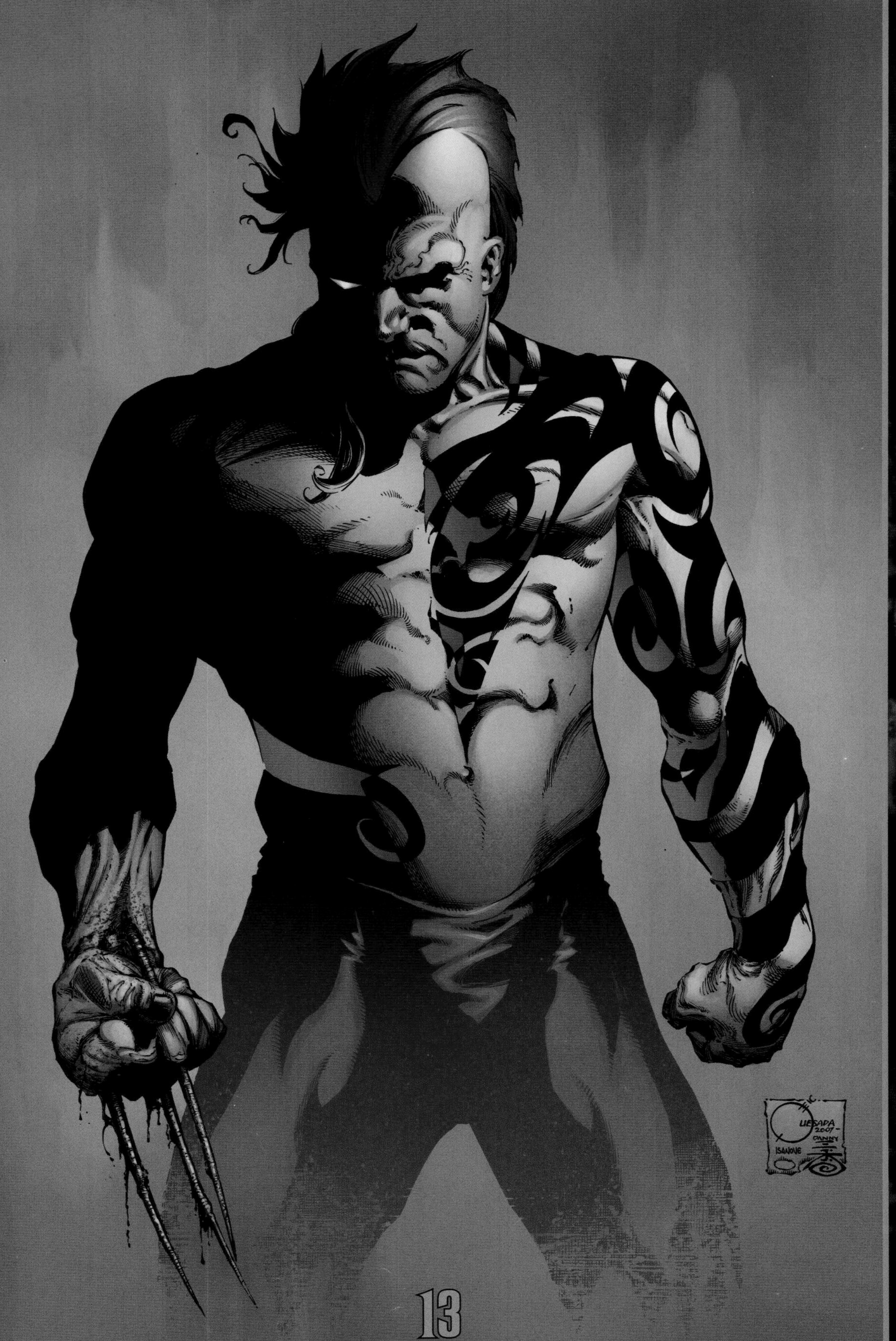
13

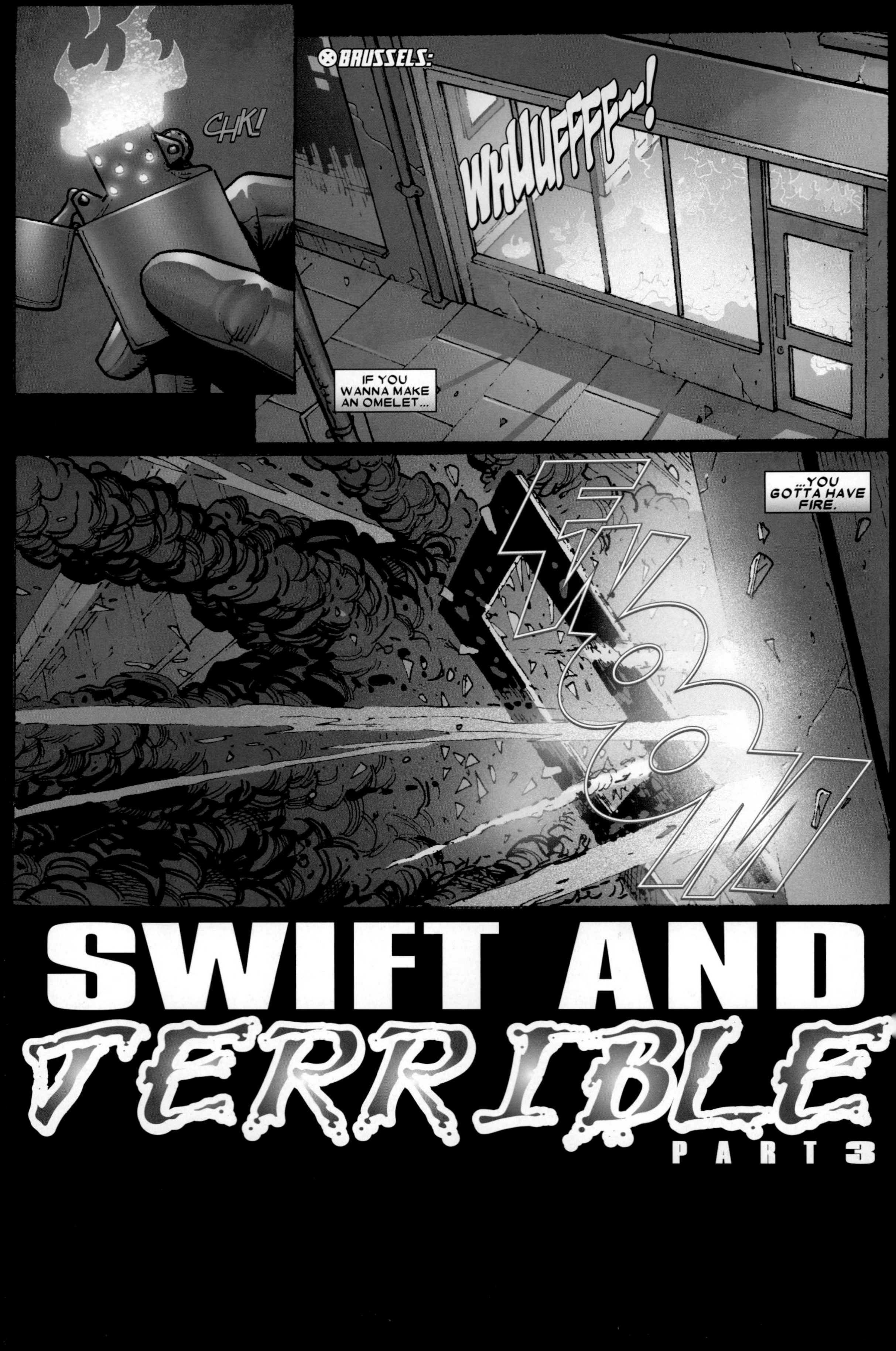
CHK!
BRUSSELS:
WHUUFFFF--!
IF YOU WANNA MAKE AN OMELET...
...YOU GOTTA HAVE FIRE.

SWIFT AND TERRIBLE
PART 3

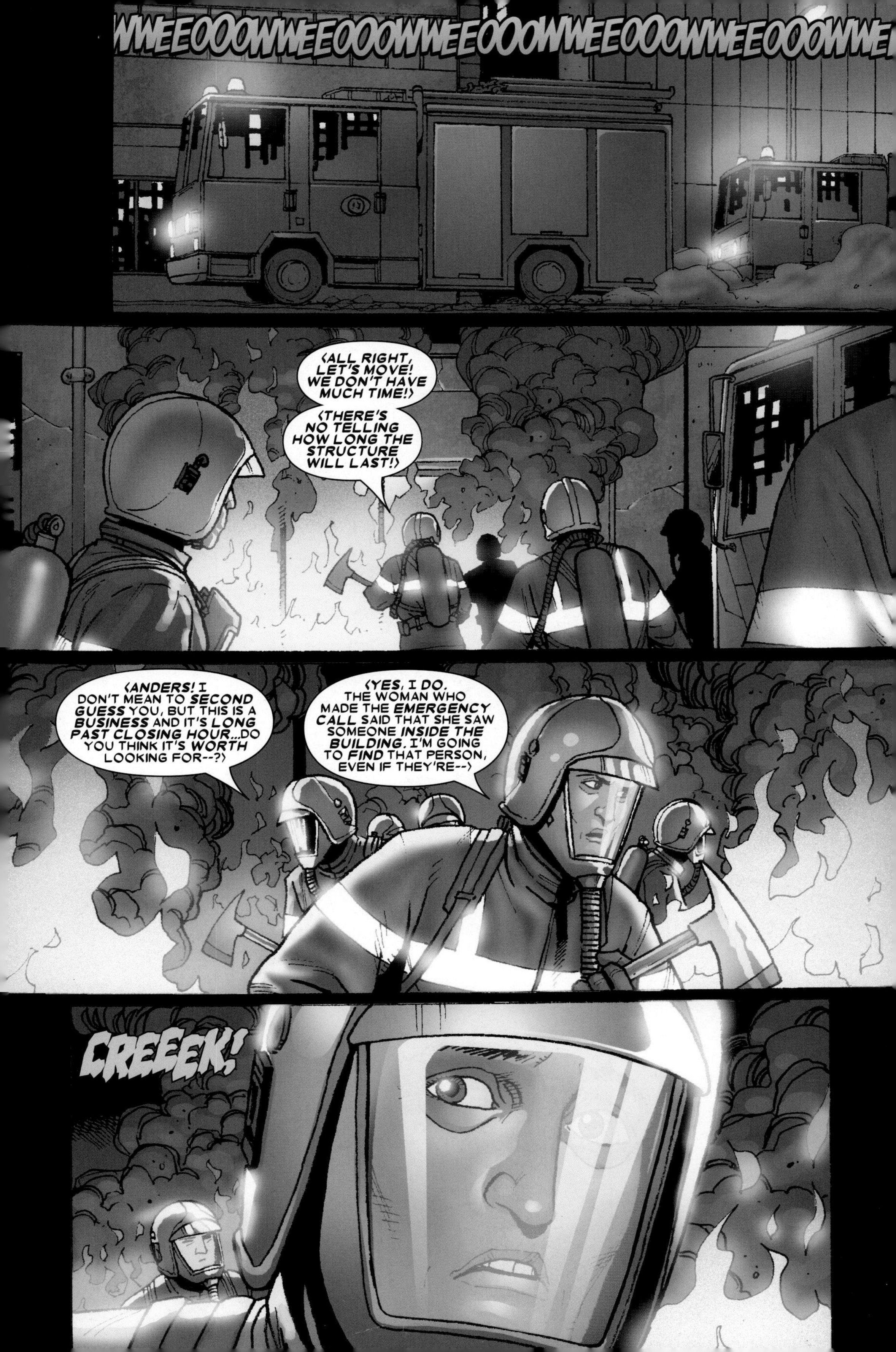
WWEEOOOWWEEOOOWWEEOOOWWEEOOOWWEEOOOWWE
‹ALL RIGHT, LET'S MOVE! WE DON'T HAVE MUCH TIME!›
‹THERE'S NO TELLING HOW LONG THE STRUCTURE WILL LAST!›
‹ANDERS! I DON'T MEAN TO SECOND GUESS YOU, BUT THIS IS A BUSINESS AND IT'S LONG PAST CLOSING HOUR...DO YOU THINK IT'S WORTH LOOKING FOR--?›
‹YES, I DO. THE WOMAN WHO MADE THE EMERGENCY CALL SAID THAT SHE SAW SOMEONE INSIDE THE BUILDING. I'M GOING TO FIND THAT PERSON, EVEN IF THEY'RE--›
CREEEK!

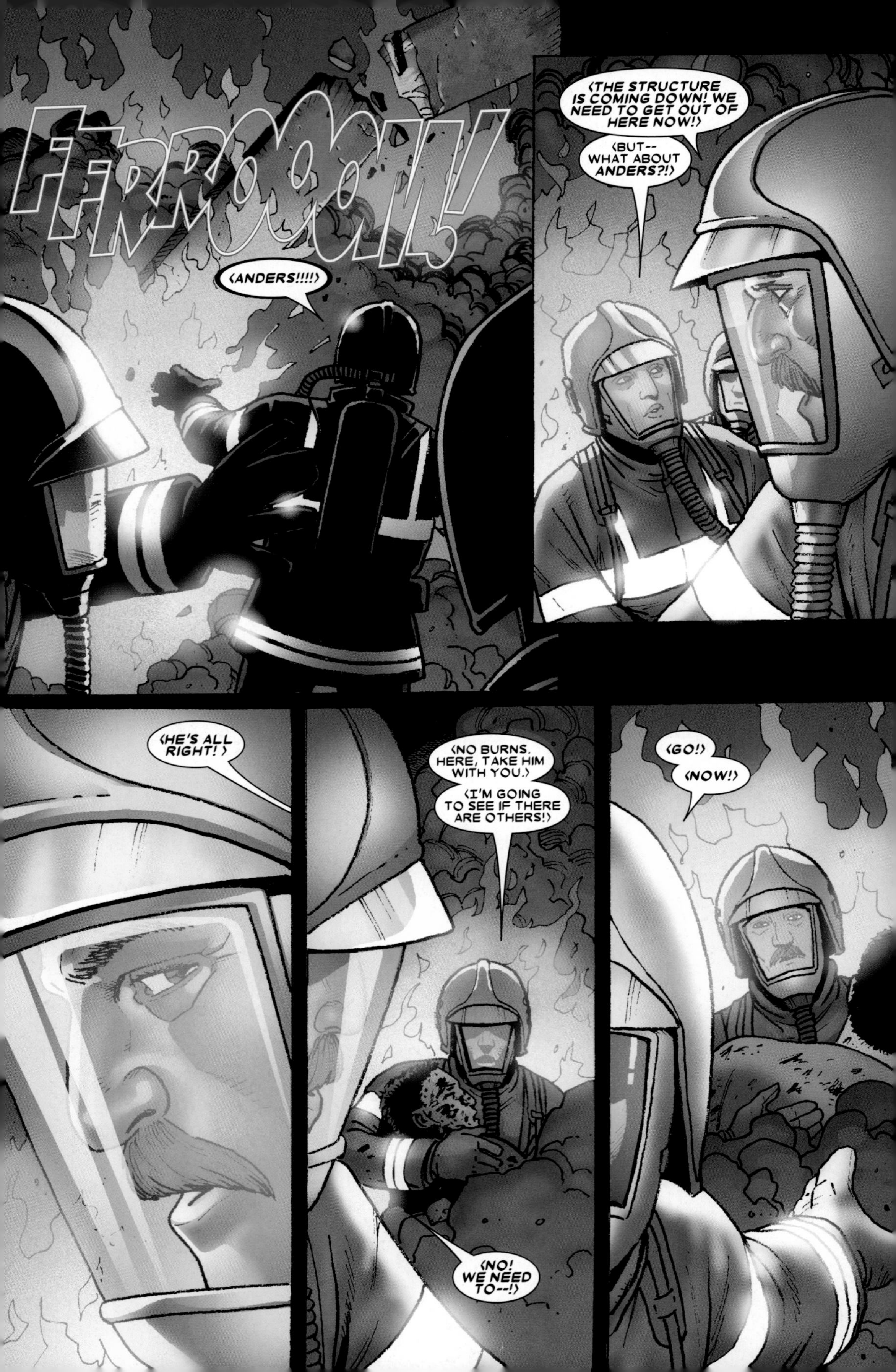
⟨ANDERS!!!!⟩
⟨THE STRUCTURE IS COMING DOWN! WE NEED TO GET OUT OF HERE NOW!⟩
⟨BUT-- WHAT ABOUT ANDERS?!⟩
⟨HE'S ALL RIGHT! ⟩
⟨NO BURNS. HERE, TAKE HIM WITH YOU.⟩
⟨I'M GOING TO SEE IF THERE ARE OTHERS!⟩
⟨NO! WE NEED TO--!⟩
⟨GO!⟩
⟨NOW!⟩

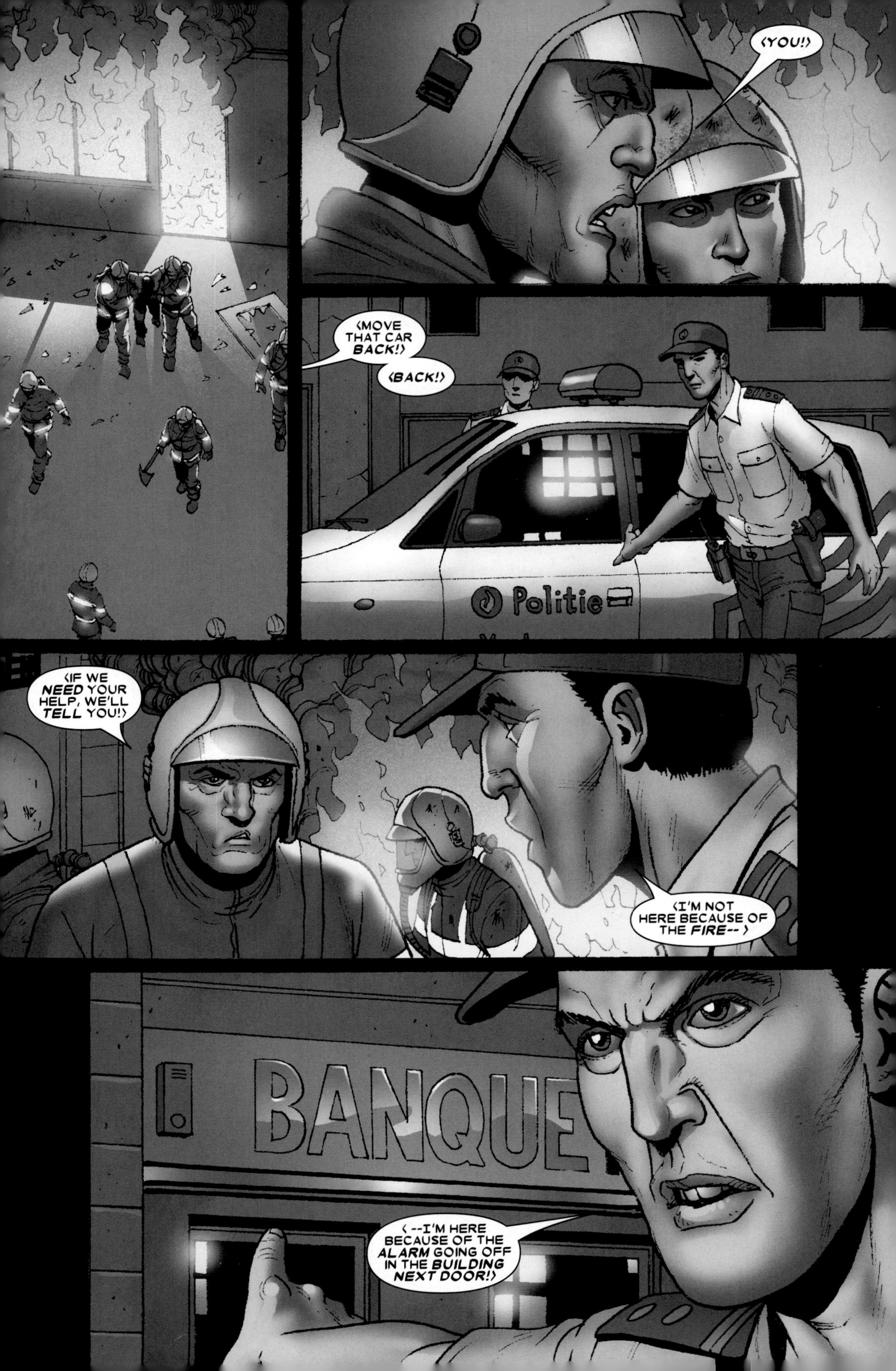
‹YOU!›
‹MOVE THAT CAR BACK!›
‹BACK!›
Politie
‹IF WE NEED YOUR HELP, WE'LL TELL YOU!›
‹I'M NOT HERE BECAUSE OF THE FIRE-- ›
BANQUE
‹ --I'M HERE BECAUSE OF THE ALARM GOING OFF IN THE BUILDING NEXT DOOR!›

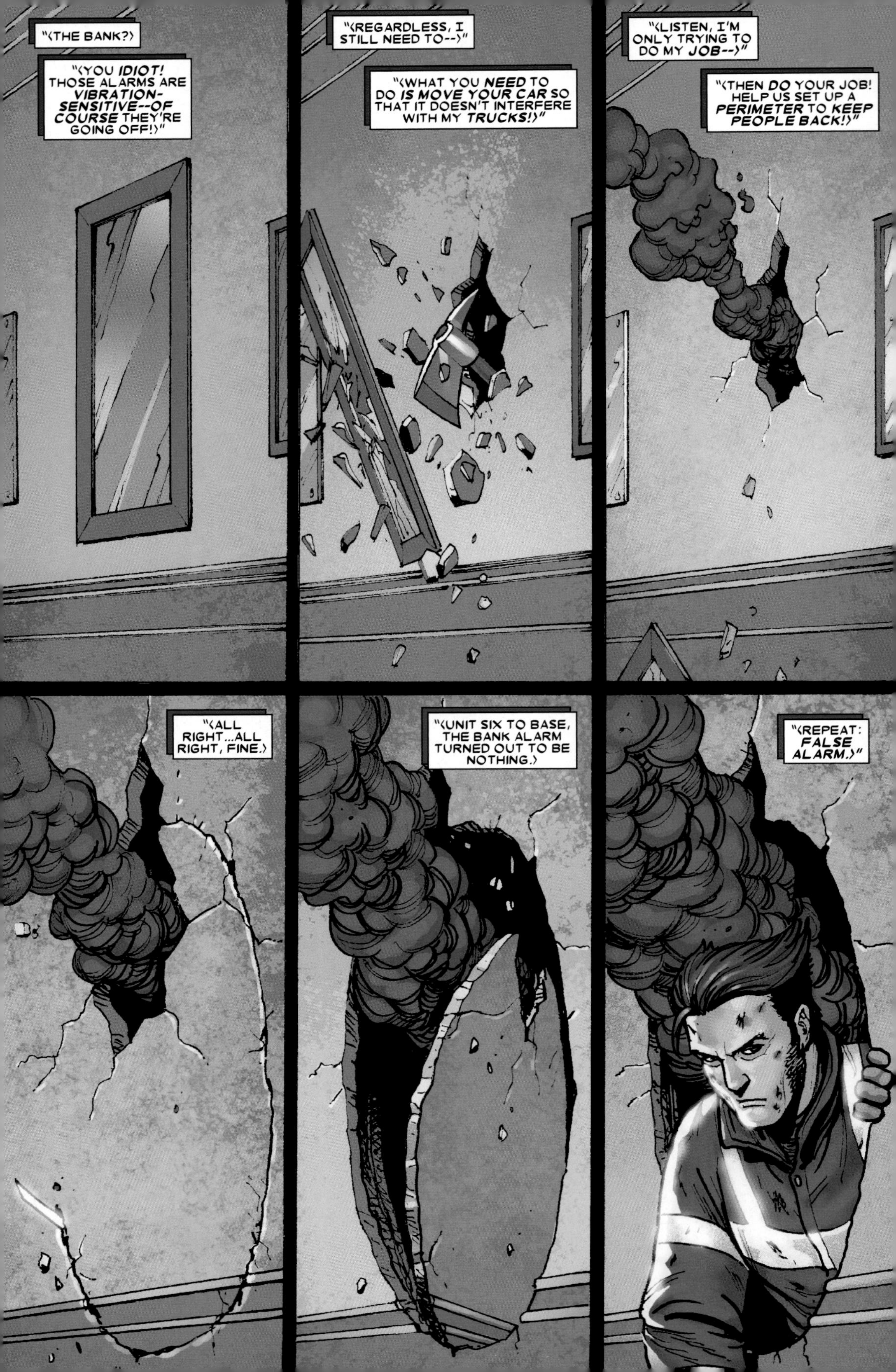
"‹THE BANK?›
"‹YOU IDIOT! THOSE ALARMS ARE VIBRATION-SENSITIVE--OF COURSE THEY'RE GOING OFF!›"
"‹REGARDLESS, I STILL NEED TO--›"
"‹WHAT YOU NEED TO DO IS MOVE YOUR CAR SO THAT IT DOESN'T INTERFERE WITH MY TRUCKS!›"
"‹LISTEN, I'M ONLY TRYING TO DO MY JOB--›"
"‹THEN DO YOUR JOB! HELP US SET UP A PERIMETER TO KEEP PEOPLE BACK!›"
"‹ALL RIGHT...ALL RIGHT, FINE.›
"‹UNIT SIX TO BASE, THE BANK ALARM TURNED OUT TO BE NOTHING.›
"‹REPEAT: FALSE ALARM.›"

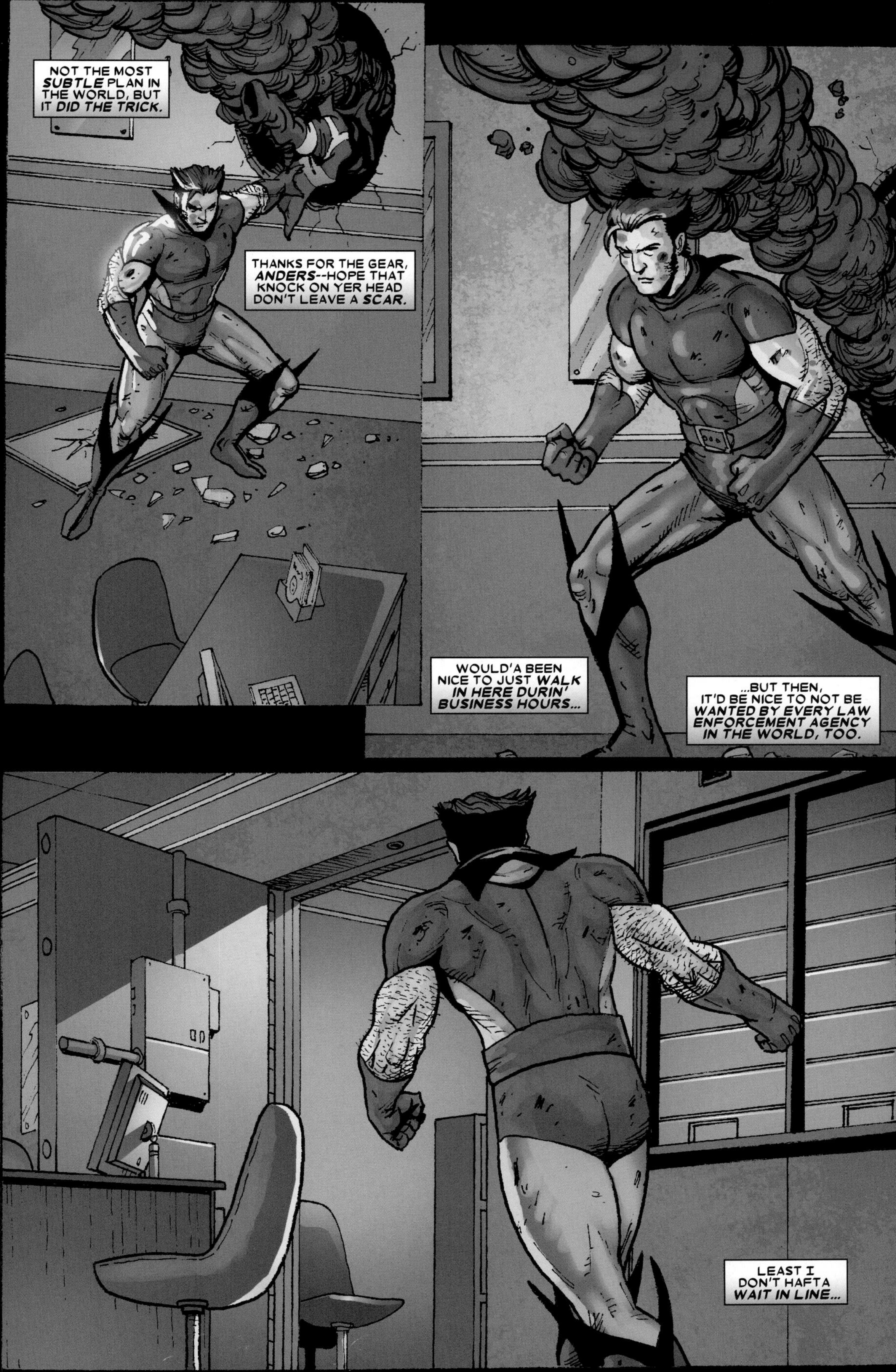

NOT THE MOST SUBTLE PLAN IN THE WORLD, BUT IT DID THE TRICK.
THANKS FOR THE GEAR, ANDERS--HOPE THAT KNOCK ON YER HEAD DON'T LEAVE A SCAR.
WOULD'A BEEN NICE TO JUST WALK IN HERE DURIN' BUSINESS HOURS...
...BUT THEN, IT'D BE NICE TO NOT BE WANTED BY EVERY LAW ENFORCEMENT AGENCY IN THE WORLD, TOO.
LEAST I DON'T HAFTA WAIT IN LINE...

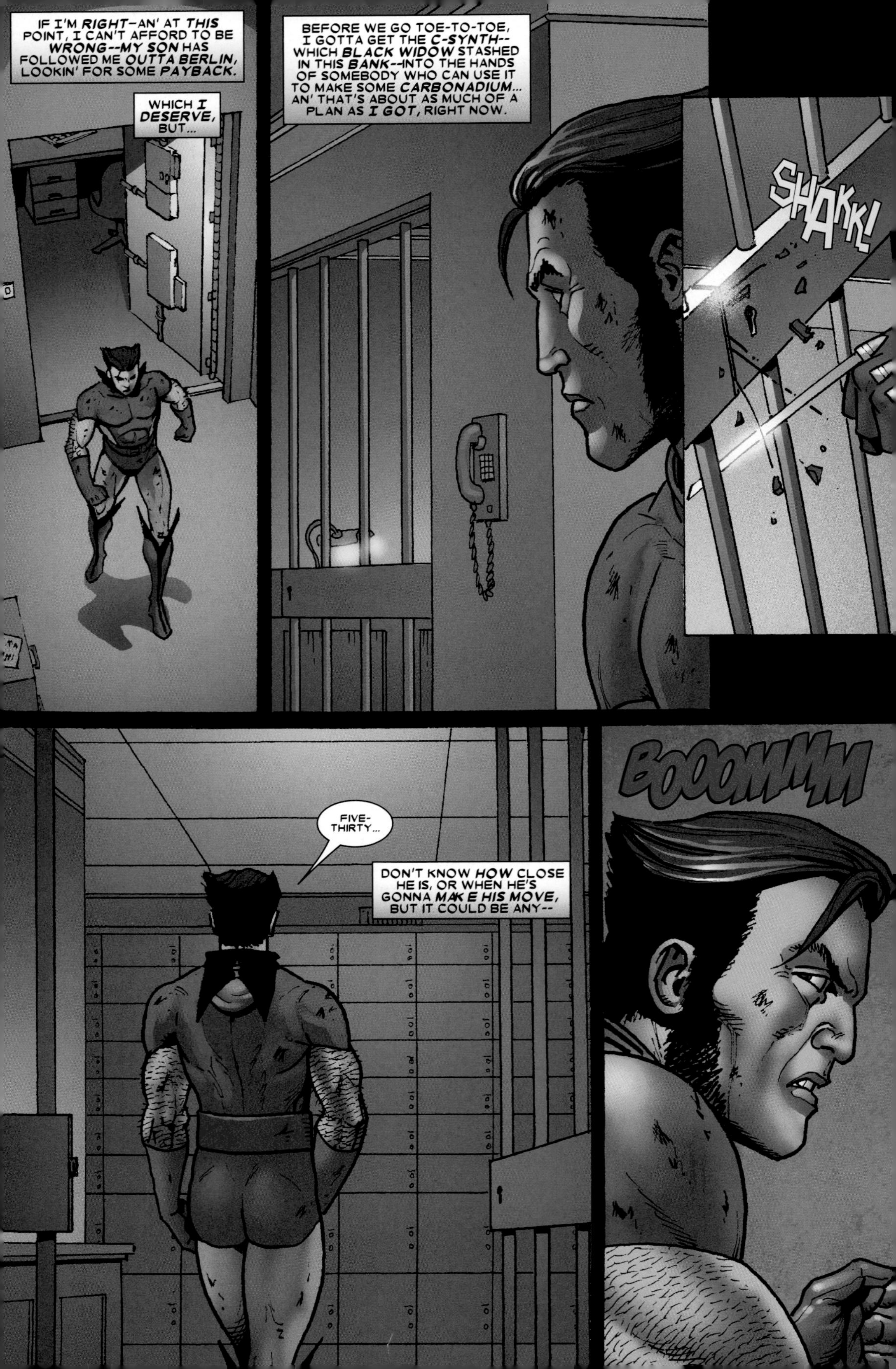
IF I'M RIGHT--AN' AT THIS POINT, I CAN'T AFFORD TO BE WRONG--MY SON HAS FOLLOWED ME OUTTA BERLIN, LOOKIN' FOR SOME PAYBACK.
WHICH I DESERVE, BUT...
BEFORE WE GO TOE-TO-TOE, I GOTTA GET THE C-SYNTH--WHICH BLACK WIDOW STASHED IN THIS BANK--INTO THE HANDS OF SOMEBODY WHO CAN USE IT TO MAKE SOME CARBONADIUM... AN' THAT'S ABOUT AS MUCH OF A PLAN AS I GOT, RIGHT NOW.
SHAKK!
FIVE-THIRTY...
DON'T KNOW HOW CLOSE HE IS, OR WHEN HE'S GONNA MAKE HIS MOVE, BUT IT COULD BE ANY--
BOOOMMM

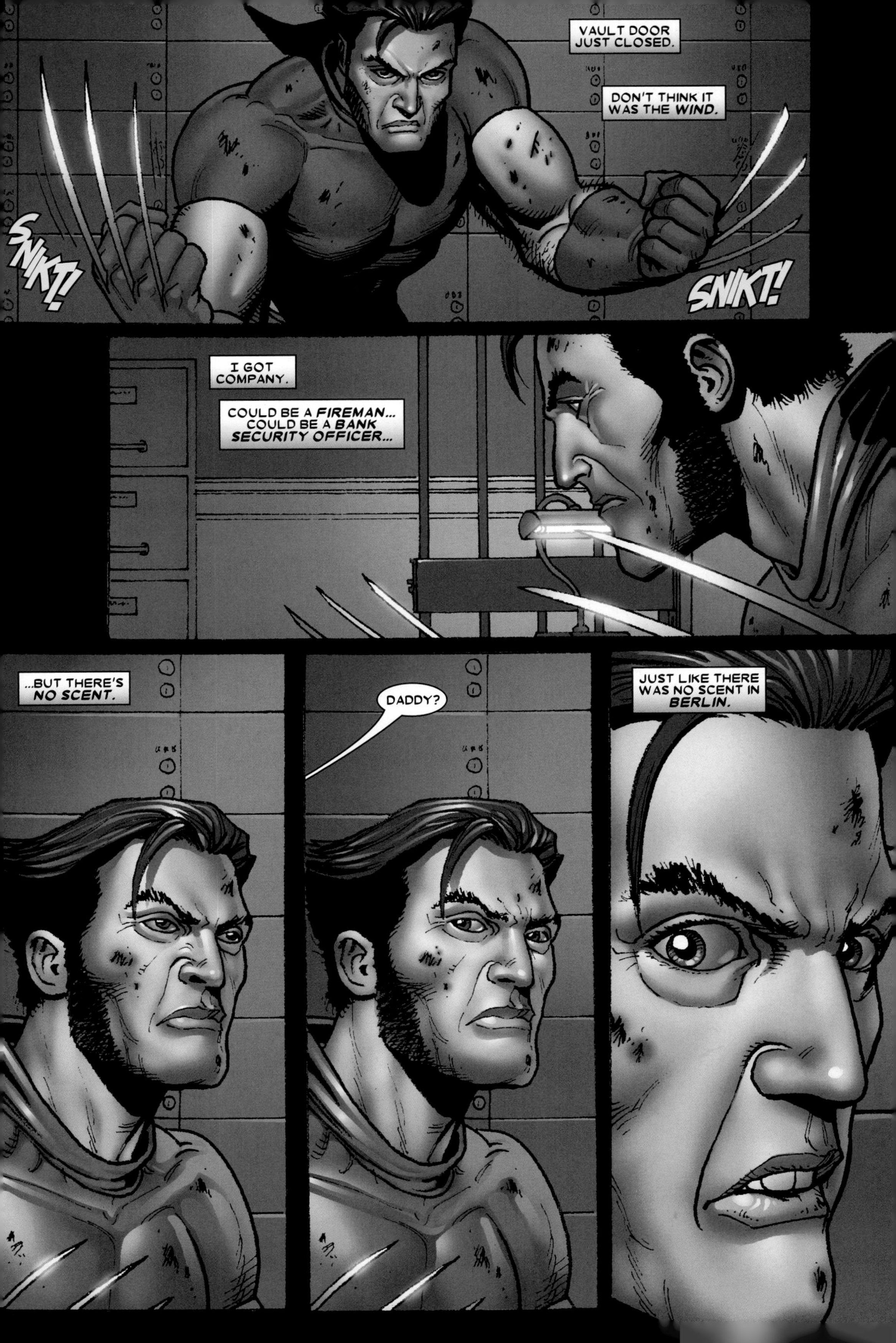
VAULT DOOR JUST CLOSED.
DON'T THINK IT WAS THE WIND.
SNIKT!
SNIKT!
I GOT COMPANY.
COULD BE A FIREMAN... COULD BE A BANK SECURITY OFFICER...
...BUT THERE'S NO SCENT.
DADDY?
JUST LIKE THERE WAS NO SCENT IN BERLIN.

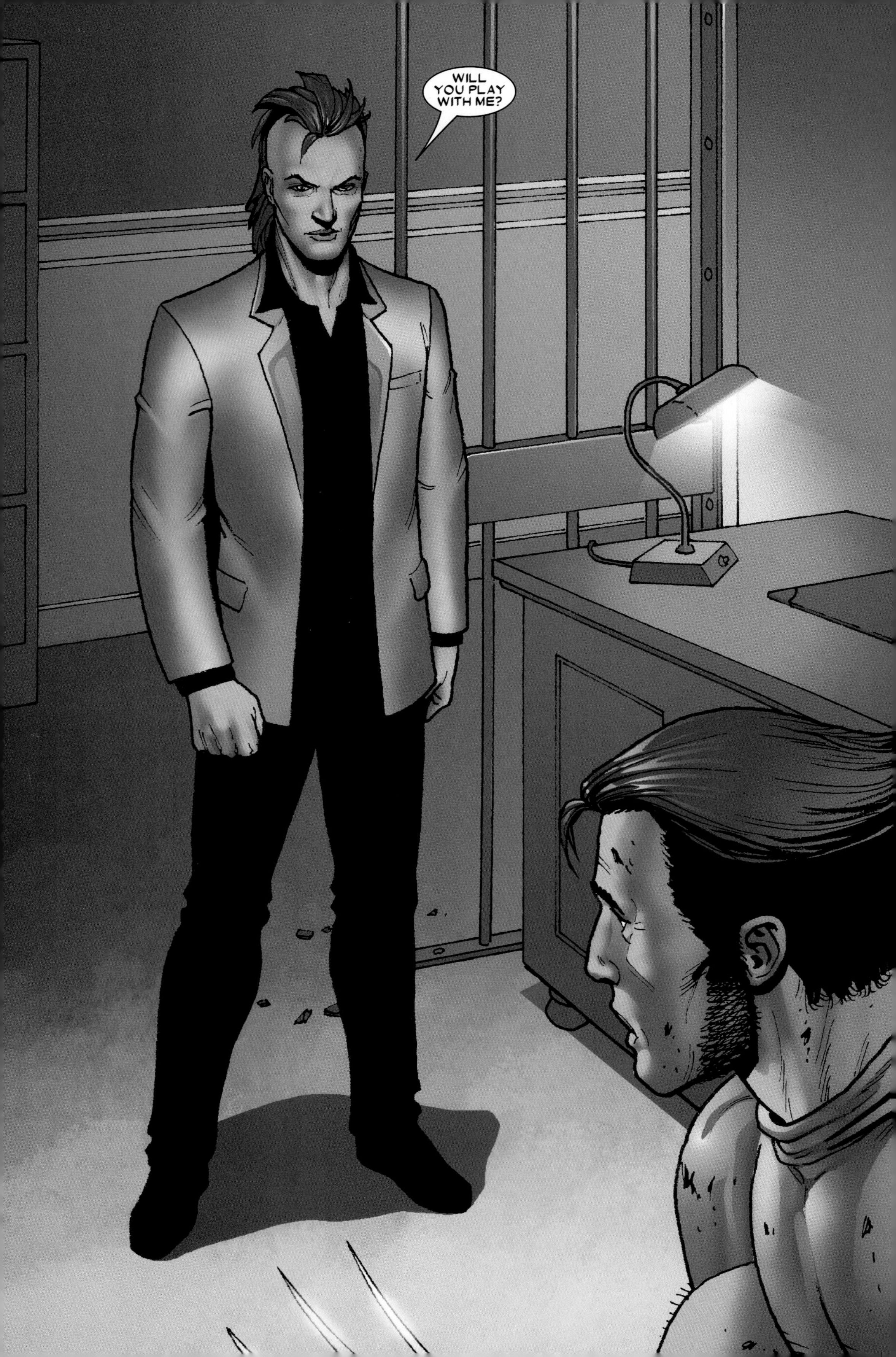
WILL YOU PLAY WITH ME?

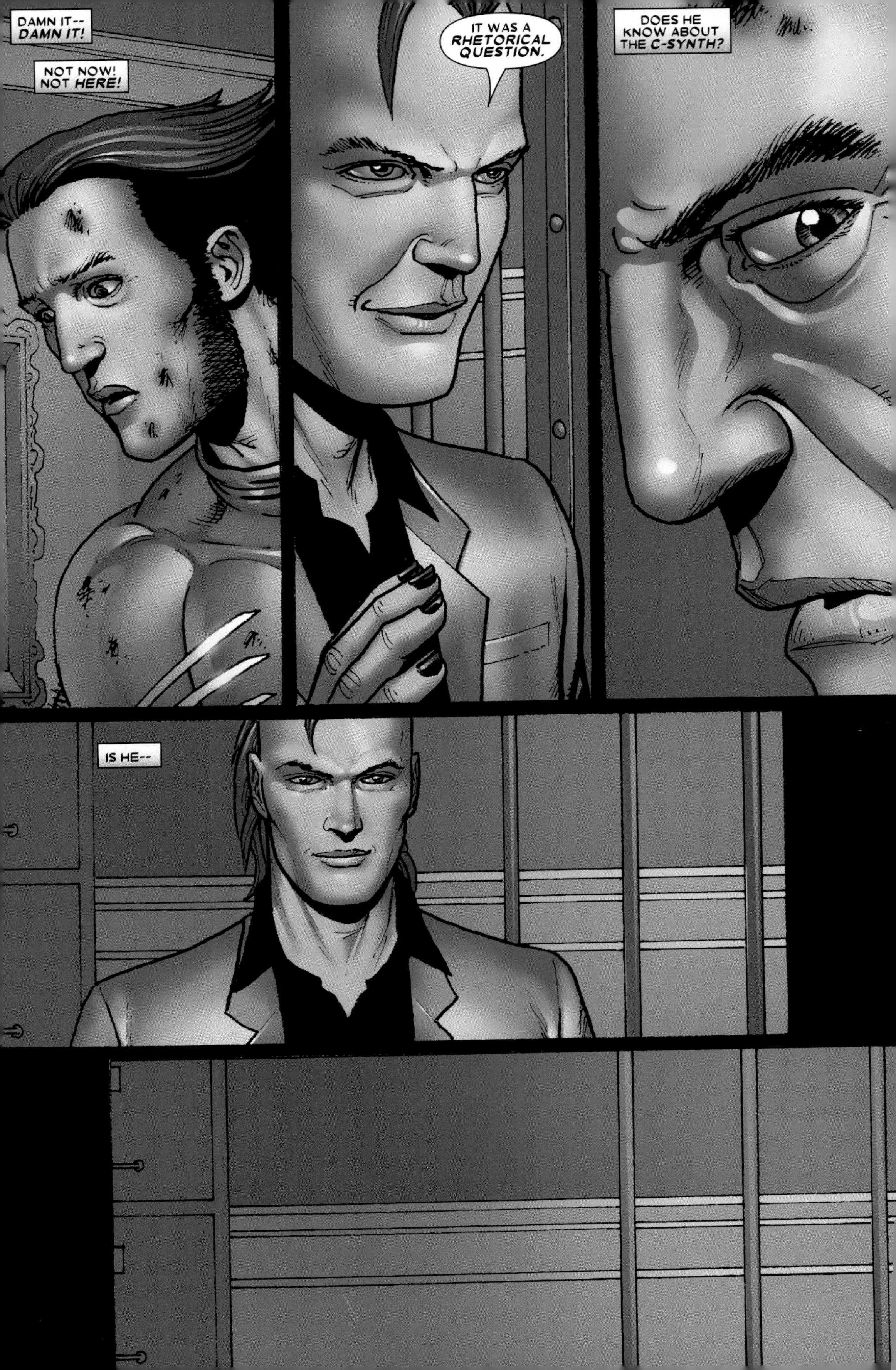
DAMN IT-- DAMN IT!
NOT NOW! NOT HERE!
IT WAS A RHETORICAL QUESTION.
DOES HE KNOW ABOUT THE C-SYNTH?
IS HE--

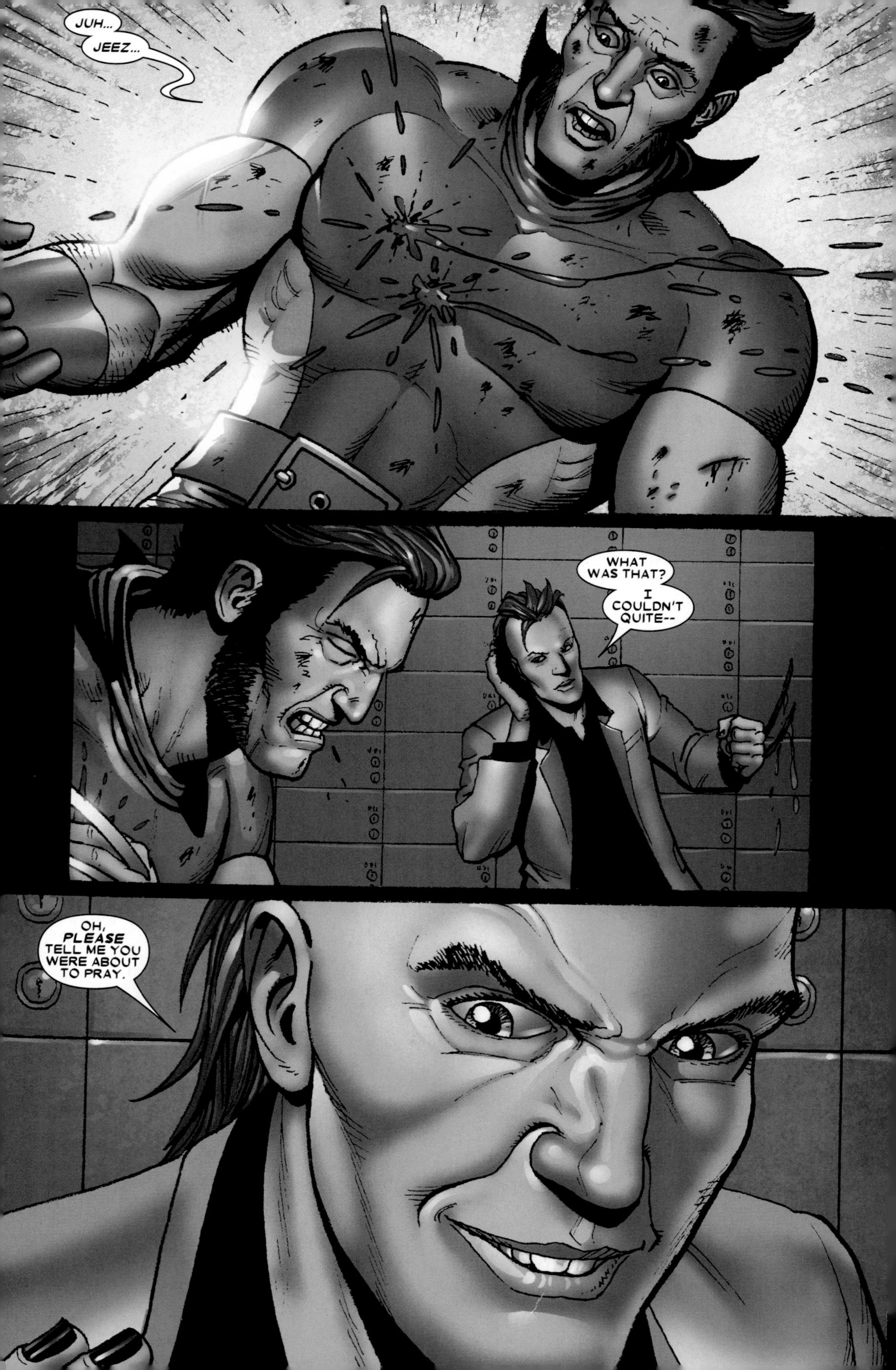

JUH... JEEZ...
WHAT WAS THAT? I COULDN'T QUITE--
OH, *PLEASE* TELL ME YOU WERE ABOUT TO PRAY.

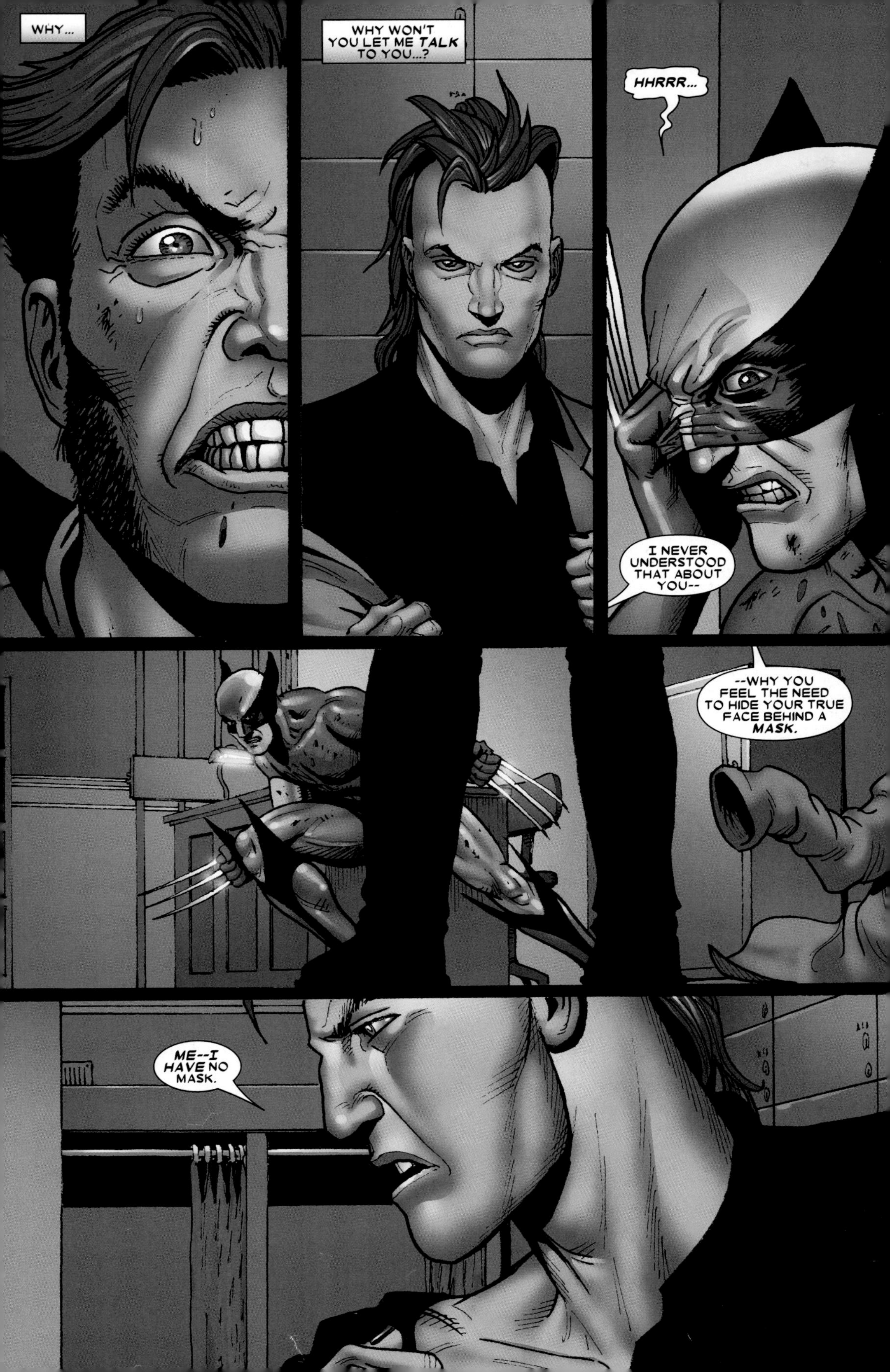
WHY...
WHY WON'T YOU LET ME *TALK* TO YOU...?
HHRRR...
I NEVER UNDERSTOOD THAT ABOUT YOU--
--WHY YOU FEEL THE NEED TO HIDE YOUR TRUE FACE BEHIND A *MASK.*
ME--I HAVE NO MASK.

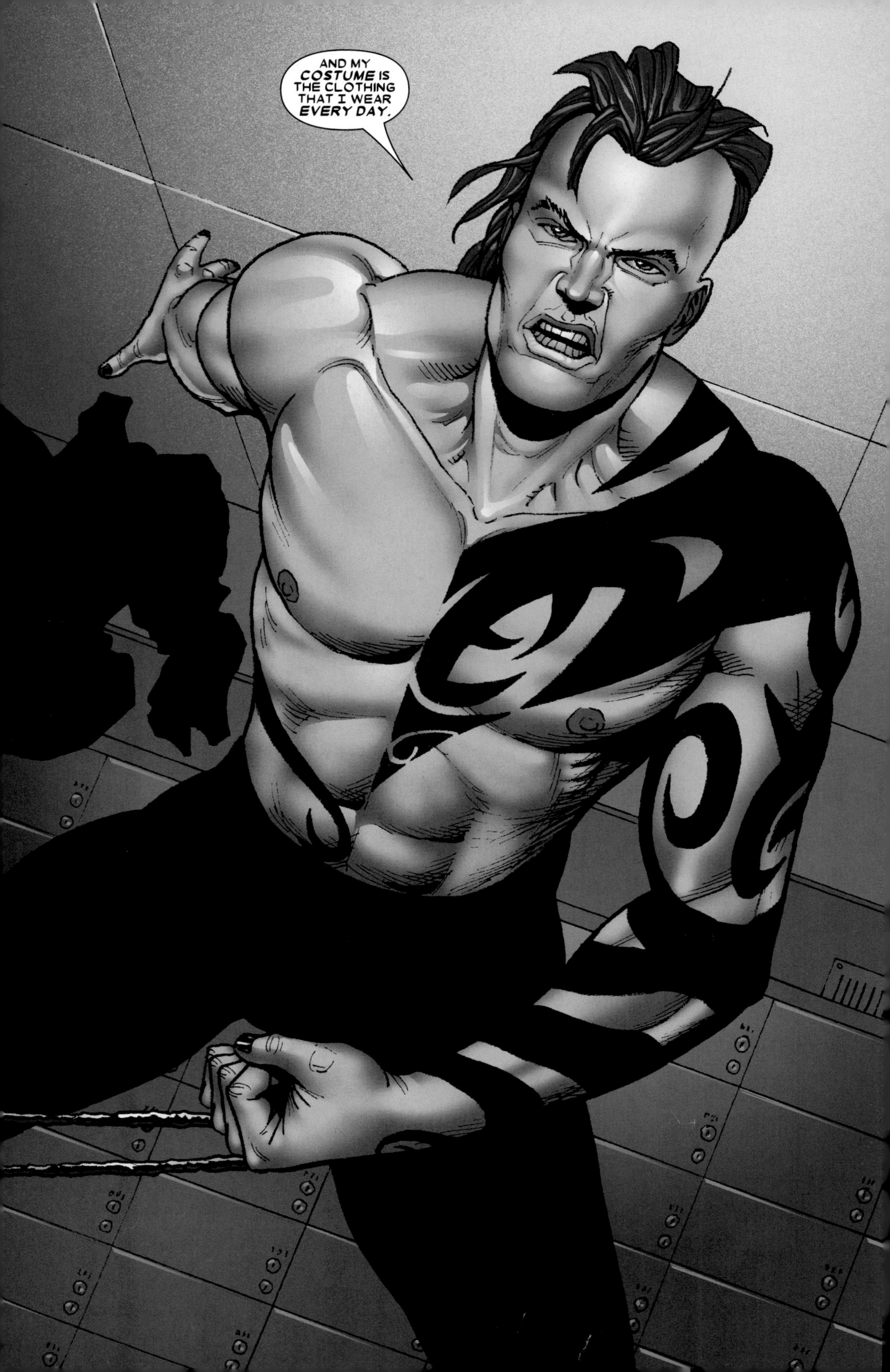
AND MY *COSTUME* IS THE CLOTHING THAT I WEAR *EVERY DAY.*

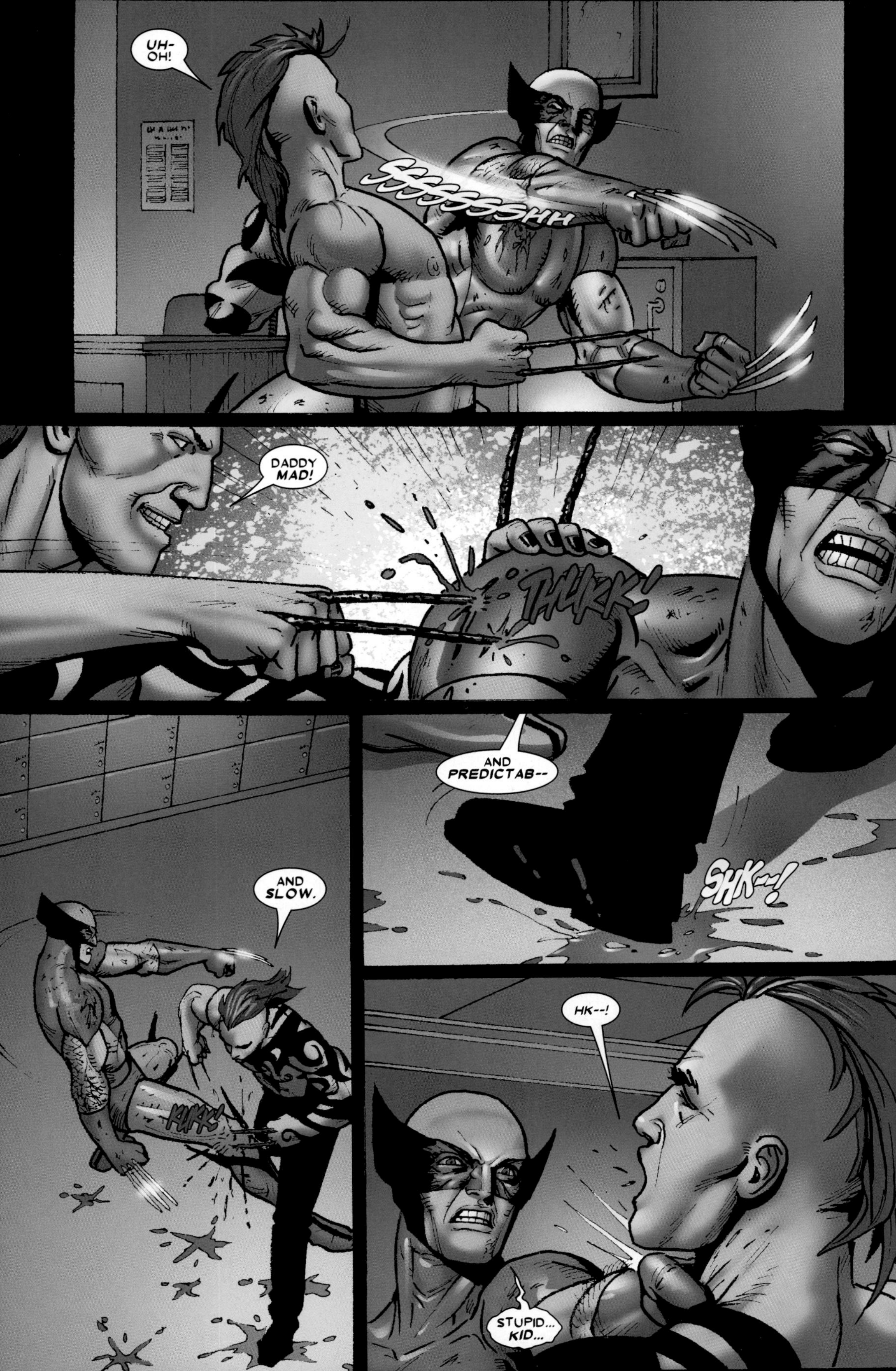

UH-OH!
SSSSSSSSHH
DADDY MAD!
THUKK!
AND PREDICTAB--
SHK--!
AND SLOW.
KLIKK!
HK--!
STUPID... KID...

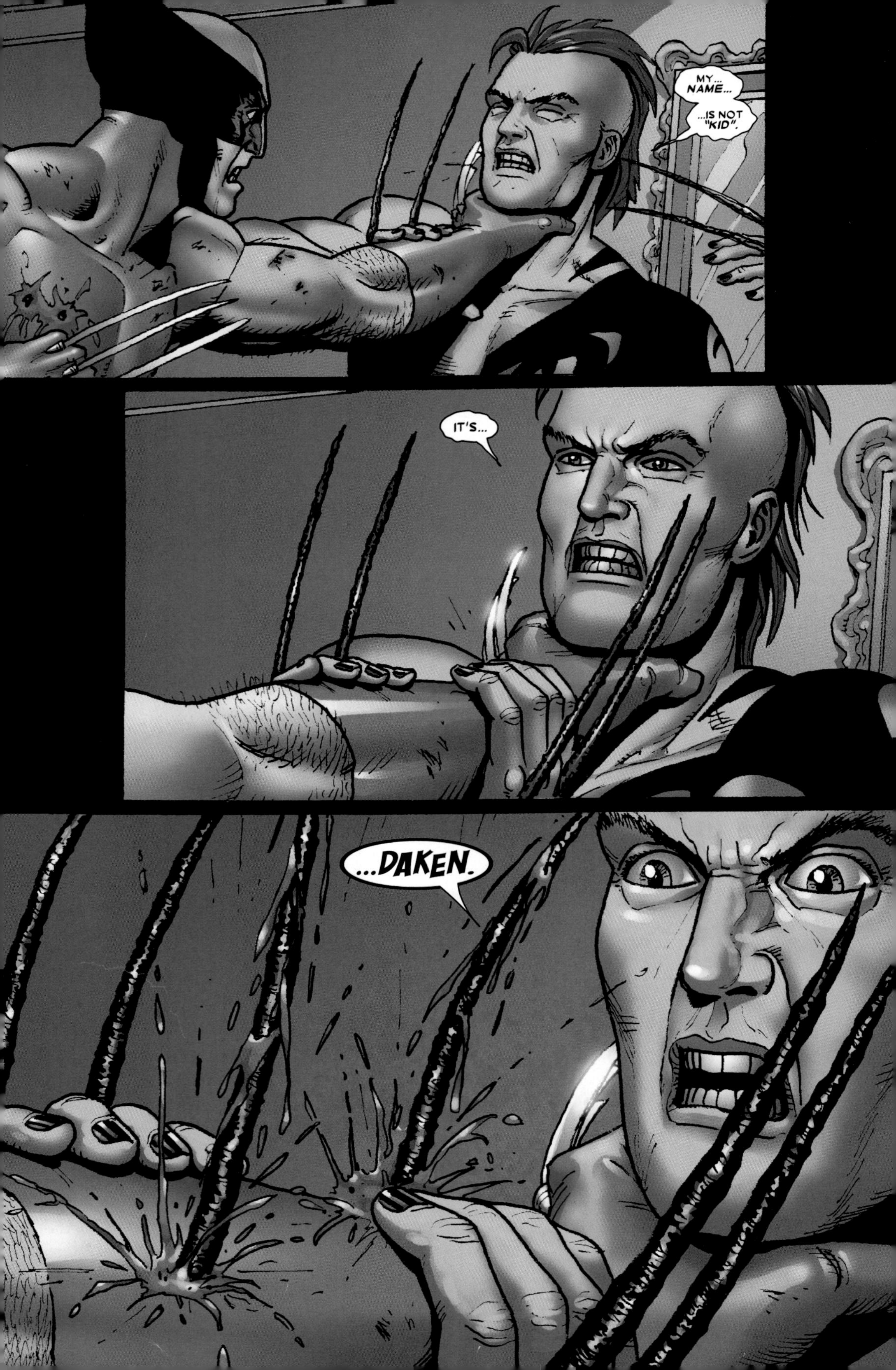
MY... NAME...
...IS NOT "KID".
IT'S...
...DAKEN.

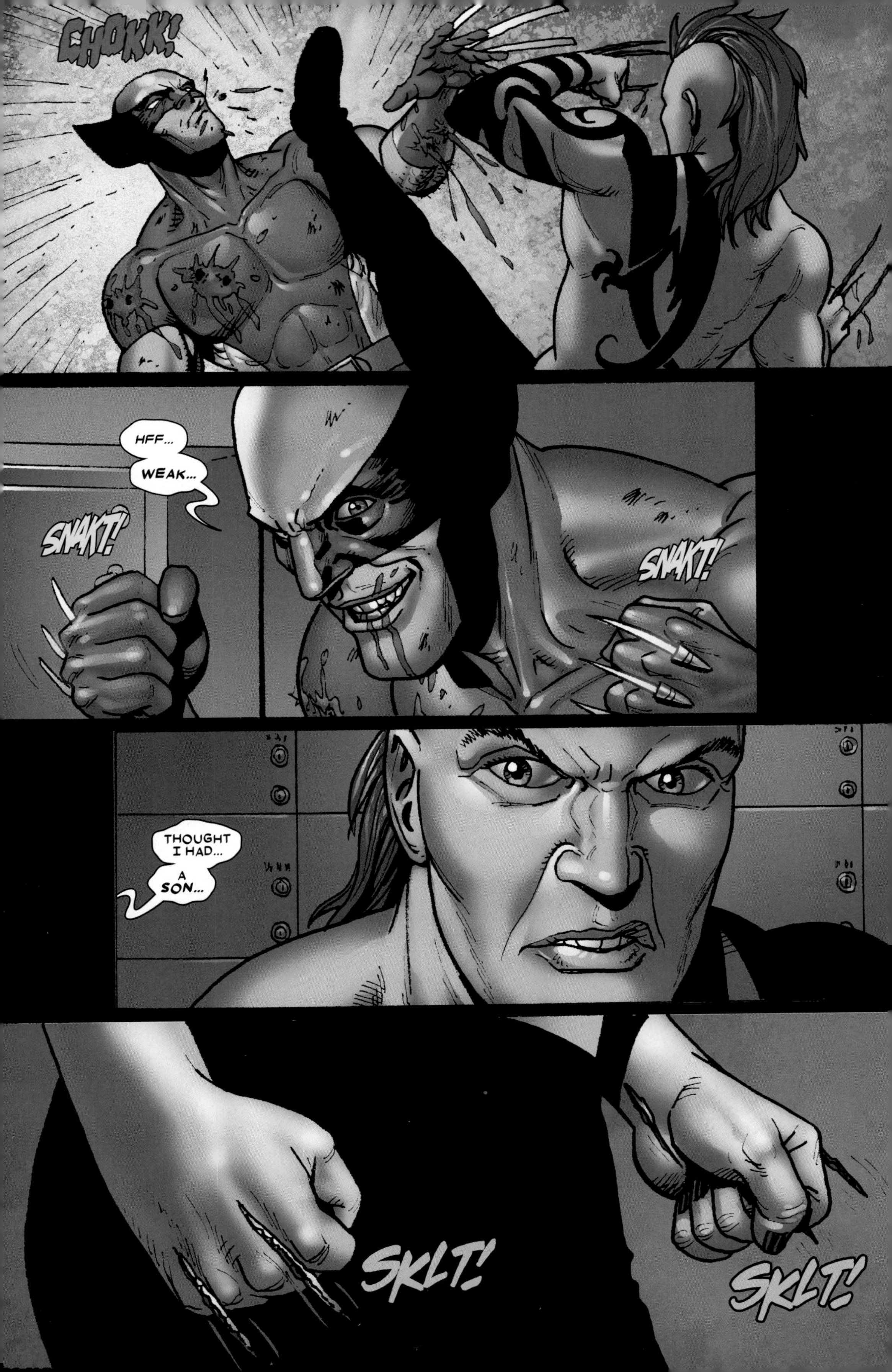
CHOKK!
HFF...
WEAK...
SNAKT!
SNAKT!
THOUGHT I HAD...
A SON...
SKLT!
SKLT!

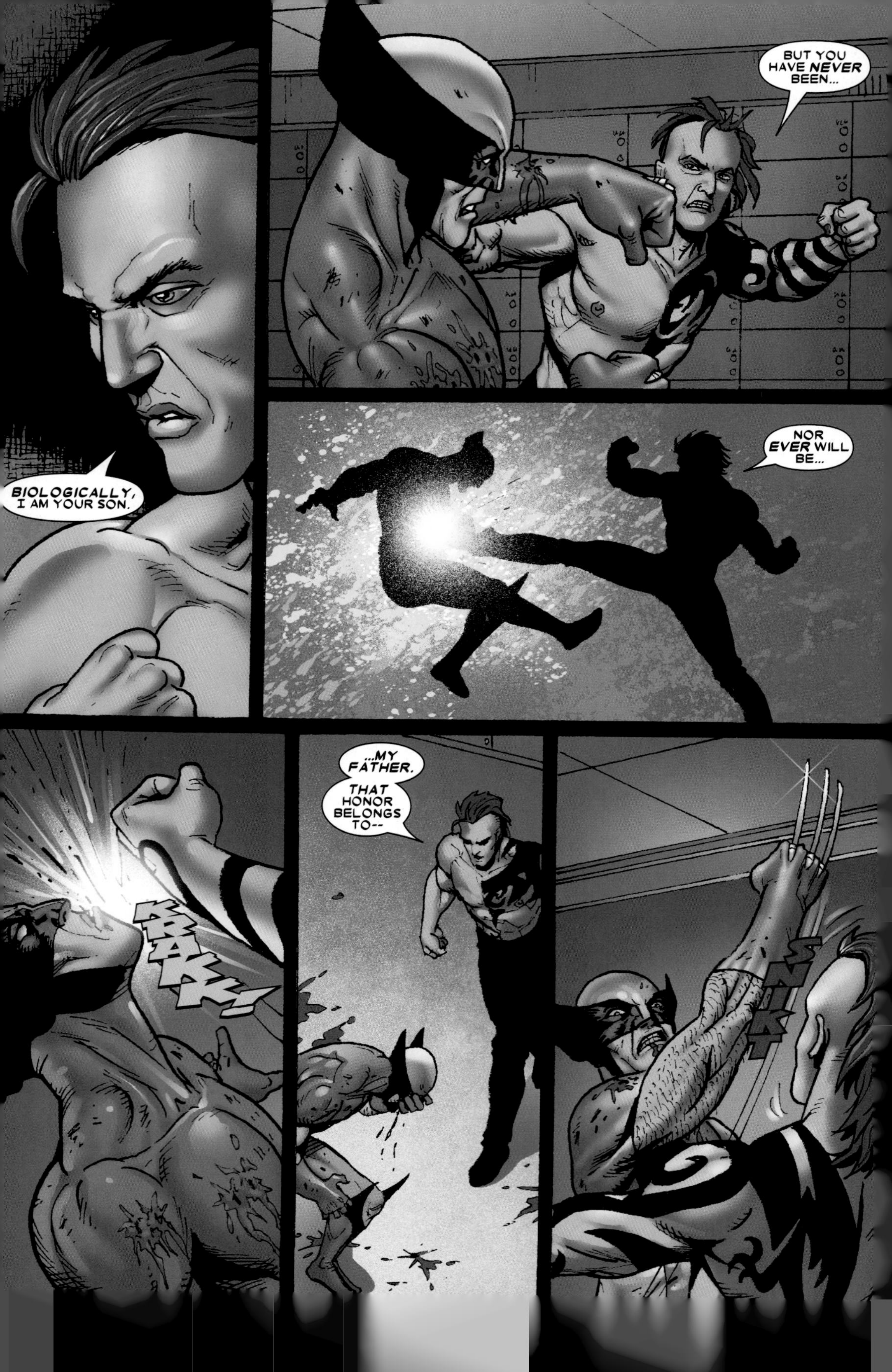
BIOLOGICALLY, I AM YOUR SON.
BUT YOU HAVE NEVER BEEN...
NOR EVER WILL BE...
KRAKK!
...MY FATHER.
THAT HONOR BELONGS TO--
SNIKT

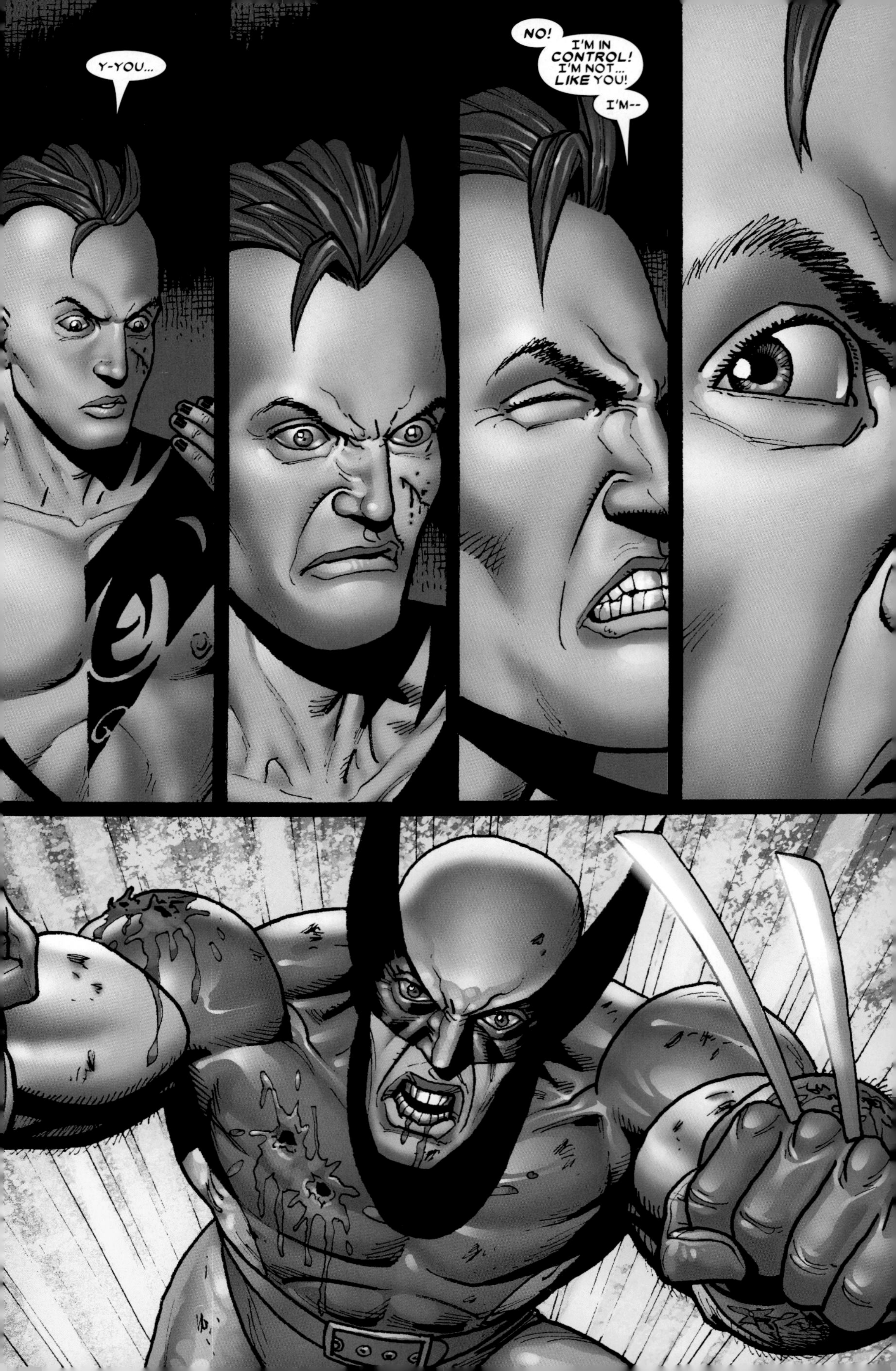
Y-YOU...
NO!
I'M IN CONTROL! I'M NOT... LIKE YOU!
I'M--

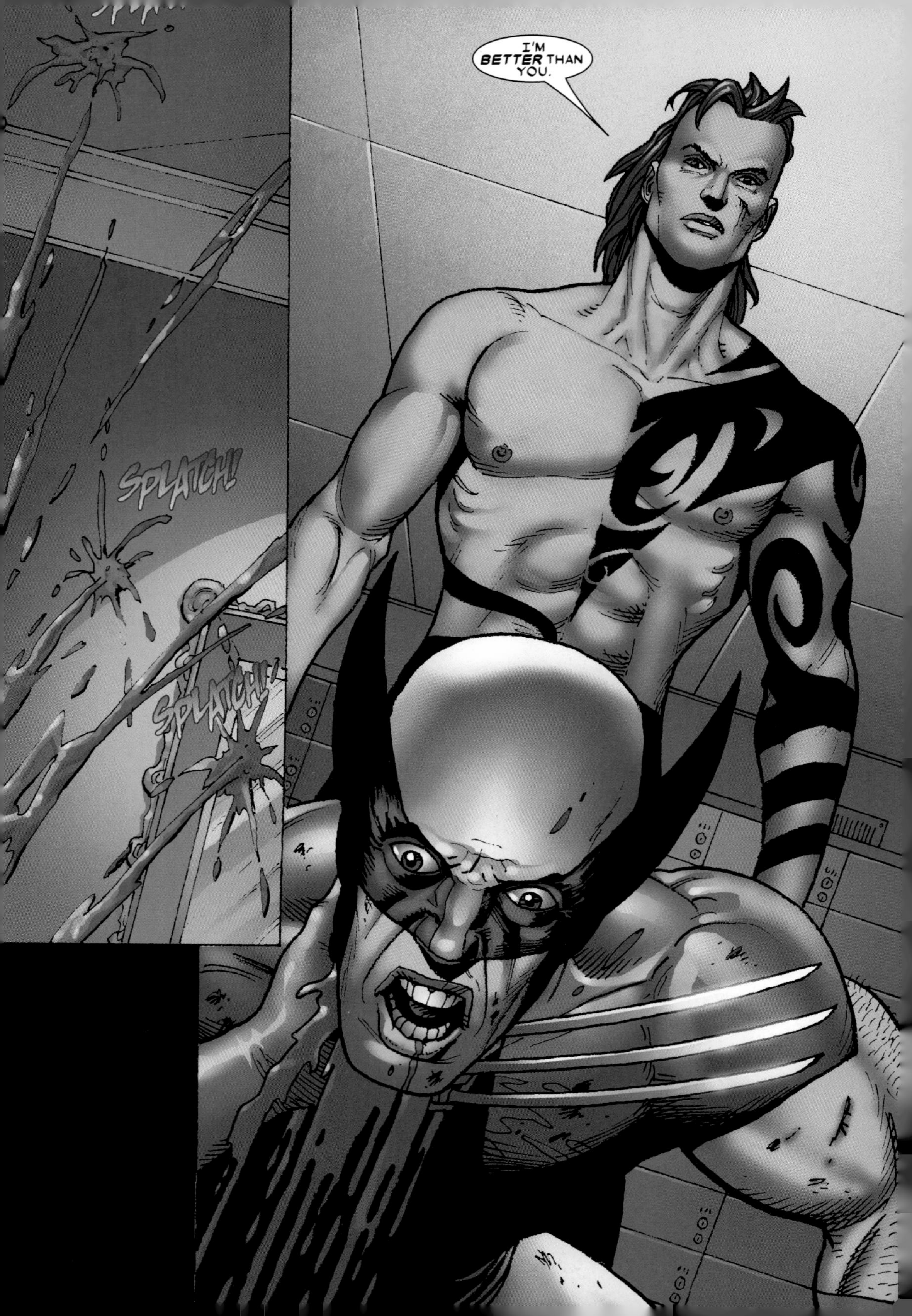

SPLATCH!
SPLATCH!
I'M BETTER THAN YOU.

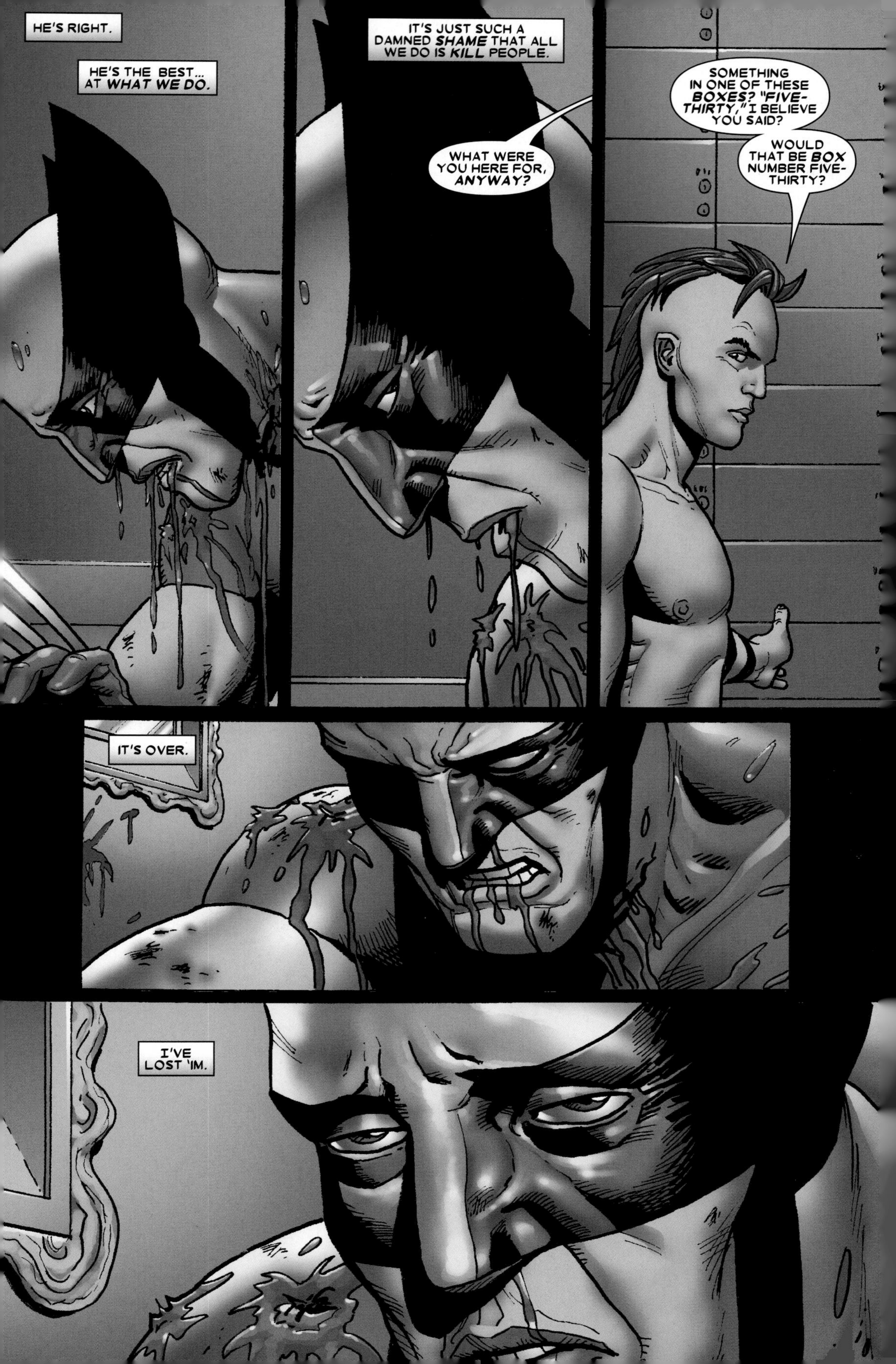
HE'S RIGHT.
HE'S THE BEST... AT WHAT WE DO.
IT'S JUST SUCH A DAMNED SHAME THAT ALL WE DO IS KILL PEOPLE.
WHAT WERE YOU HERE FOR, ANYWAY?
SOMETHING IN ONE OF THESE BOXES? "FIVE-THIRTY," I BELIEVE YOU SAID?
WOULD THAT BE BOX NUMBER FIVE-THIRTY?
IT'S OVER.
I'VE LOST 'IM.

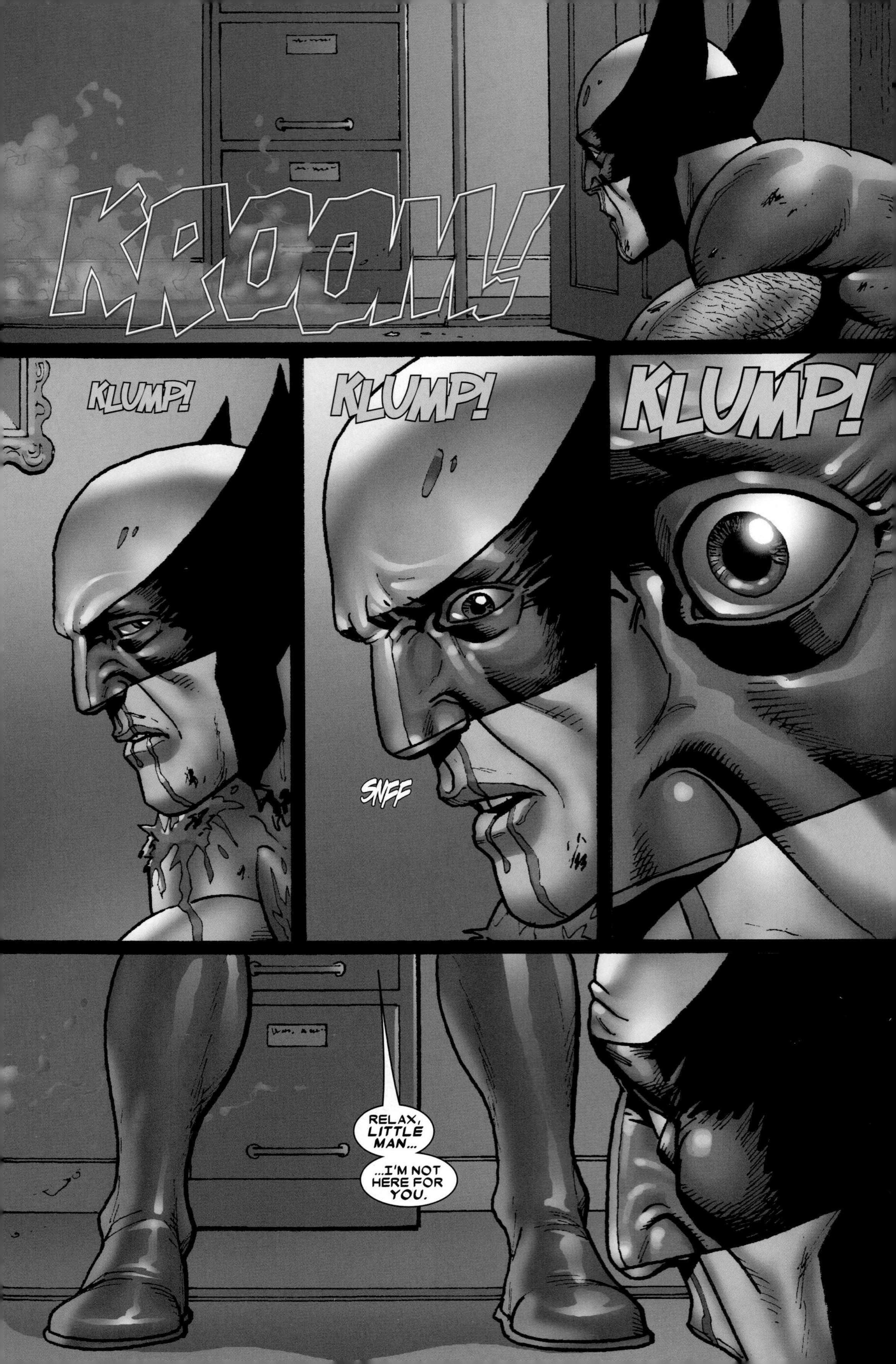
KROOM!
KLUMP!
KLUMP!
SNFF
KLUMP!
RELAX, LITTLE MAN...
...I'M NOT HERE FOR YOU.

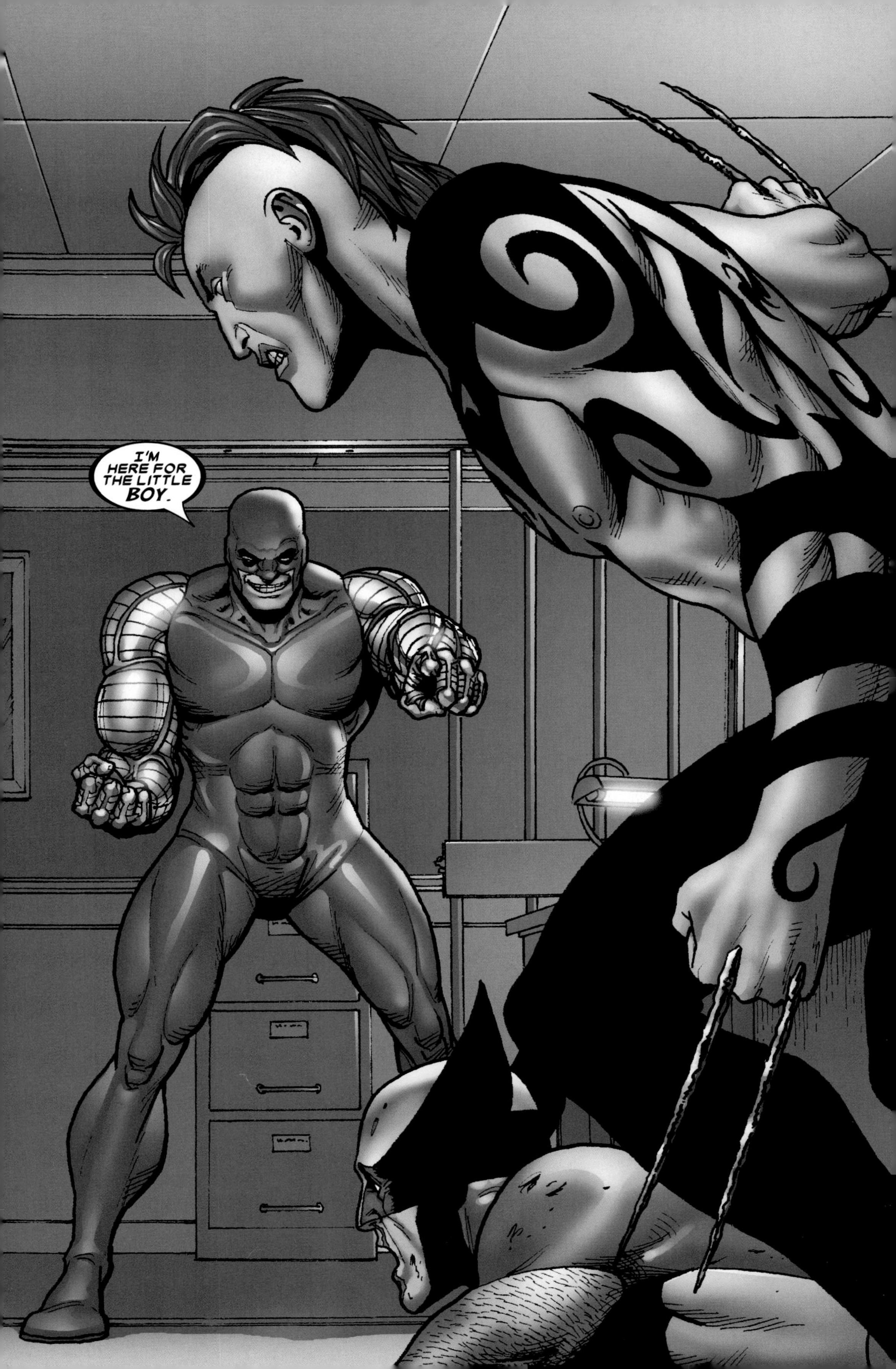
I'M HERE FOR THE LITTLE BOY.

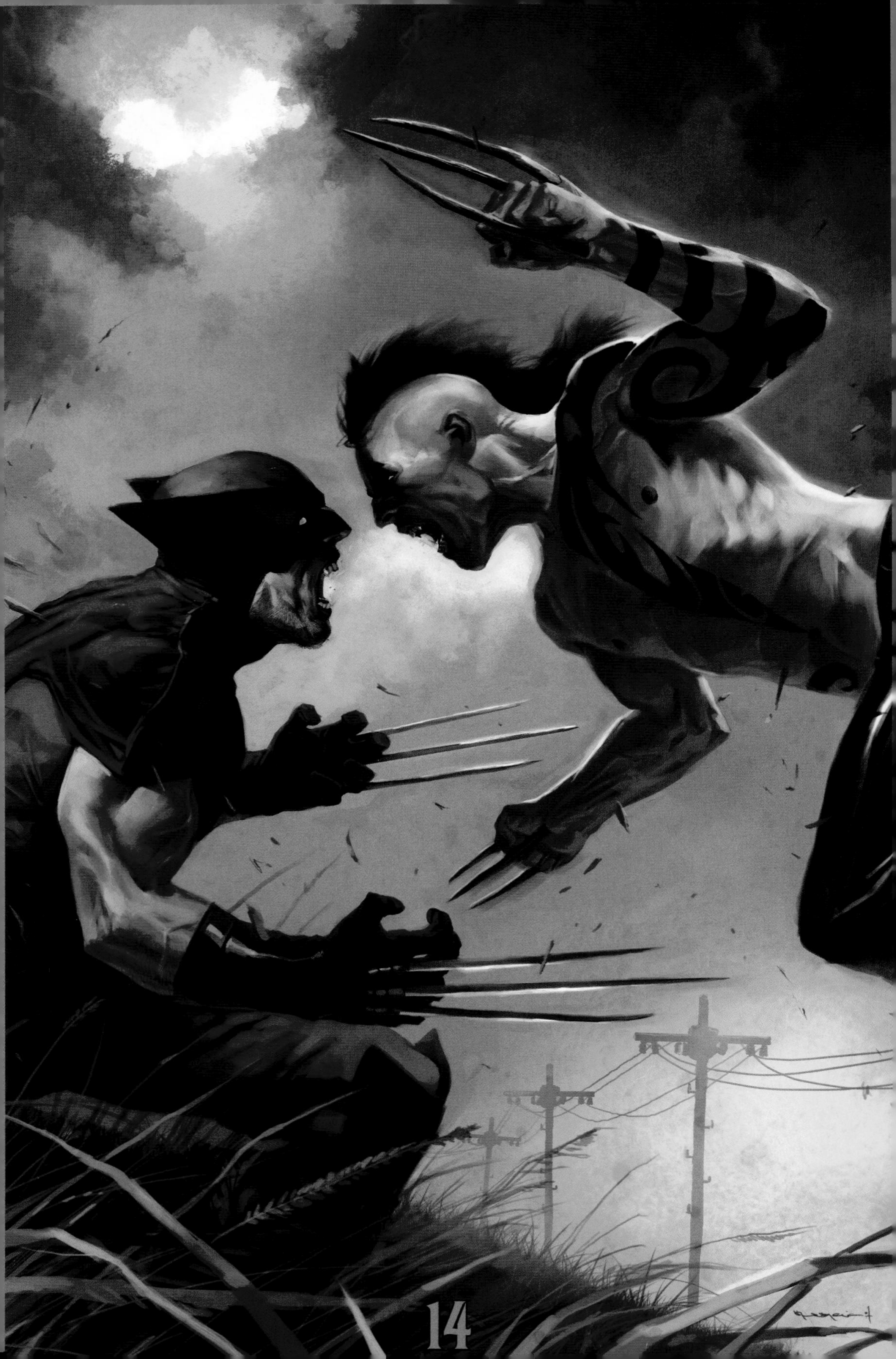

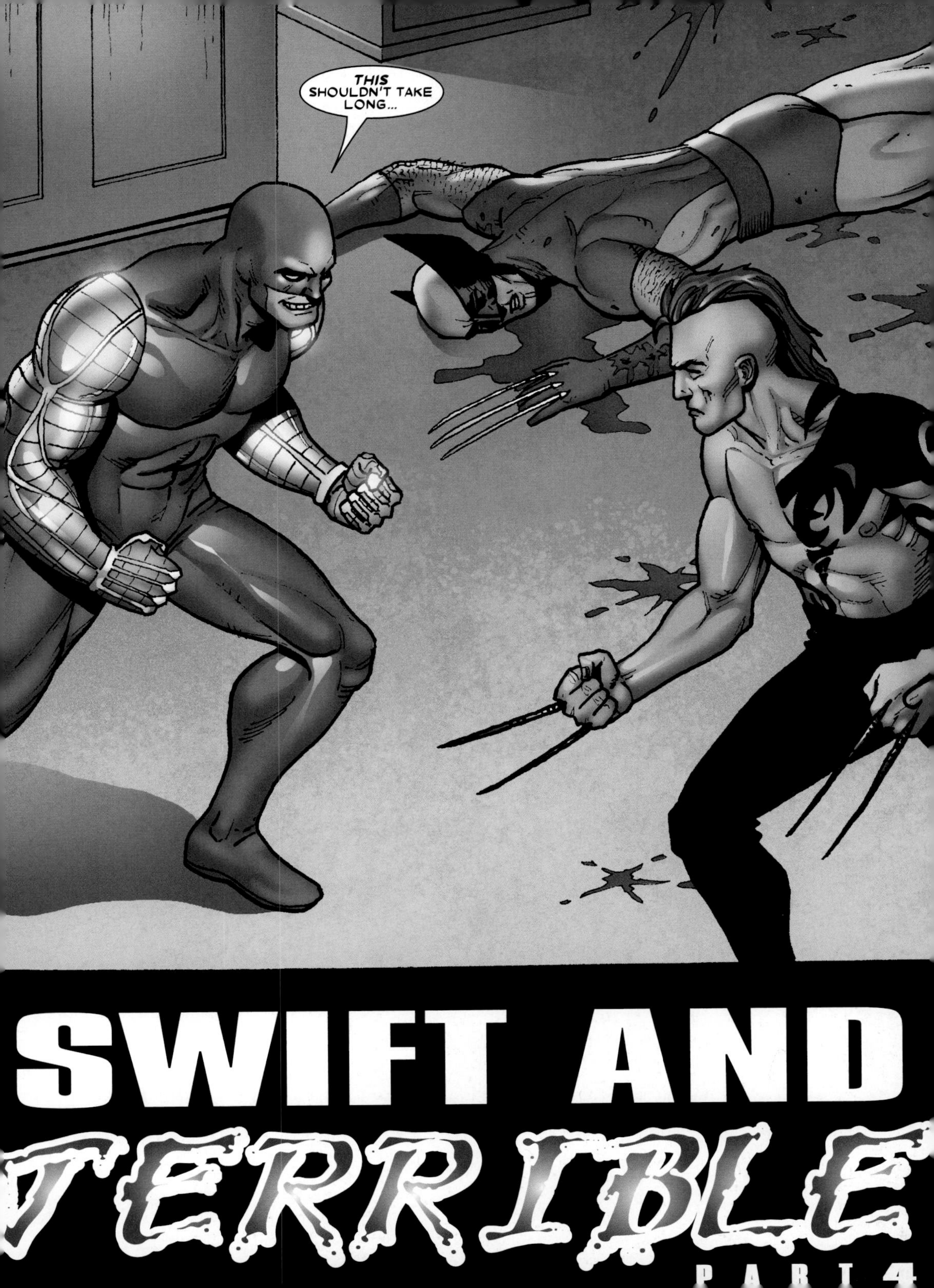
THIS SHOULDN'T TAKE LONG...

SWIFT AND TERRIBLE

PART 4

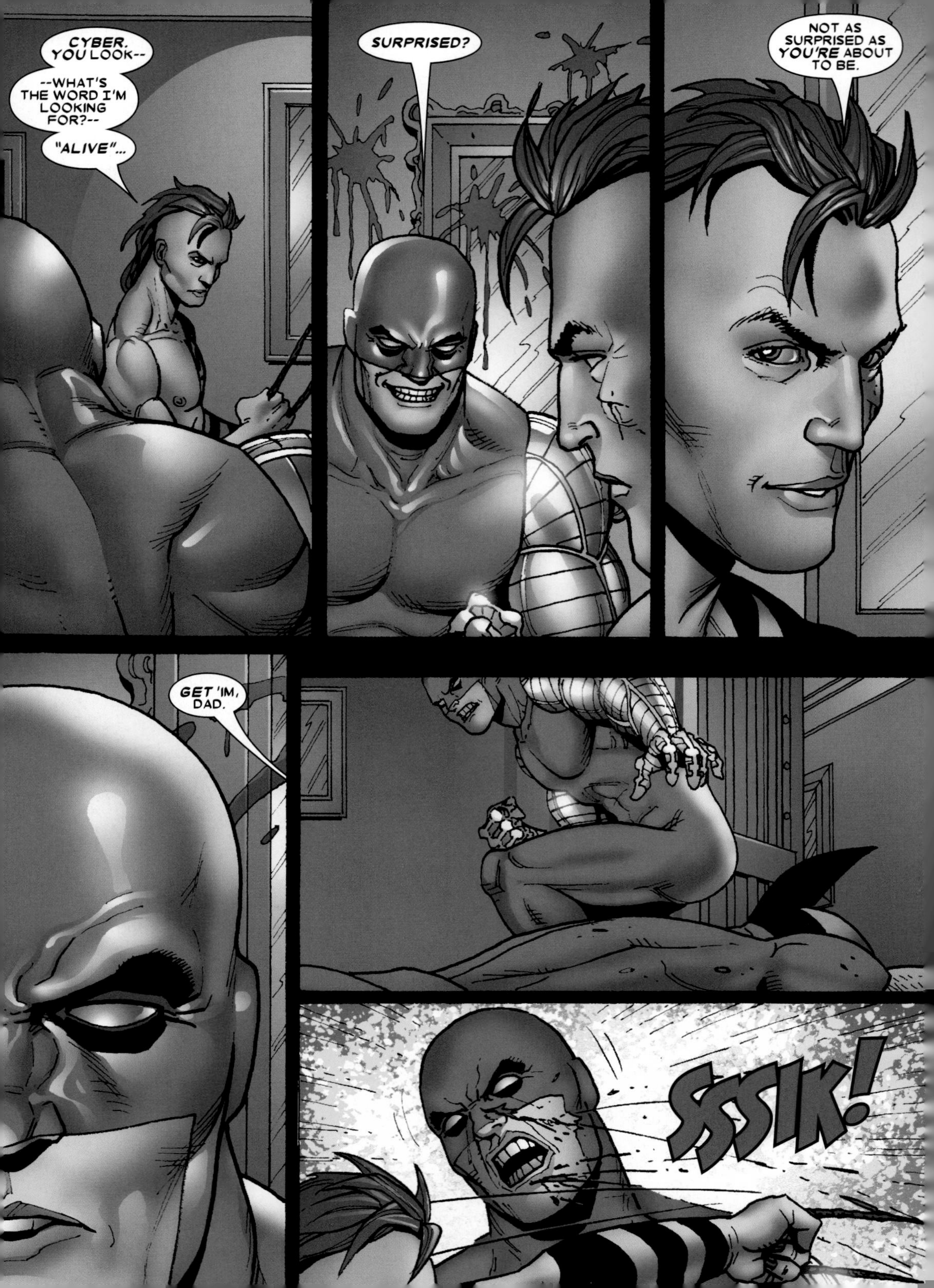
CYBER. YOU LOOK--
--WHAT'S THE WORD I'M LOOKING FOR?--
"ALIVE"...
SURPRISED?
NOT AS SURPRISED AS YOU'RE ABOUT TO BE.
GET 'IM, DAD.
SSSIK!

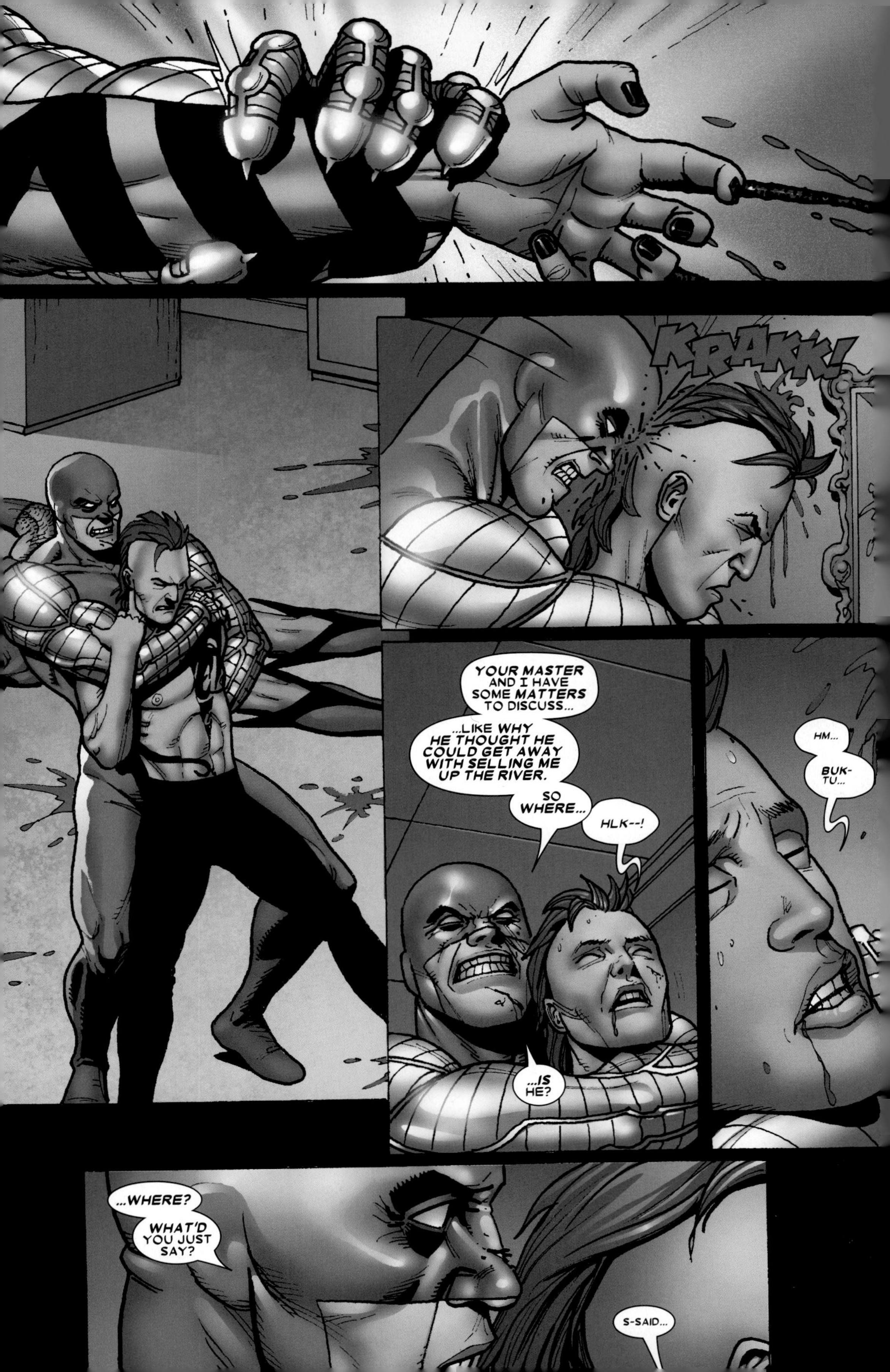
KRAKK!
YOUR MASTER AND I HAVE SOME MATTERS TO DISCUSS...
...LIKE WHY HE THOUGHT HE COULD GET AWAY WITH SELLING ME UP THE RIVER.
SO WHERE...
HLK--!
...IS HE?
HM...
BUK-TU...
...WHERE?
WHAT'D YOU JUST SAY?
S-SAID...

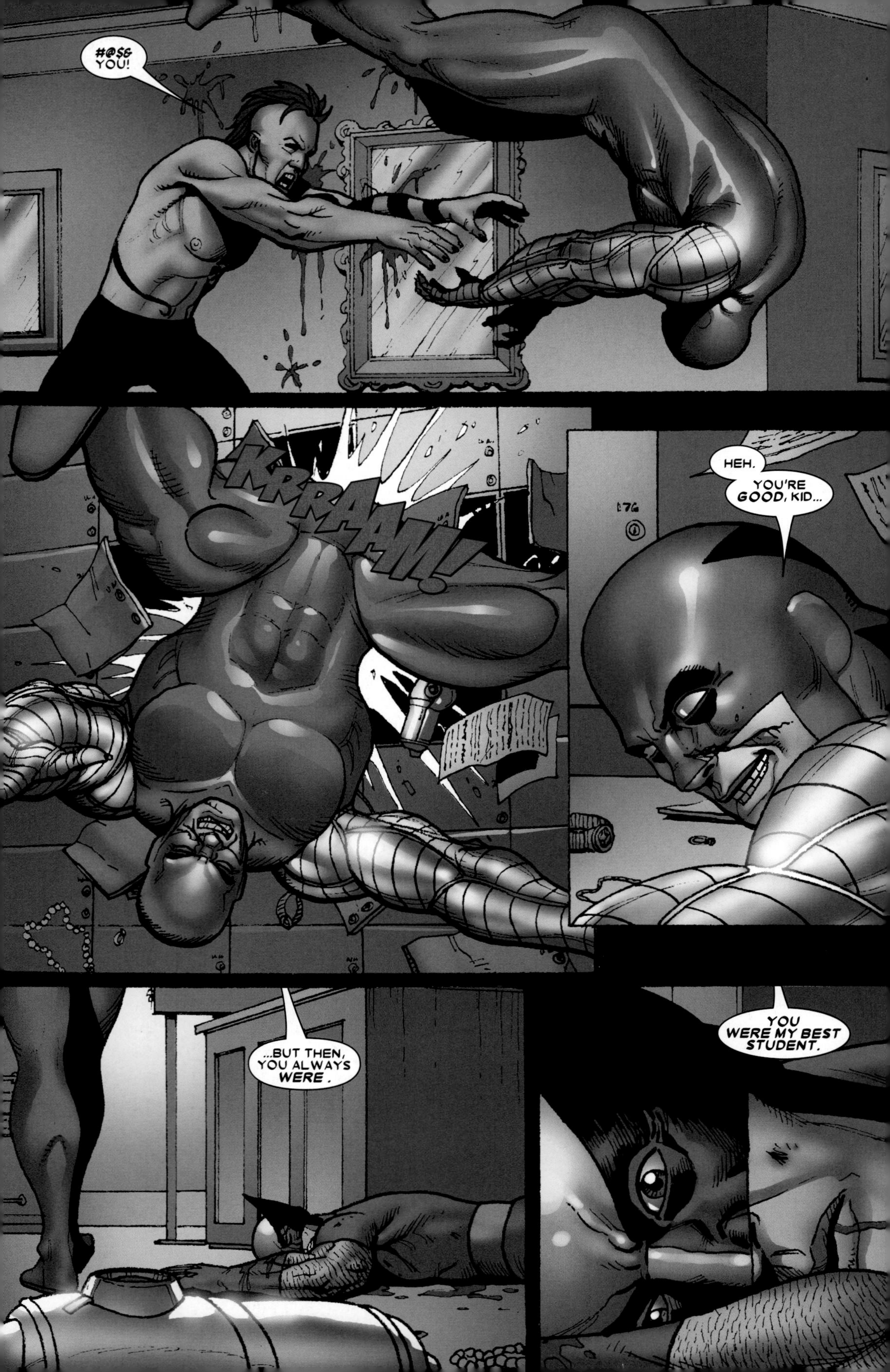
#@$&
YOU!
KRRAAAM!
HEH.
YOU'RE GOOD, KID...
...BUT THEN, YOU ALWAYS WERE.
YOU WERE MY BEST STUDENT.

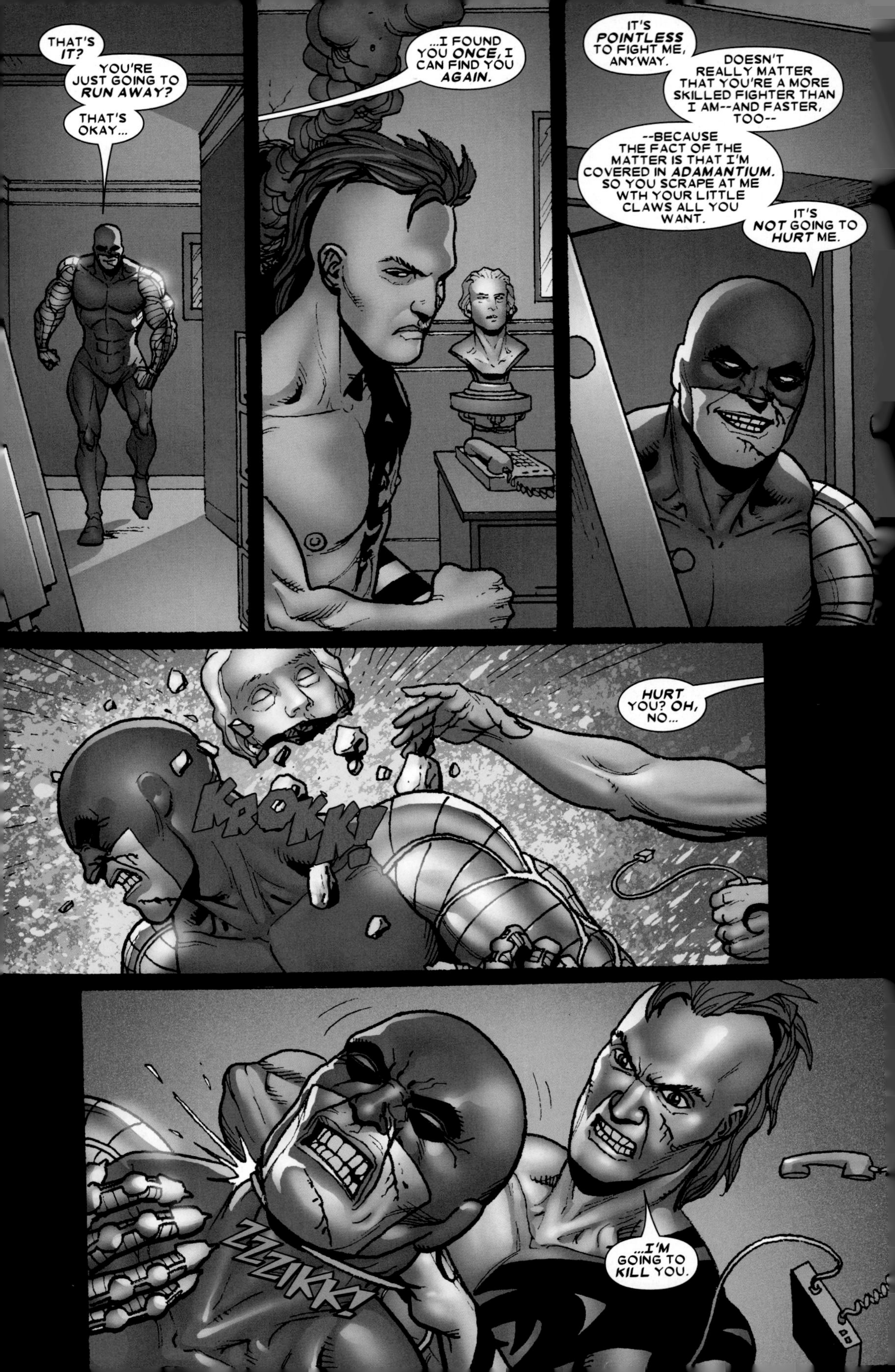
THAT'S IT?
YOU'RE JUST GOING TO RUN AWAY?
THAT'S OKAY...
...I FOUND YOU ONCE, I CAN FIND YOU AGAIN.
IT'S POINTLESS TO FIGHT ME, ANYWAY.
DOESN'T REALLY MATTER THAT YOU'RE A MORE SKILLED FIGHTER THAN I AM--AND FASTER, TOO--
--BECAUSE THE FACT OF THE MATTER IS THAT I'M COVERED IN ADAMANTIUM. SO YOU SCRAPE AT ME WTH YOUR LITTLE CLAWS ALL YOU WANT.
IT'S NOT GOING TO HURT ME.
HURT YOU? OH, NO...
KROKK!
...I'M GOING TO KILL YOU.
ZZZIKK!

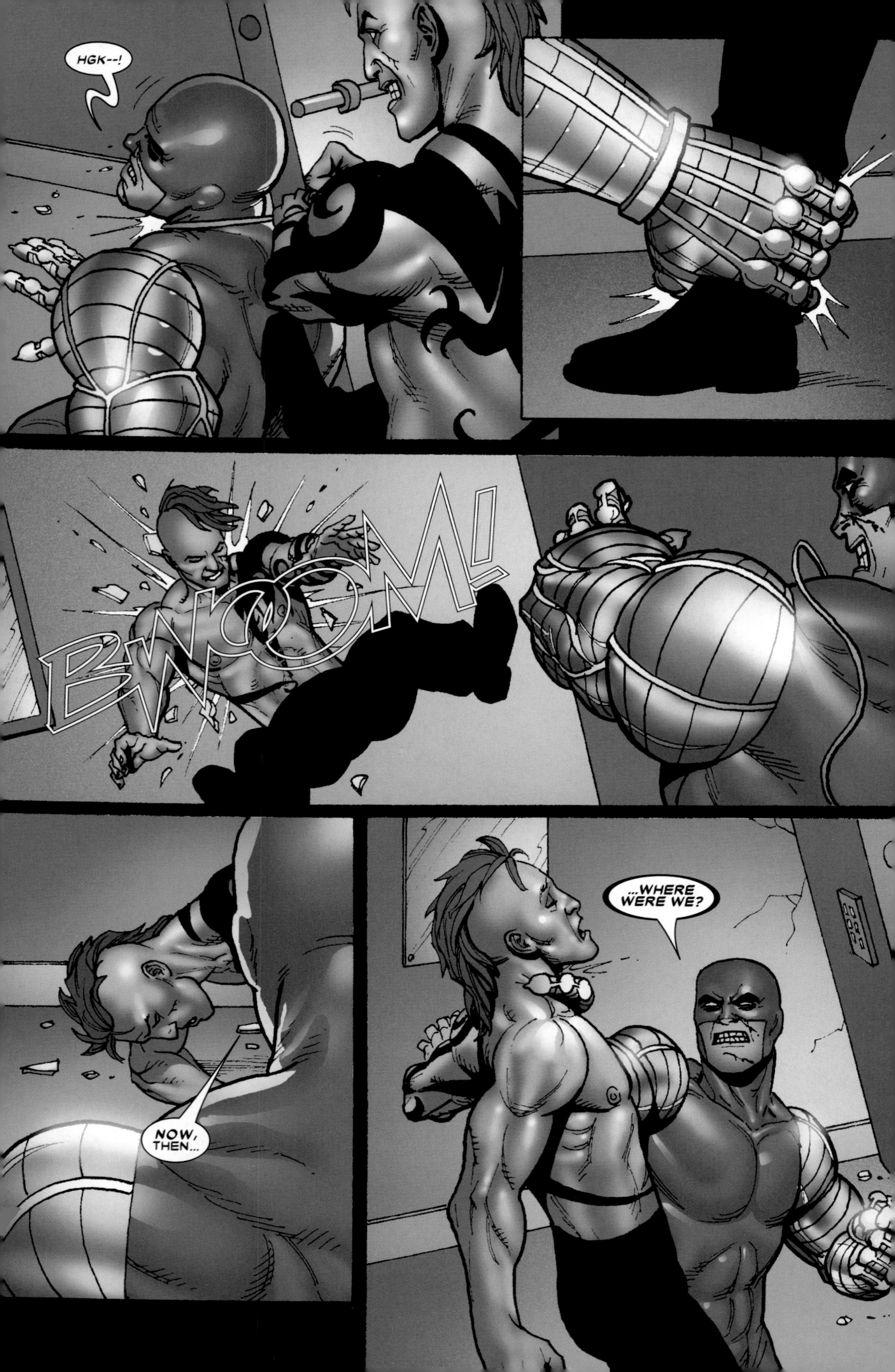
HGK--!
BWOOM!
NOW, THEN...
...WHERE WERE WE?

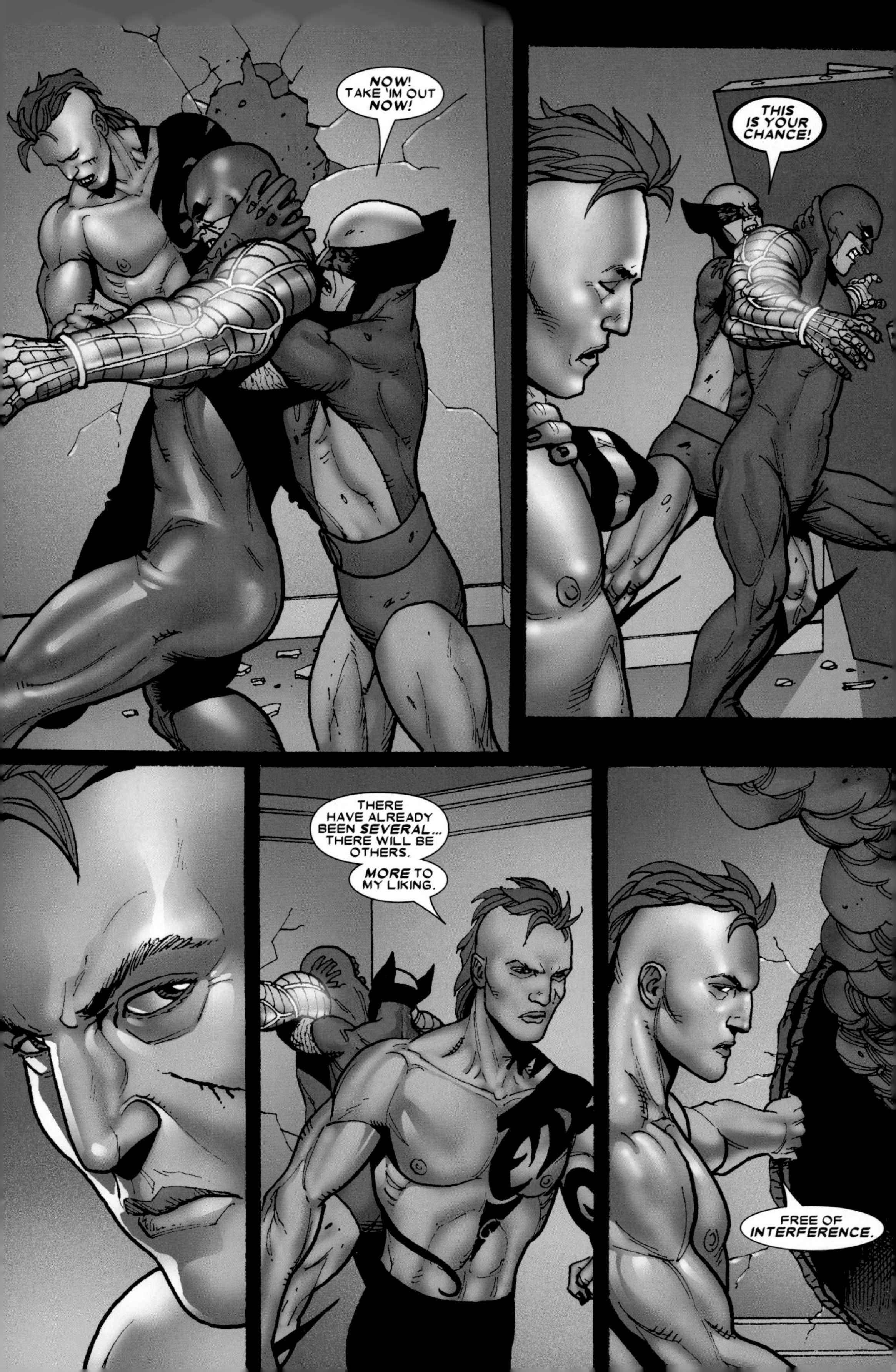
NOW! TAKE 'IM OUT NOW!
THIS IS YOUR CHANCE!
THERE HAVE ALREADY BEEN SEVERAL... THERE WILL BE OTHERS.
MORE TO MY LIKING.
FREE OF INTERFERENCE.

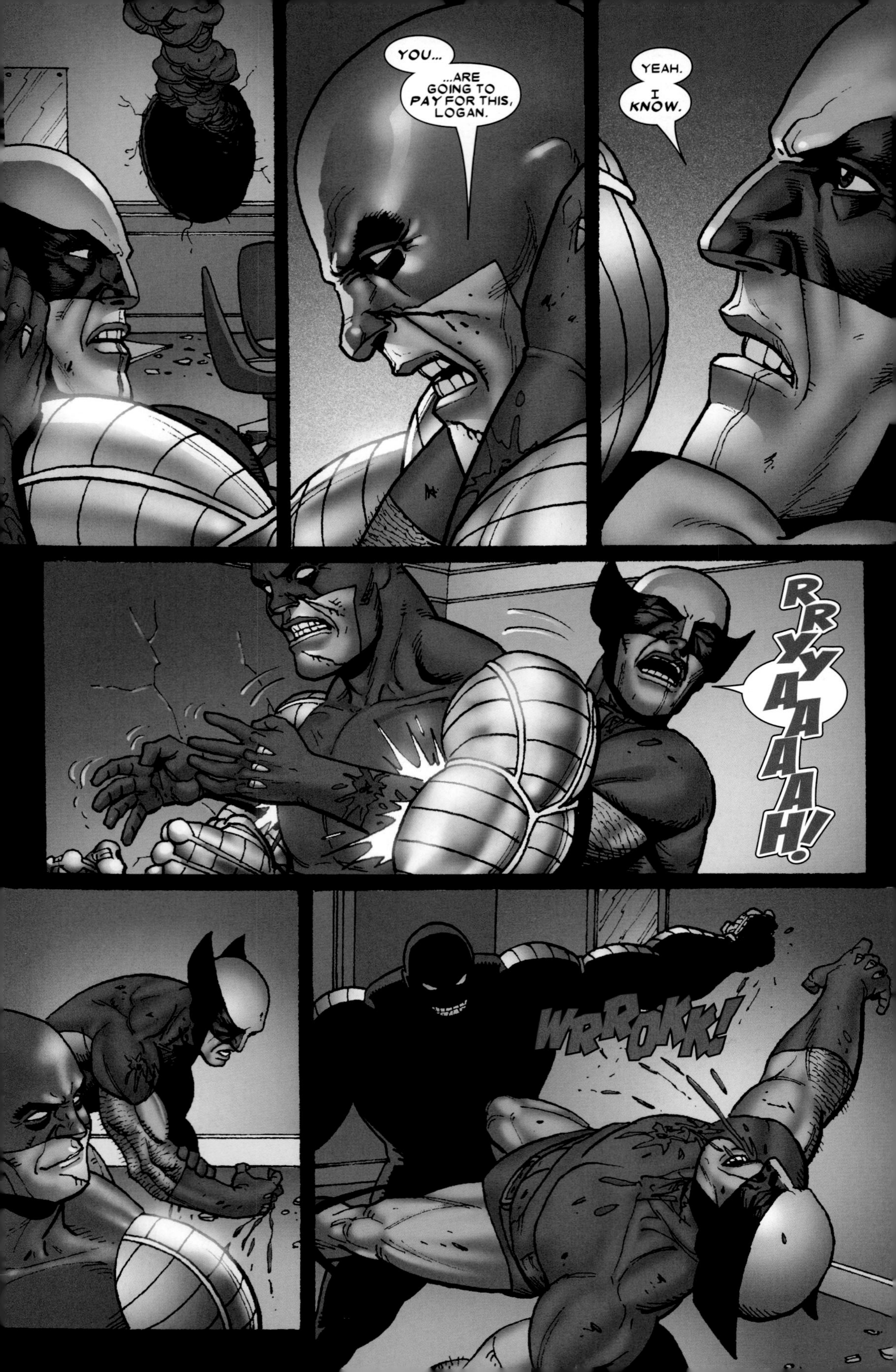
YOU...
...ARE GOING TO PAY FOR THIS, LOGAN.
YEAH.
I KNOW.
RRYAAAAH!
WRROKK!

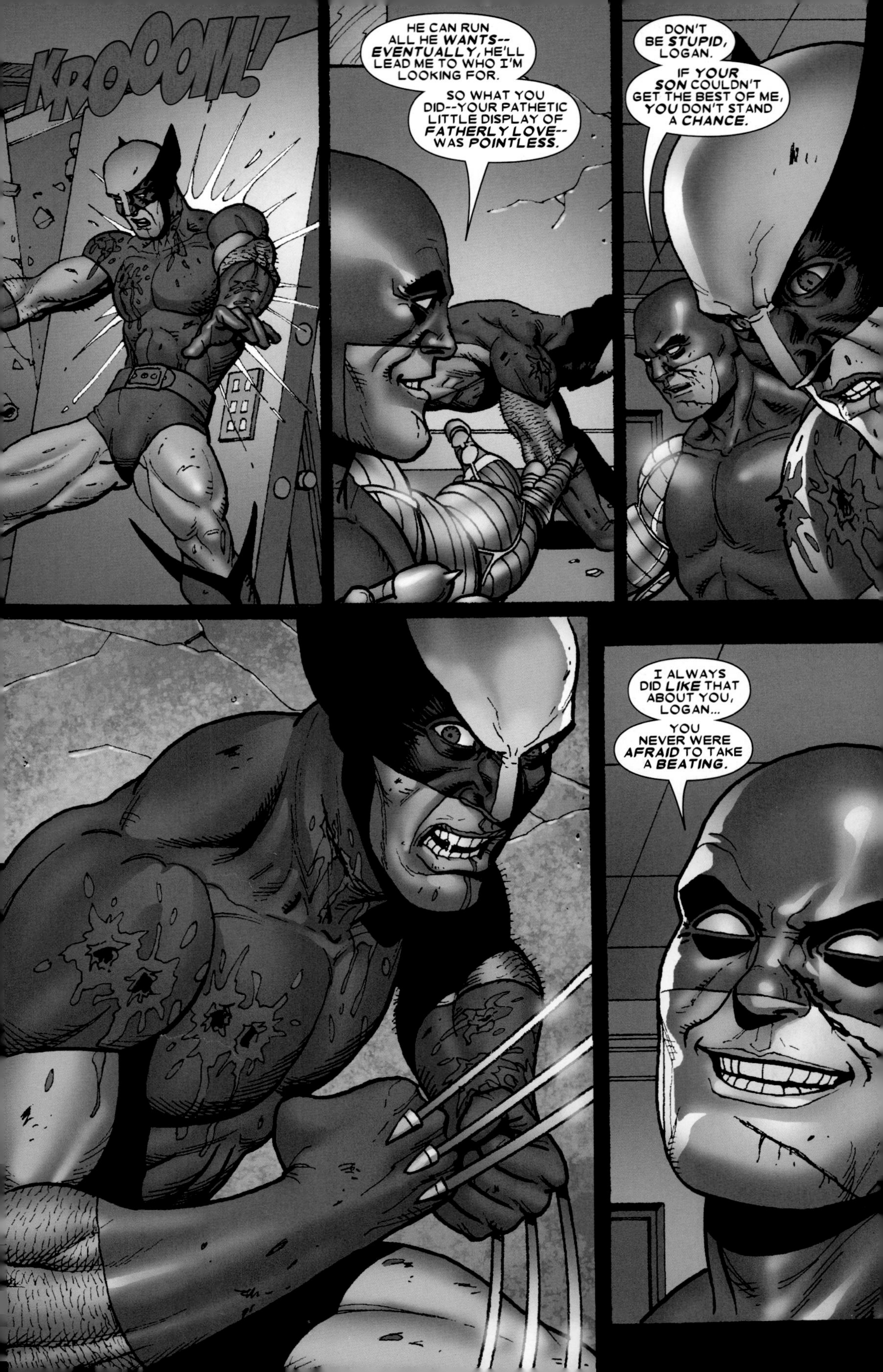

KROOOM!
HE CAN RUN ALL HE WANTS-- EVENTUALLY, HE'LL LEAD ME TO WHO I'M LOOKING FOR.
SO WHAT YOU DID--YOUR PATHETIC LITTLE DISPLAY OF FATHERLY LOVE-- WAS POINTLESS.
DON'T BE STUPID, LOGAN.
IF YOUR SON COULDN'T GET THE BEST OF ME, YOU DON'T STAND A CHANCE.
I ALWAYS DID LIKE THAT ABOUT YOU, LOGAN...
YOU NEVER WERE AFRAID TO TAKE A BEATING.

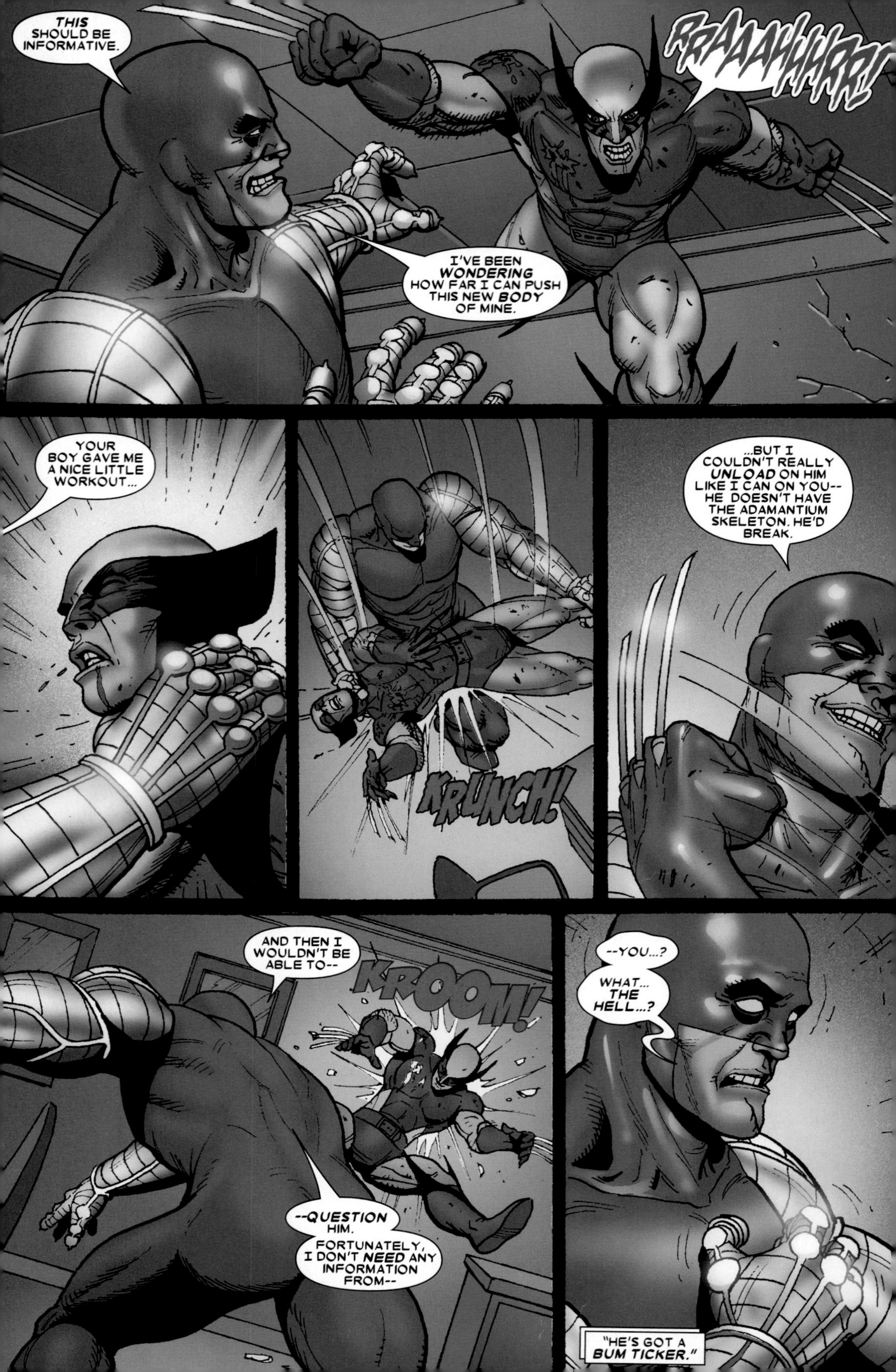
THIS SHOULD BE INFORMATIVE.
RRAAAHHHRR!
I'VE BEEN WONDERING HOW FAR I CAN PUSH THIS NEW BODY OF MINE.
YOUR BOY GAVE ME A NICE LITTLE WORKOUT...
KRUNCH!
...BUT I COULDN'T REALLY UNLOAD ON HIM LIKE I CAN ON YOU-- HE DOESN'T HAVE THE ADAMANTIUM SKELETON. HE'D BREAK.
AND THEN I WOULDN'T BE ABLE TO--
KROOOM!
--QUESTION HIM. FORTUNATELY, I DON'T NEED ANY INFORMATION FROM--
--YOU...?
WHAT... THE HELL...?
"HE'S GOT A BUM TICKER."

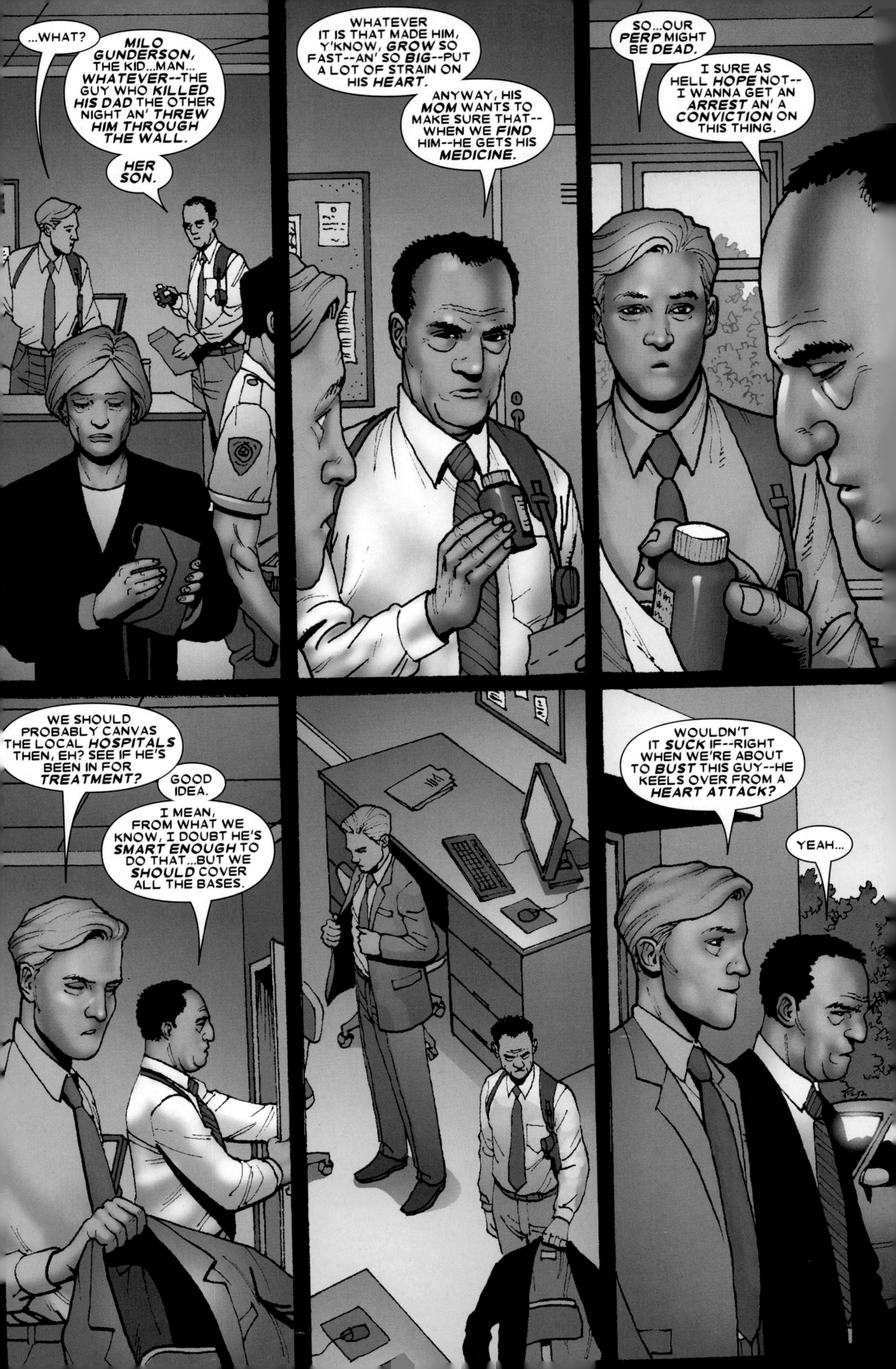
...WHAT?
MILO GUNDERSON, THE KID...MAN... WHATEVER--THE GUY WHO KILLED HIS DAD THE OTHER NIGHT AN' THREW HIM THROUGH THE WALL.
HER SON.
WHATEVER IT IS THAT MADE HIM, Y'KNOW, GROW SO FAST--AN' SO BIG--PUT A LOT OF STRAIN ON HIS HEART.
ANYWAY, HIS MOM WANTS TO MAKE SURE THAT--WHEN WE FIND HIM--HE GETS HIS MEDICINE.
SO...OUR PERP MIGHT BE DEAD.
I SURE AS HELL HOPE NOT--I WANNA GET AN ARREST AN' A CONVICTION ON THIS THING.
WE SHOULD PROBABLY CANVAS THE LOCAL HOSPITALS THEN, EH? SEE IF HE'S BEEN IN FOR TREATMENT?
GOOD IDEA.
I MEAN, FROM WHAT WE KNOW, I DOUBT HE'S SMART ENOUGH TO DO THAT...BUT WE SHOULD COVER ALL THE BASES.
WOULDN'T IT SUCK IF--RIGHT WHEN WE'RE ABOUT TO BUST THIS GUY--HE KEELS OVER FROM A HEART ATTACK?
YEAH...

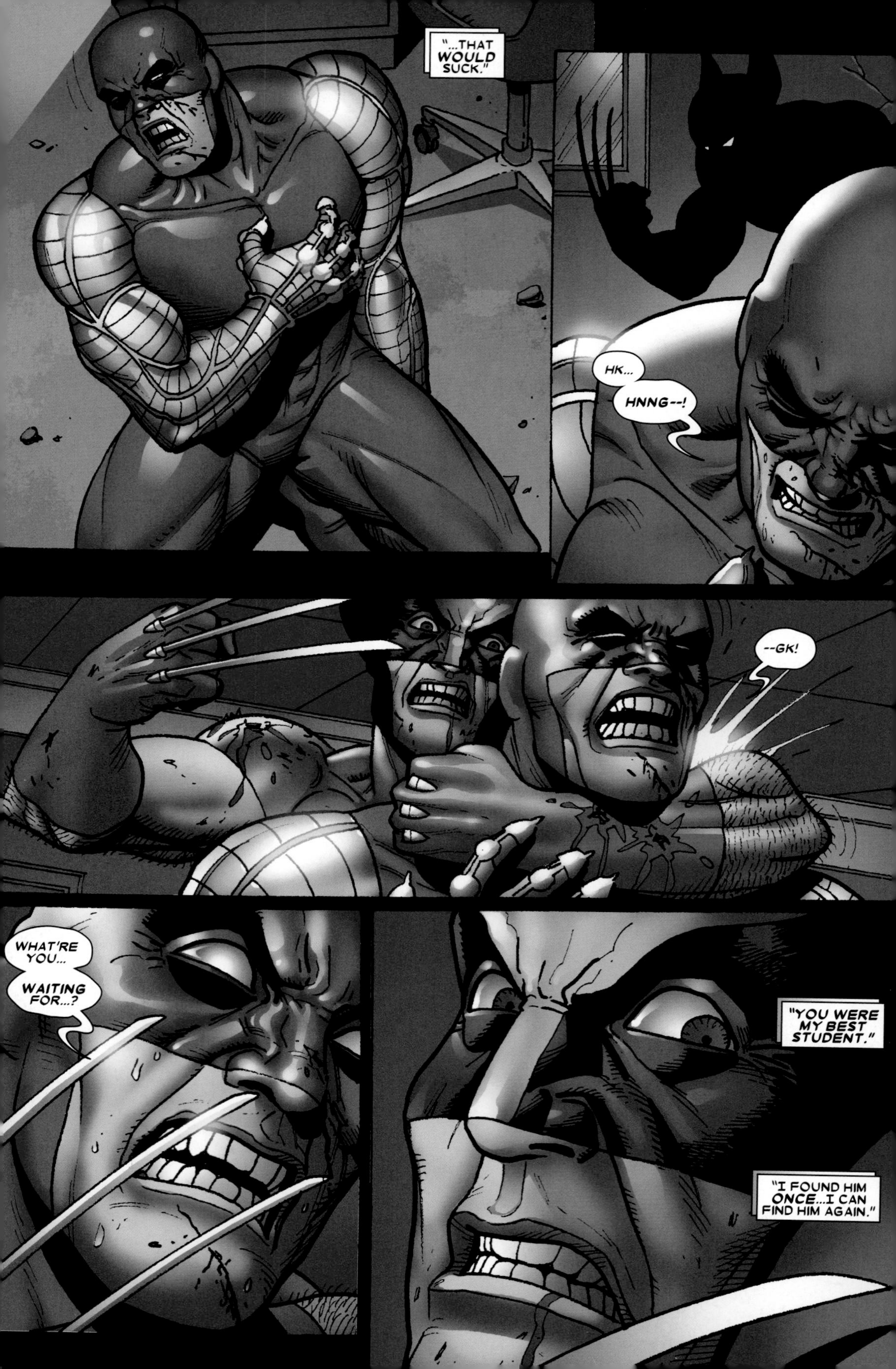

"...THAT WOULD SUCK."
HK...
HNNG--!
--GK!
WHAT'RE YOU...
WAITING FOR...?
"YOU WERE MY BEST STUDENT."
"I FOUND HIM ONCE...I CAN FIND HIM AGAIN."

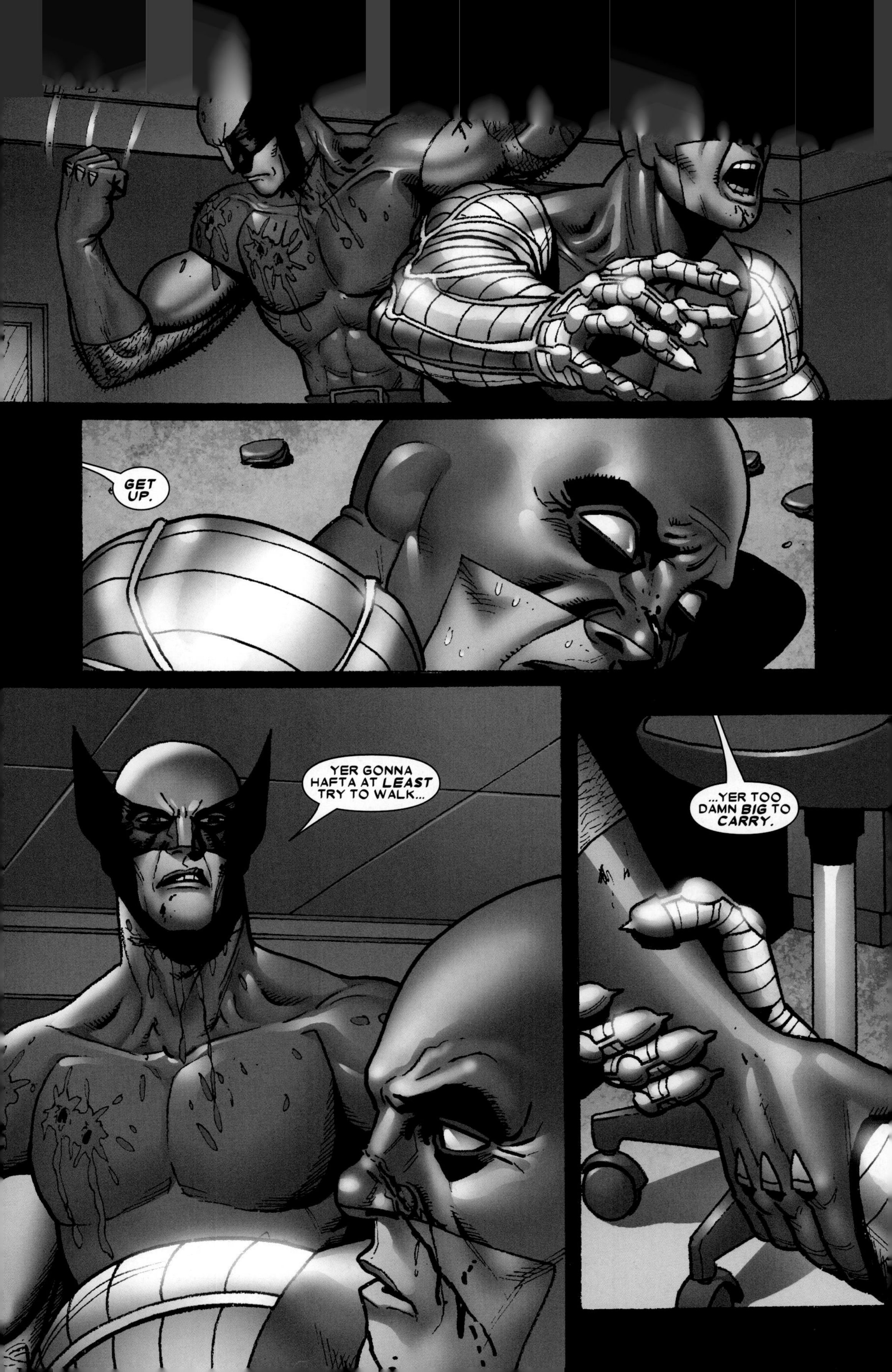
GET UP.
YER GONNA HAFTA AT LEAST TRY TO WALK...
...YER TOO DAMN BIG TO CARRY.

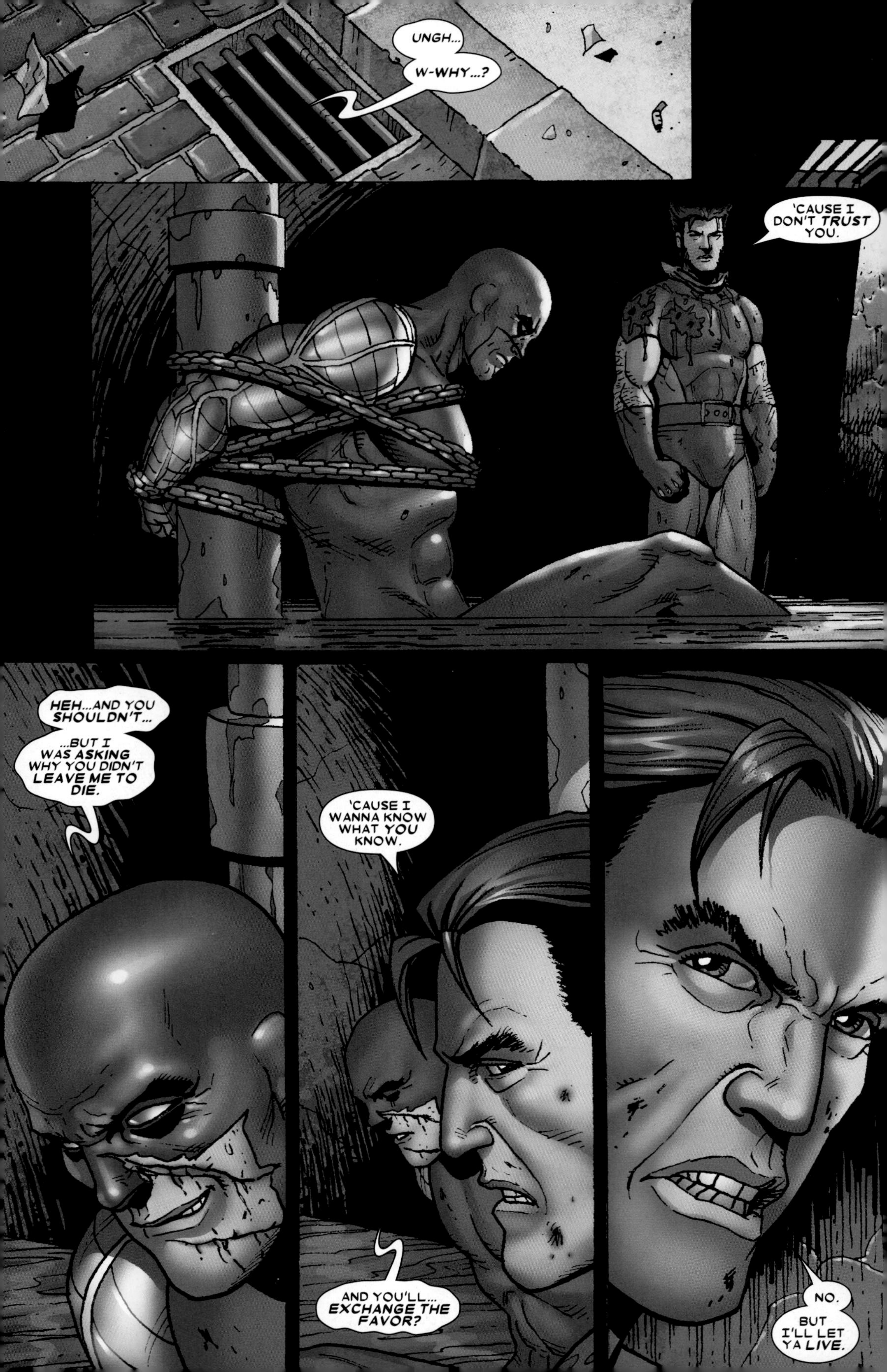
UNGH...
W-WHY...?
'CAUSE I DON'T TRUST YOU.
HEH...AND YOU SHOULDN'T...
...BUT I WAS ASKING WHY YOU DIDN'T LEAVE ME TO DIE.
'CAUSE I WANNA KNOW WHAT YOU KNOW.
AND YOU'LL... EXCHANGE THE FAVOR?
NO.
BUT I'LL LET YA LIVE.

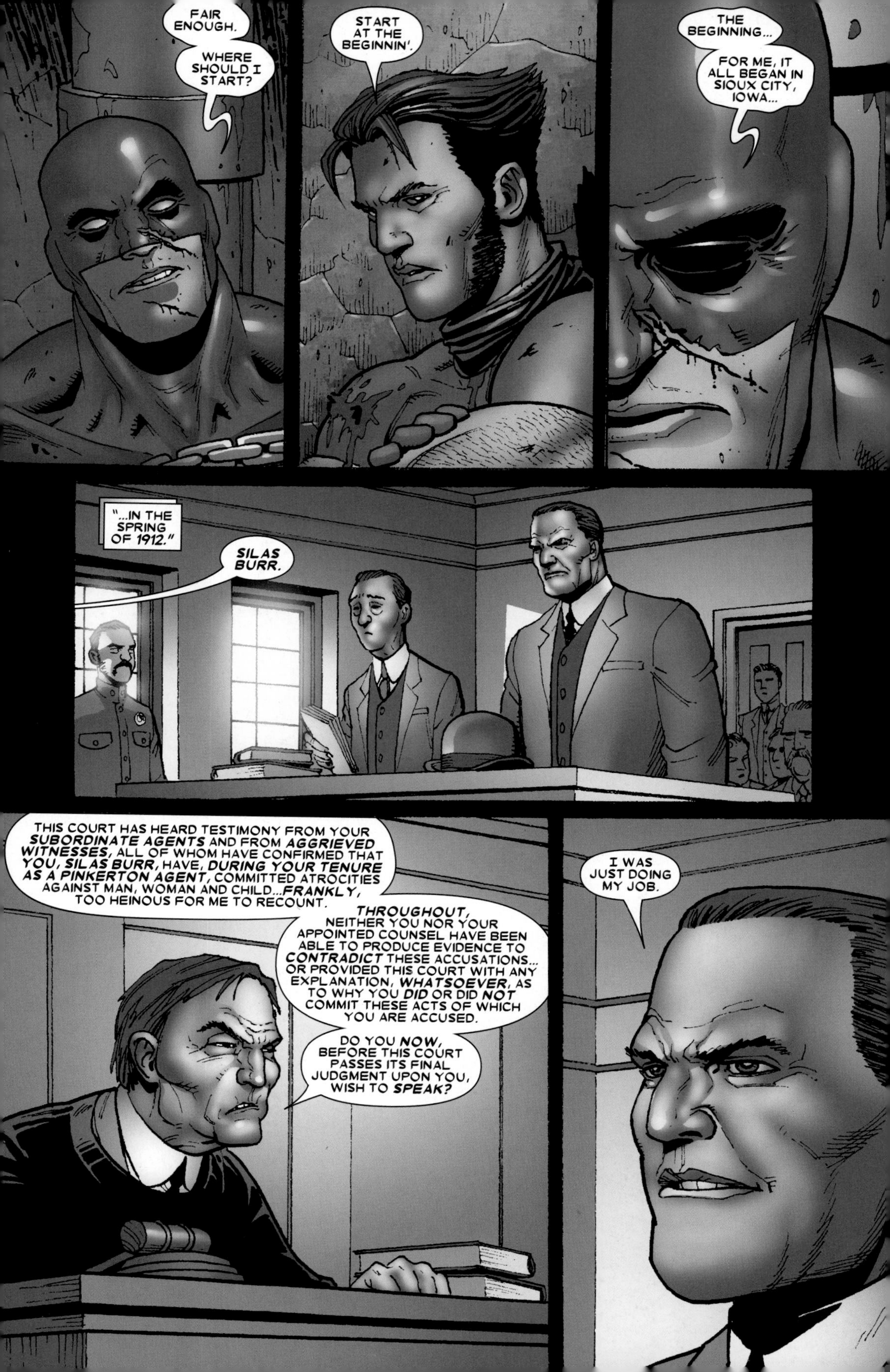
FAIR ENOUGH.
WHERE SHOULD I START?
START AT THE BEGINNIN'.
THE BEGINNING...
FOR ME, IT ALL BEGAN IN SIOUX CITY, IOWA...
"...IN THE SPRING OF 1912."
SILAS BURR.
THIS COURT HAS HEARD TESTIMONY FROM YOUR SUBORDINATE AGENTS AND FROM AGGRIEVED WITNESSES, ALL OF WHOM HAVE CONFIRMED THAT YOU, SILAS BURR, HAVE, DURING YOUR TENURE AS A PINKERTON AGENT, COMMITTED ATROCITIES AGAINST MAN, WOMAN AND CHILD...FRANKLY, TOO HEINOUS FOR ME TO RECOUNT.
THROUGHOUT, NEITHER YOU NOR YOUR APPOINTED COUNSEL HAVE BEEN ABLE TO PRODUCE EVIDENCE TO CONTRADICT THESE ACCUSATIONS... OR PROVIDED THIS COURT WITH ANY EXPLANATION, WHATSOEVER, AS TO WHY YOU DID OR DID NOT COMMIT THESE ACTS OF WHICH YOU ARE ACCUSED.
DO YOU NOW, BEFORE THIS COURT PASSES ITS FINAL JUDGMENT UPON YOU, WISH TO SPEAK?
I WAS JUST DOING MY JOB.

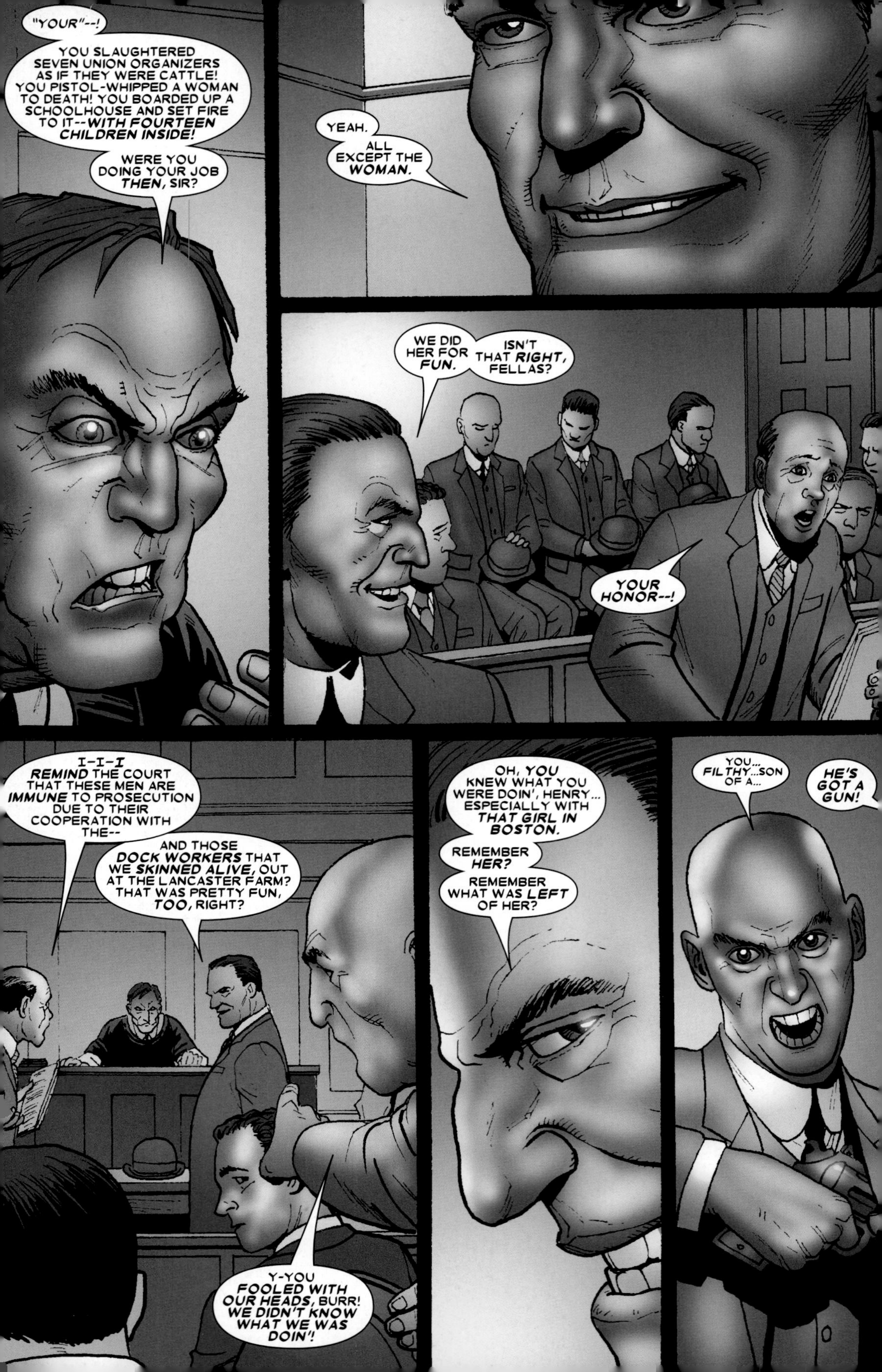
"YOUR"--!
YOU SLAUGHTERED SEVEN UNION ORGANIZERS AS IF THEY WERE CATTLE! YOU PISTOL-WHIPPED A WOMAN TO DEATH! YOU BOARDED UP A SCHOOLHOUSE AND SET FIRE TO IT--WITH FOURTEEN CHILDREN INSIDE!
WERE YOU DOING YOUR JOB THEN, SIR?
YEAH.
ALL EXCEPT THE WOMAN.
WE DID HER FOR FUN.
ISN'T THAT RIGHT, FELLAS?
YOUR HONOR--!
I-I-I REMIND THE COURT THAT THESE MEN ARE IMMUNE TO PROSECUTION DUE TO THEIR COOPERATION WITH THE--
AND THOSE DOCK WORKERS THAT WE SKINNED ALIVE, OUT AT THE LANCASTER FARM? THAT WAS PRETTY FUN, TOO, RIGHT?
Y-YOU FOOLED WITH OUR HEADS, BURR! WE DIDN'T KNOW WHAT WE WAS DOIN'!
OH, YOU KNEW WHAT YOU WERE DOIN', HENRY... ESPECIALLY WITH THAT GIRL IN BOSTON.
REMEMBER HER?
REMEMBER WHAT WAS LEFT OF HER?
YOU... FILTHY...SON OF A...
HE'S GOT A GUN!

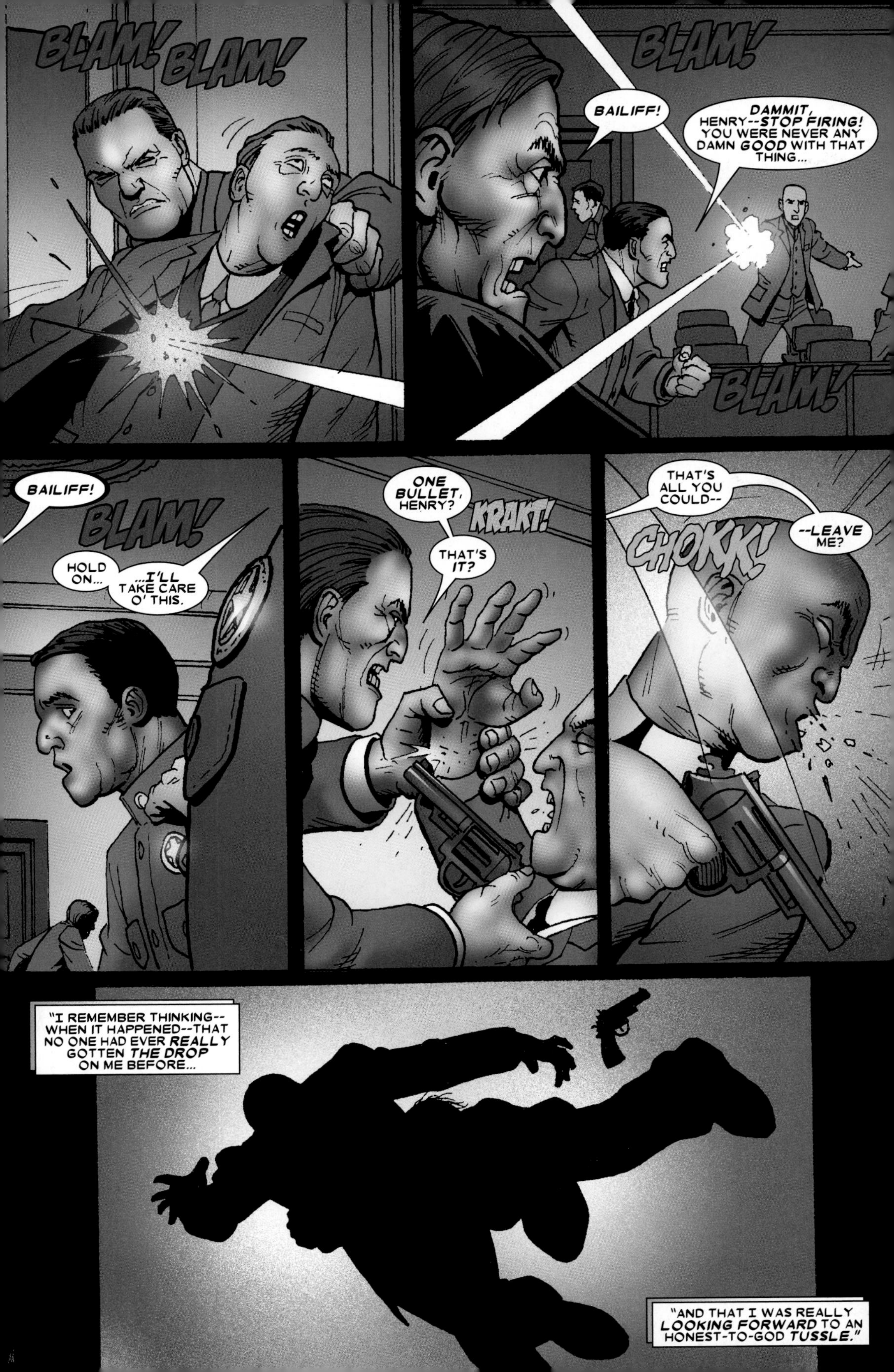
BLAM! BLAM!
BLAM!
BAILIFF!
DAMMIT, HENRY--STOP FIRING! YOU WERE NEVER ANY DAMN GOOD WITH THAT THING...
BLAM!
BAILIFF!
BLAM!
HOLD ON...
...I'LL TAKE CARE O' THIS.
ONE BULLET, HENRY?
KRAKT!
THAT'S IT?
THAT'S ALL YOU COULD--
CHOKK!
--LEAVE ME?
"I REMEMBER THINKING--WHEN IT HAPPENED--THAT NO ONE HAD EVER REALLY GOTTEN THE DROP ON ME BEFORE...
"AND THAT I WAS REALLY LOOKING FORWARD TO AN HONEST-TO-GOD TUSSLE."

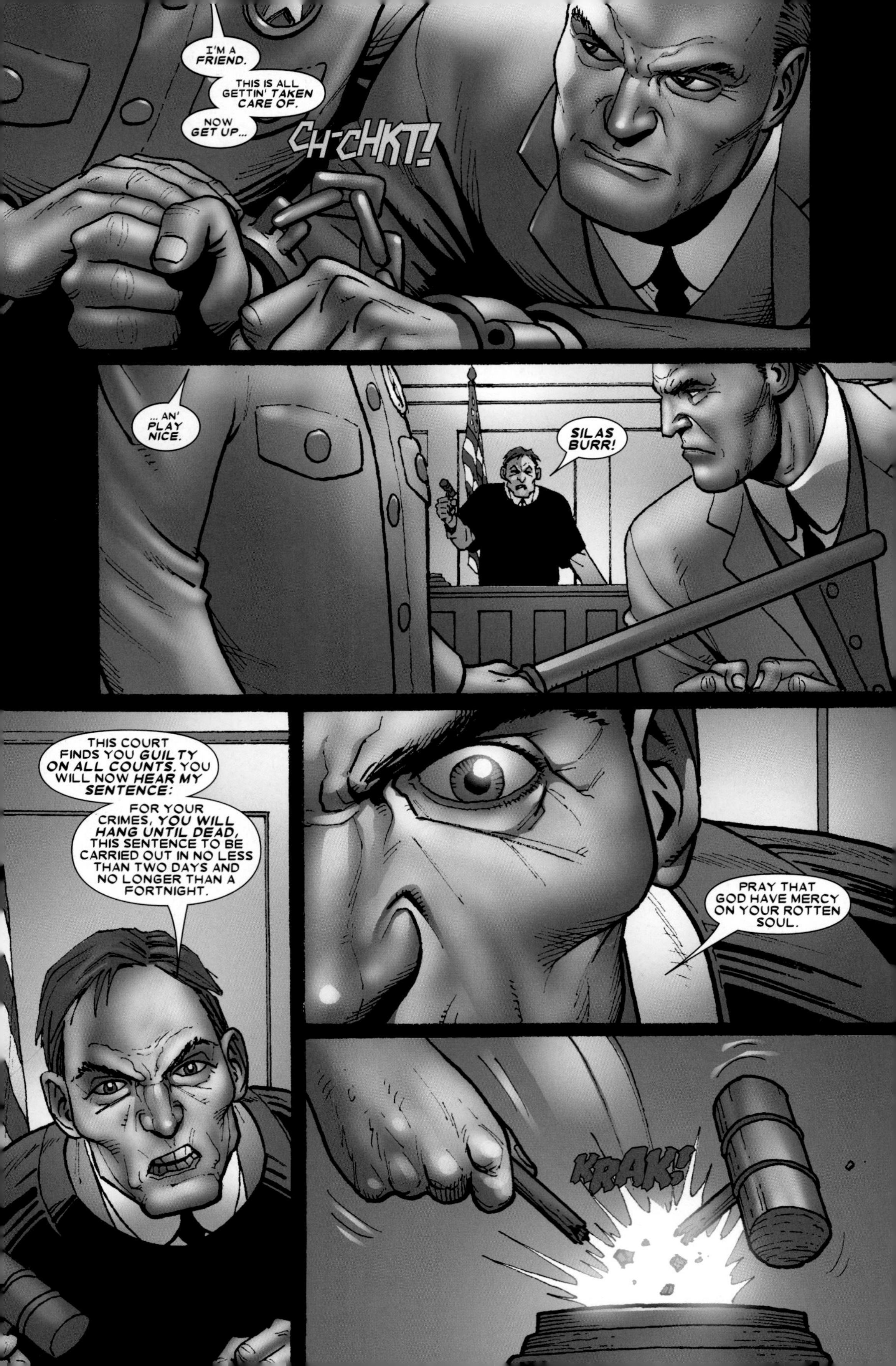
I'M A FRIEND.
THIS IS ALL GETTIN' TAKEN CARE OF.
NOW GET UP...
CH-CHKT!
...AN' PLAY NICE.
SILAS BURR!
THIS COURT FINDS YOU GUILTY ON ALL COUNTS. YOU WILL NOW HEAR MY SENTENCE:
FOR YOUR CRIMES, YOU WILL HANG UNTIL DEAD, THIS SENTENCE TO BE CARRIED OUT IN NO LESS THAN TWO DAYS AND NO LONGER THAN A FORTNIGHT.
PRAY THAT GOD HAVE MERCY ON YOUR ROTTEN SOUL.
KRAK!

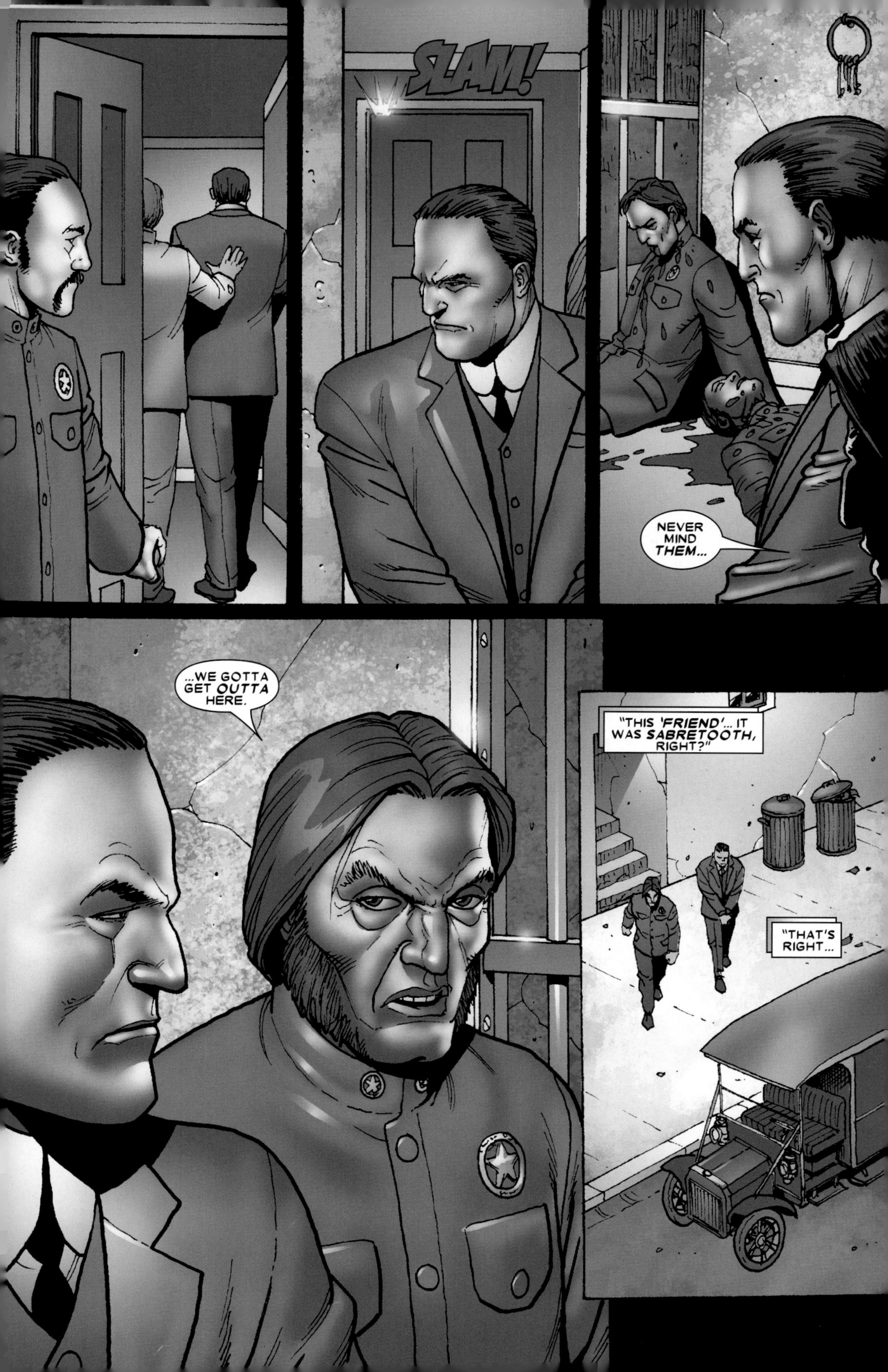
SLAM!
NEVER MIND THEM...
...WE GOTTA GET OUTTA HERE.
"THIS 'FRIEND'... IT WAS SABRETOOTH, RIGHT?"
"THAT'S RIGHT...

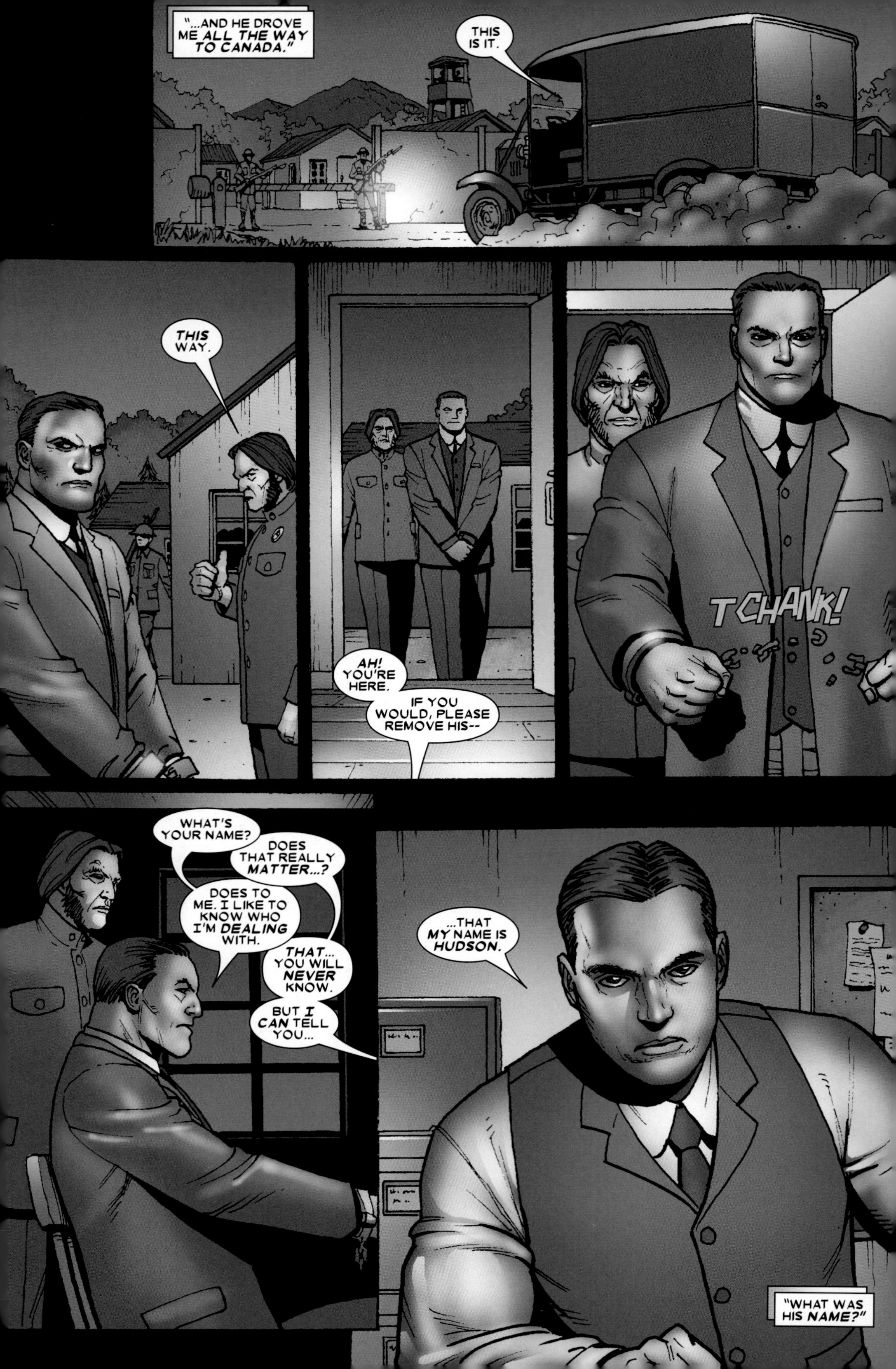
"...AND HE DROVE ME ALL THE WAY TO CANADA."
THIS IS IT.
THIS WAY.
AH! YOU'RE HERE.
IF YOU WOULD, PLEASE REMOVE HIS--
T CHANK!
WHAT'S YOUR NAME?
DOES THAT REALLY MATTER...?
DOES TO ME. I LIKE TO KNOW WHO I'M DEALING WITH.
THAT... YOU WILL NEVER KNOW.
BUT I CAN TELL YOU...
...THAT MY NAME IS HUDSON.
"WHAT WAS HIS NAME?"

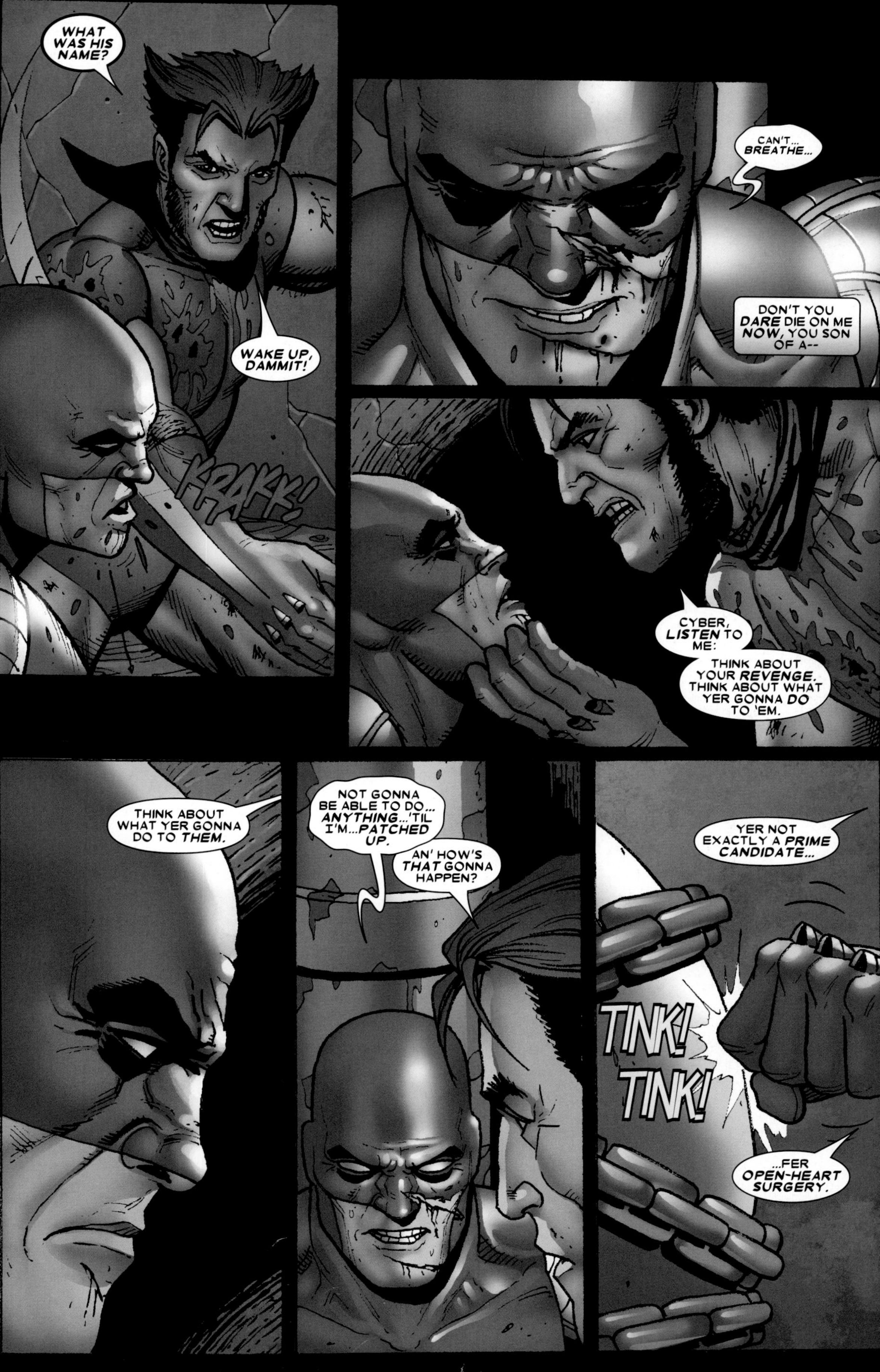
WHAT WAS HIS NAME?
WAKE UP, DAMMIT!
KRAKK!
CAN'T... BREATHE...
DON'T YOU DARE DIE ON ME NOW, YOU SON OF A--
CYBER, LISTEN TO ME:
THINK ABOUT YOUR REVENGE. THINK ABOUT WHAT YER GONNA DO TO 'EM.
THINK ABOUT WHAT YER GONNA DO TO THEM.
NOT GONNA BE ABLE TO DO... ANYTHING...'TIL I'M...PATCHED UP.
AN' HOW'S THAT GONNA HAPPEN?
YER NOT EXACTLY A PRIME CANDIDATE...
TINK! TINK!
...FER OPEN-HEART SURGERY.

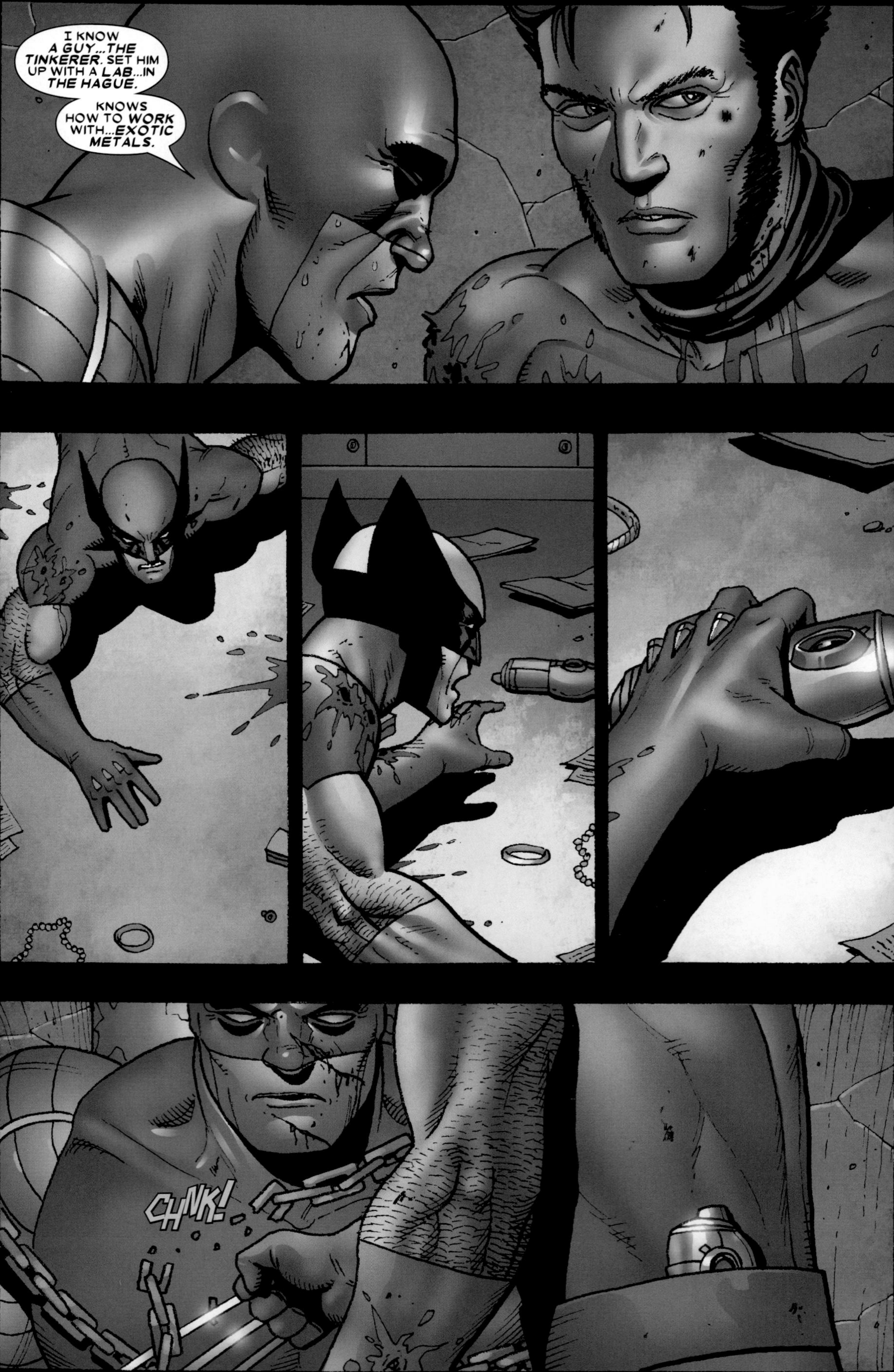
I KNOW A GUY...THE TINKERER. SET HIM UP WITH A LAB...IN THE HAGUE.
KNOWS HOW TO WORK WITH...EXOTIC METALS.
CHNK!

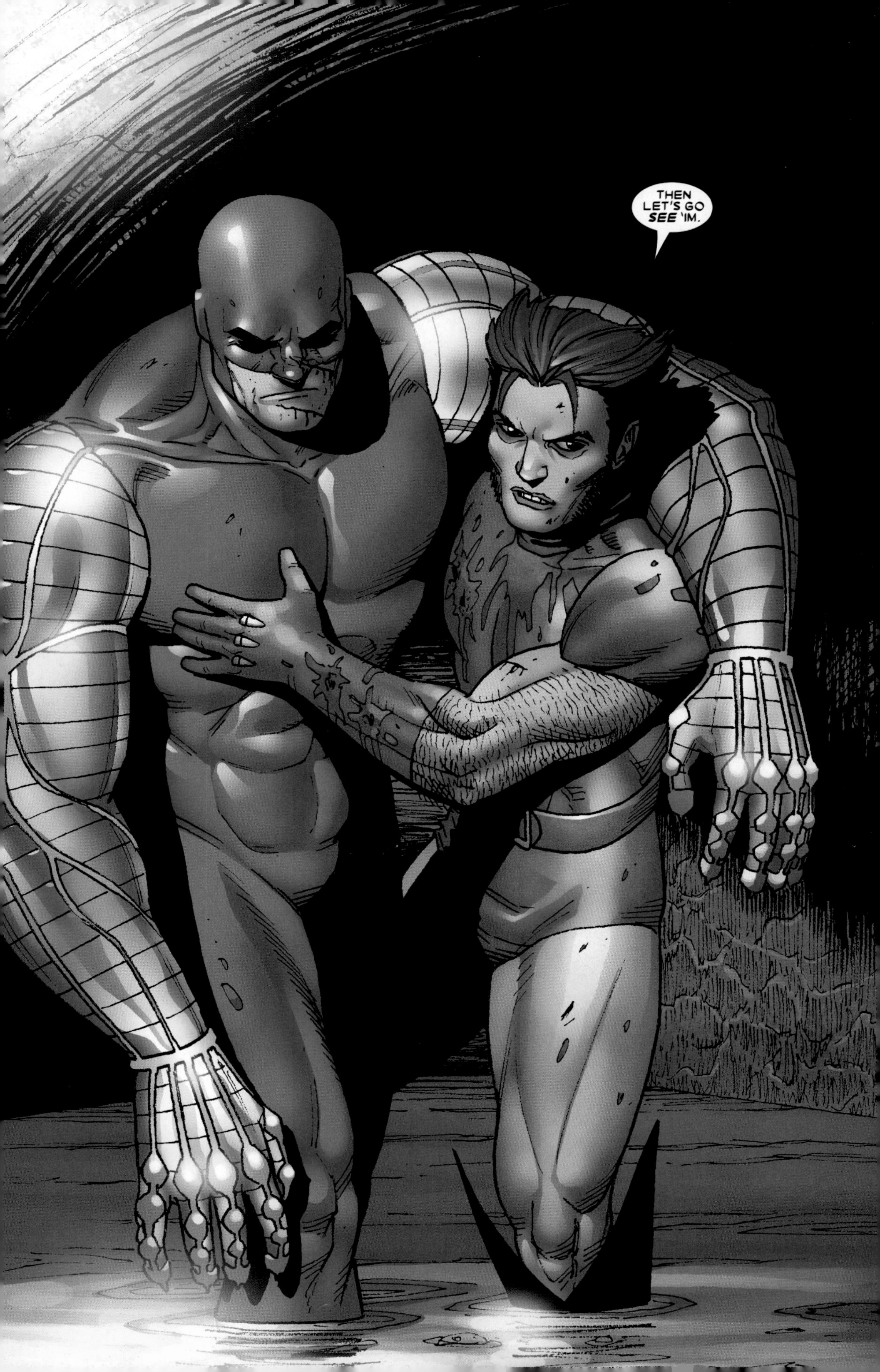
THEN LET'S GO SEE 'IM.

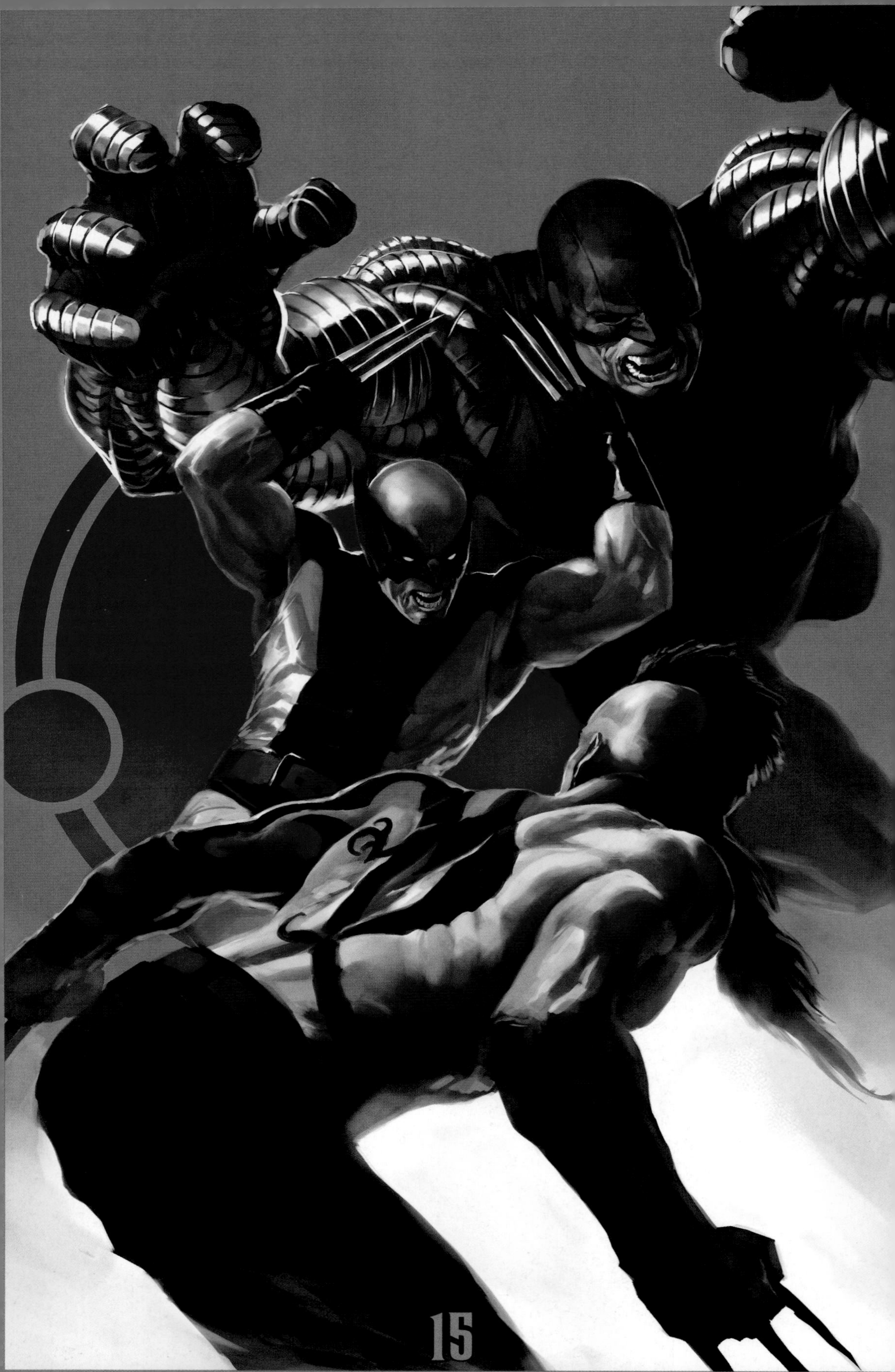

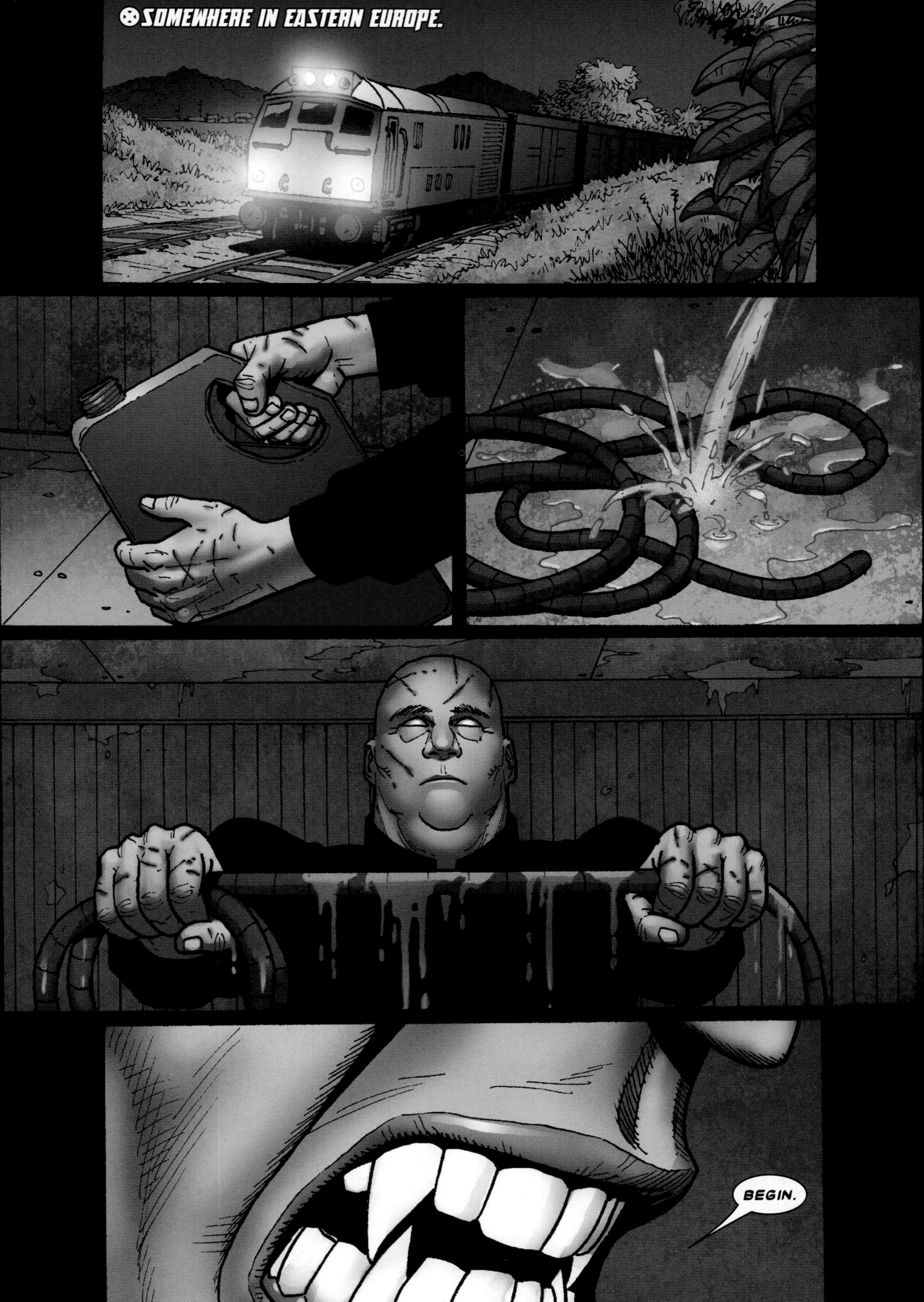
SOMEWHERE IN EASTERN EUROPE.
BEGIN.

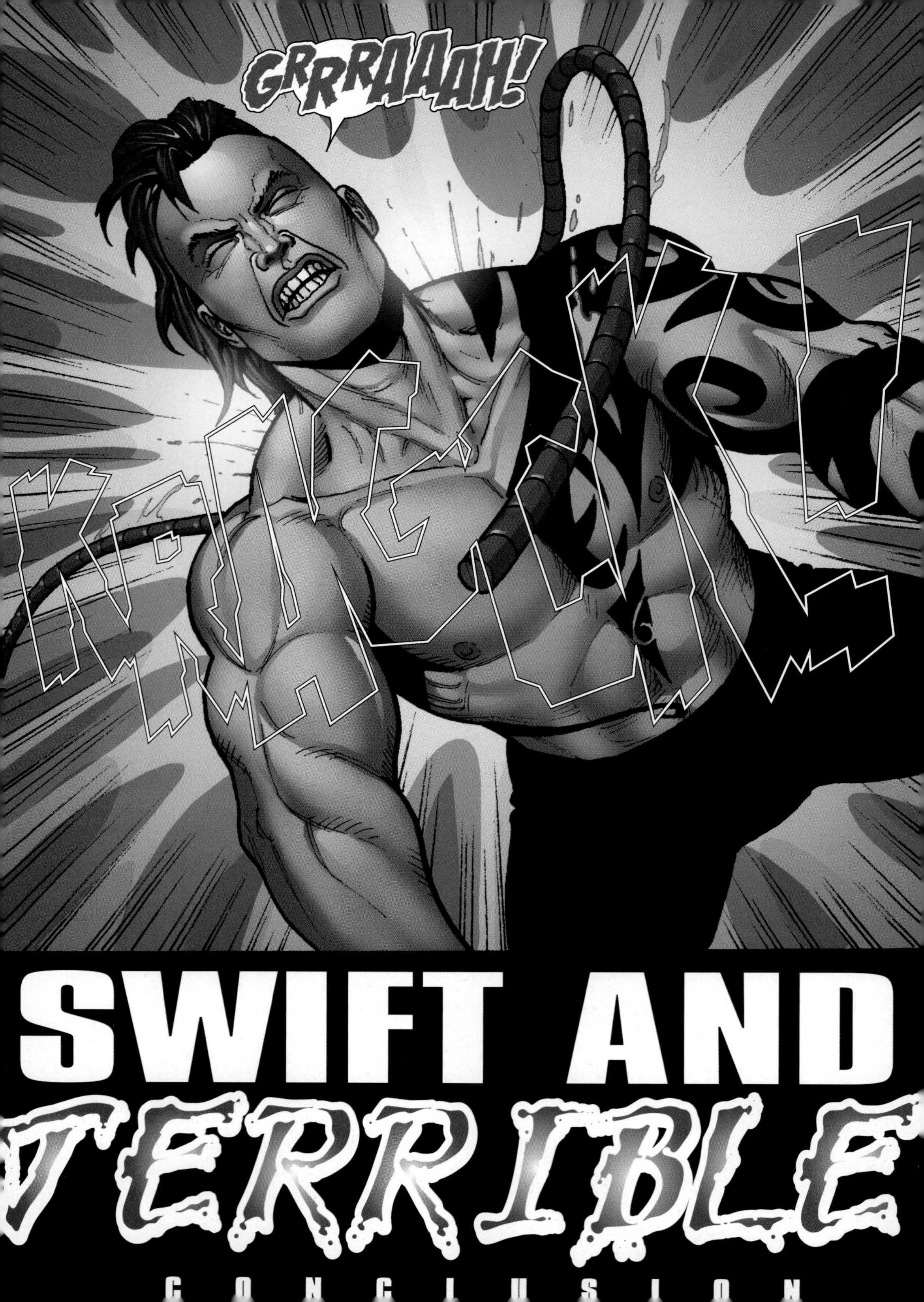
GRRRAAAH!

SWIFT AND TERRIBLE

C O N C L U S I O N

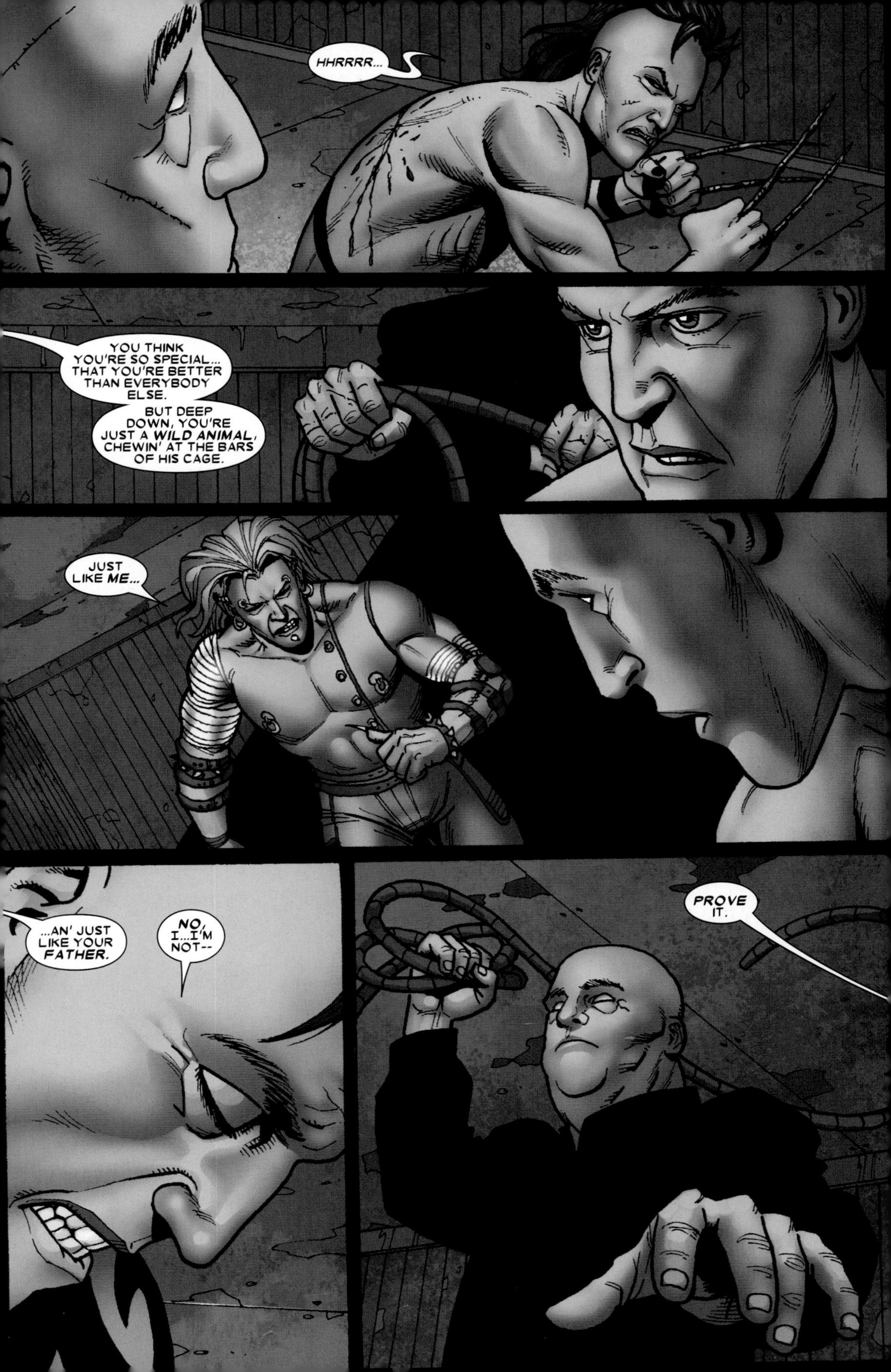
HHRRRR...
YOU THINK YOU'RE SO SPECIAL... THAT YOU'RE BETTER THAN EVERYBODY ELSE.
BUT DEEP DOWN, YOU'RE JUST A *WILD ANIMAL*, CHEWIN' AT THE BARS OF HIS CAGE.
JUST LIKE *ME*...
...AN' JUST LIKE YOUR *FATHER*.
NO, I...I'M NOT--
PROVE IT.

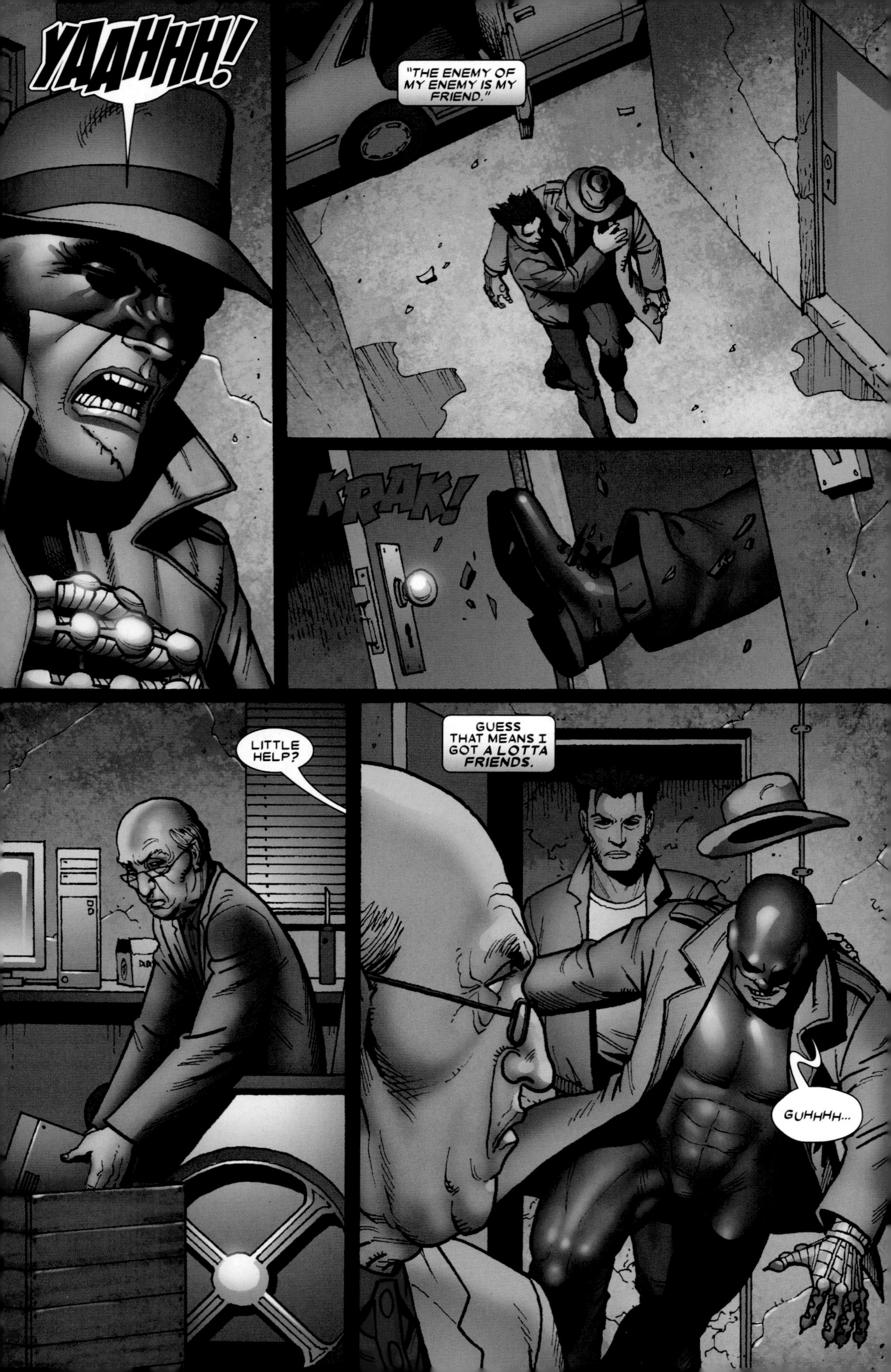
YAAHHH!
"THE ENEMY OF MY ENEMY IS MY FRIEND."
KRAK!
LITTLE HELP?
GUESS THAT MEANS I GOT A LOTTA FRIENDS.
GUHHHH...

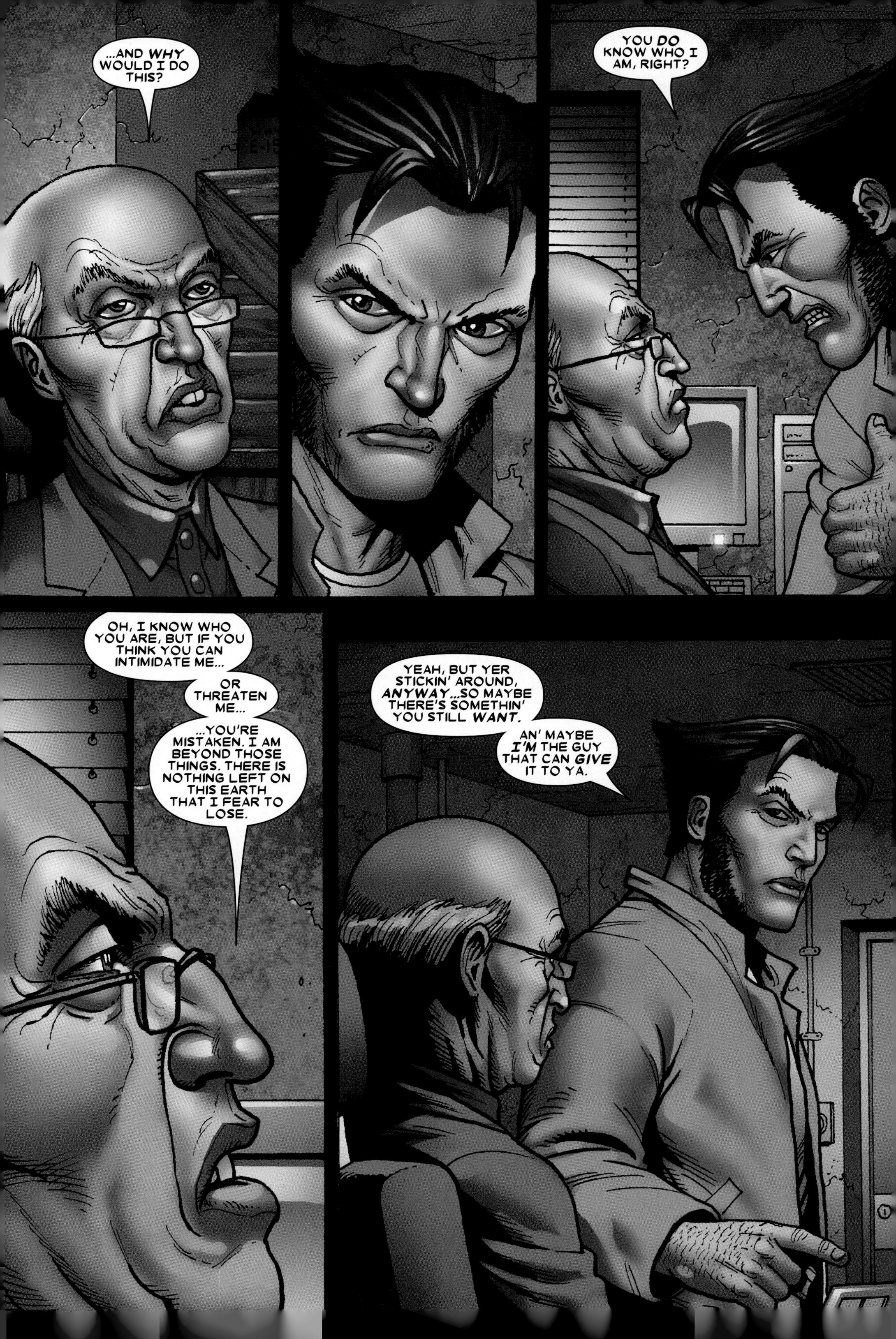
...AND WHY WOULD I DO THIS?
YOU DO KNOW WHO I AM, RIGHT?
OH, I KNOW WHO YOU ARE, BUT IF YOU THINK YOU CAN INTIMIDATE ME...
OR THREATEN ME...
...YOU'RE MISTAKEN. I AM BEYOND THOSE THINGS. THERE IS NOTHING LEFT ON THIS EARTH THAT I FEAR TO LOSE.
YEAH, BUT YER STICKIN' AROUND, ANYWAY...SO MAYBE THERE'S SOMETHIN' YOU STILL WANT.
AN' MAYBE I'M THE GUY THAT CAN GIVE IT TO YA.

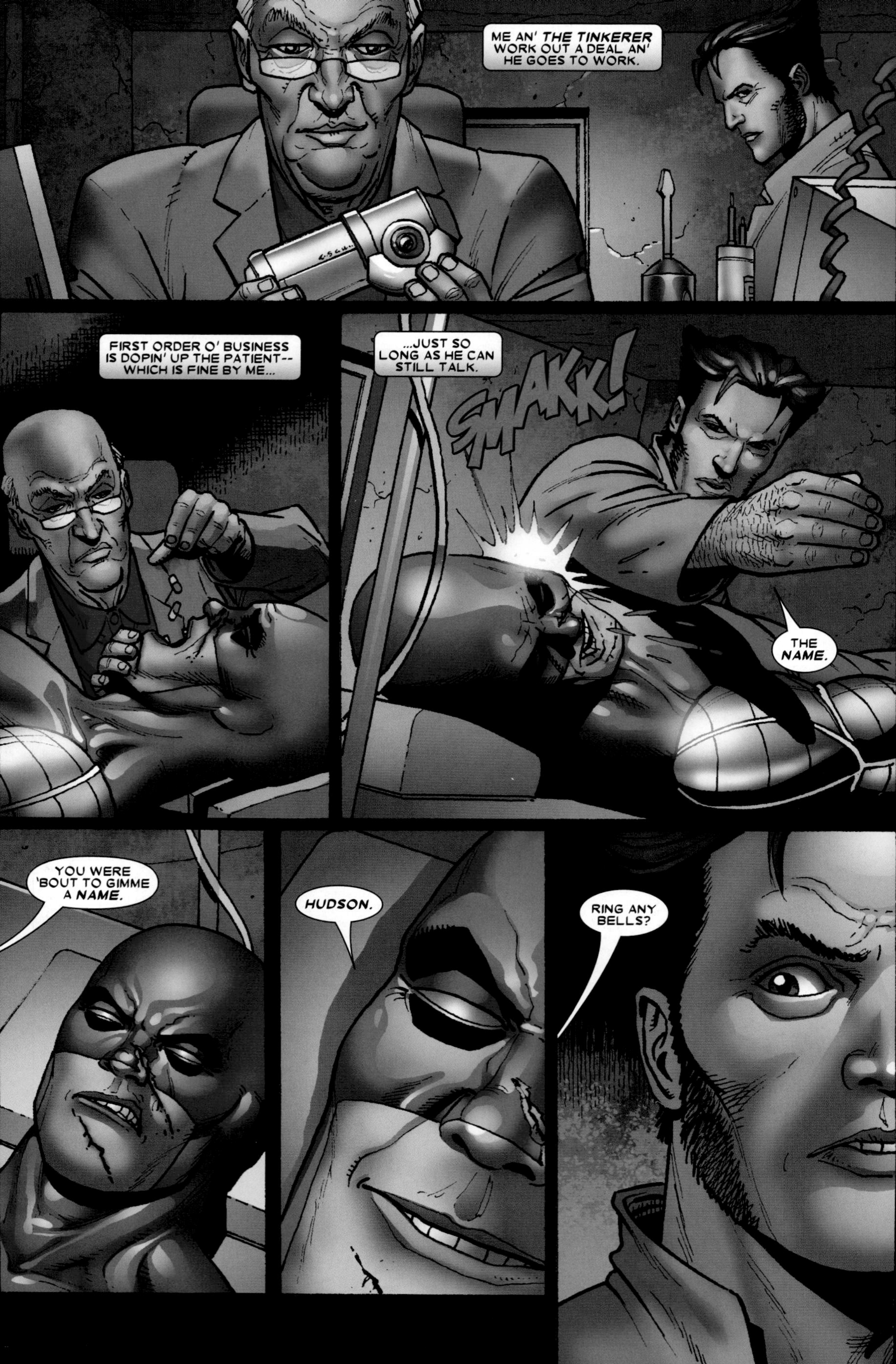
ME AN' THE TINKERER WORK OUT A DEAL AN' HE GOES TO WORK.
FIRST ORDER O' BUSINESS IS DOPIN' UP THE PATIENT-- WHICH IS FINE BY ME...
...JUST SO LONG AS HE CAN STILL TALK.
SHAKK!
THE NAME.
YOU WERE 'BOUT TO GIMME A NAME.
HUDSON.
RING ANY BELLS?

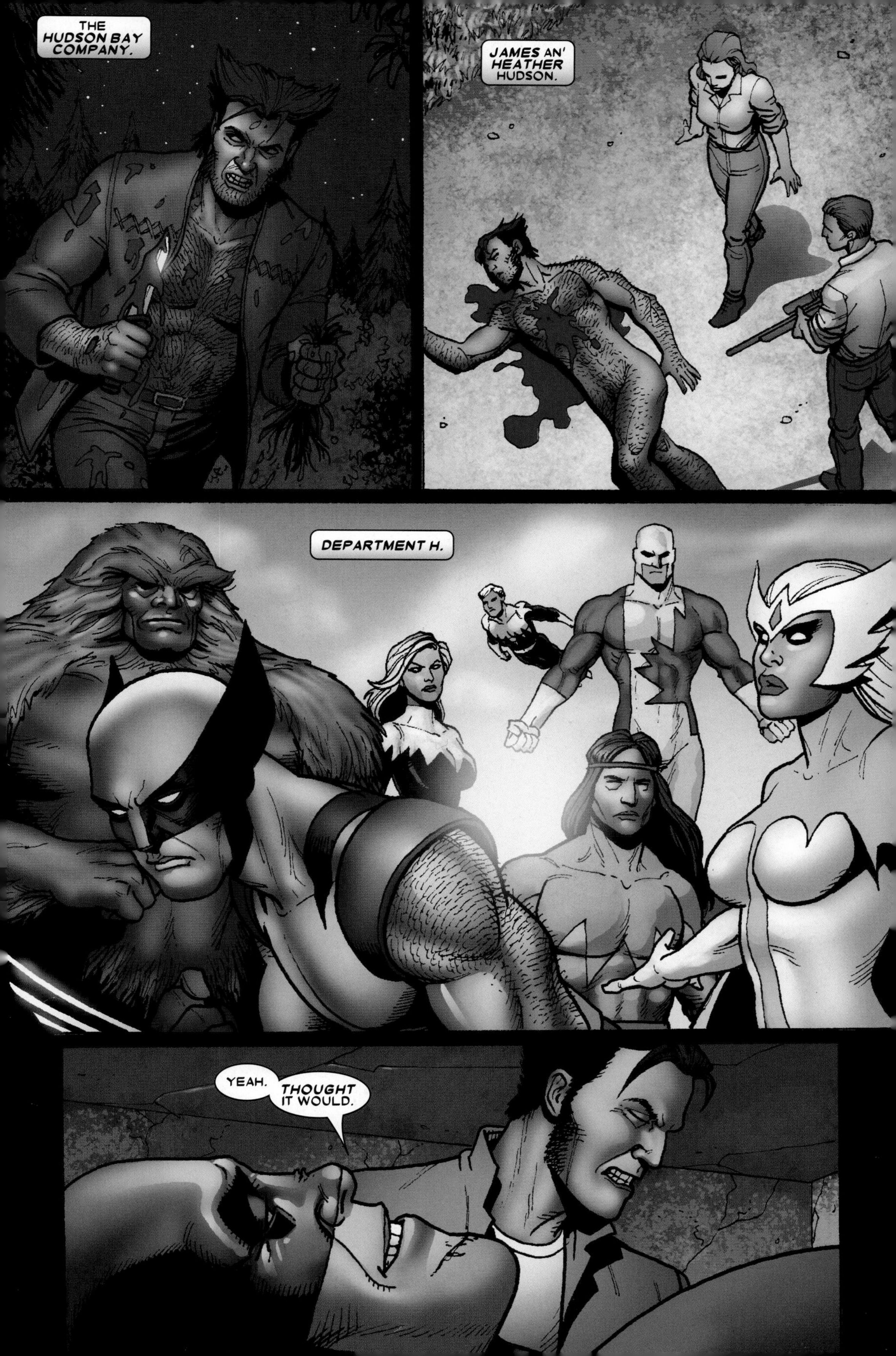
THE HUDSON BAY COMPANY.
JAMES AN' HEATHER HUDSON.
DEPARTMENT H.
YEAH.
THOUGHT IT WOULD.

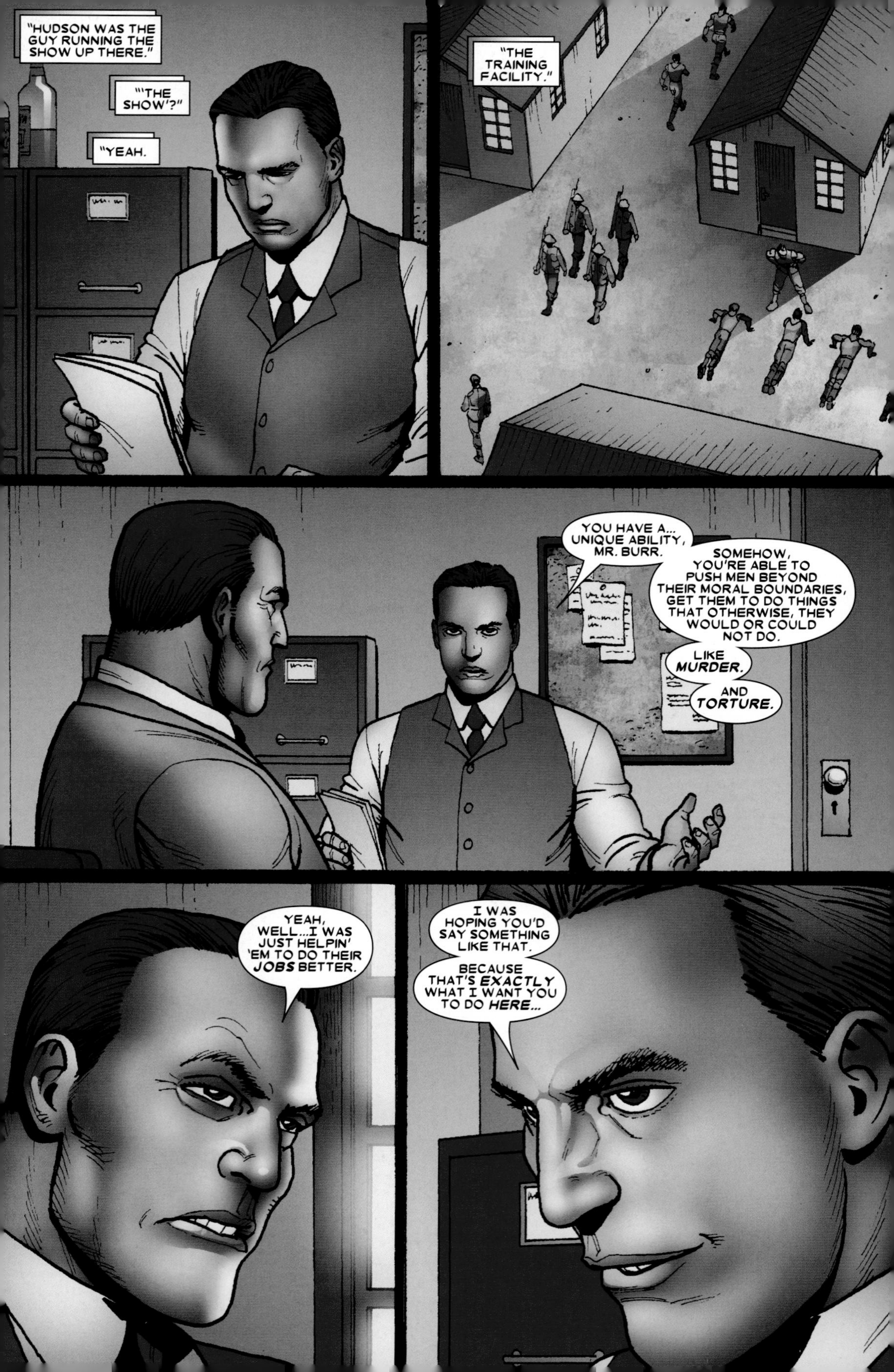

"HUDSON WAS THE GUY RUNNING THE SHOW UP THERE."
"'THE SHOW'?"
"YEAH.
"THE TRAINING FACILITY."
YOU HAVE A... UNIQUE ABILITY, MR. BURR.
SOMEHOW, YOU'RE ABLE TO PUSH MEN BEYOND THEIR MORAL BOUNDARIES, GET THEM TO DO THINGS THAT OTHERWISE, THEY WOULD OR COULD NOT DO.
LIKE *MURDER*.
AND *TORTURE*.
YEAH, WELL...I WAS JUST HELPIN' 'EM TO DO THEIR *JOBS* BETTER.
I WAS HOPING YOU'D SAY SOMETHING LIKE THAT.
BECAUSE THAT'S *EXACTLY* WHAT I WANT YOU TO DO *HERE*...

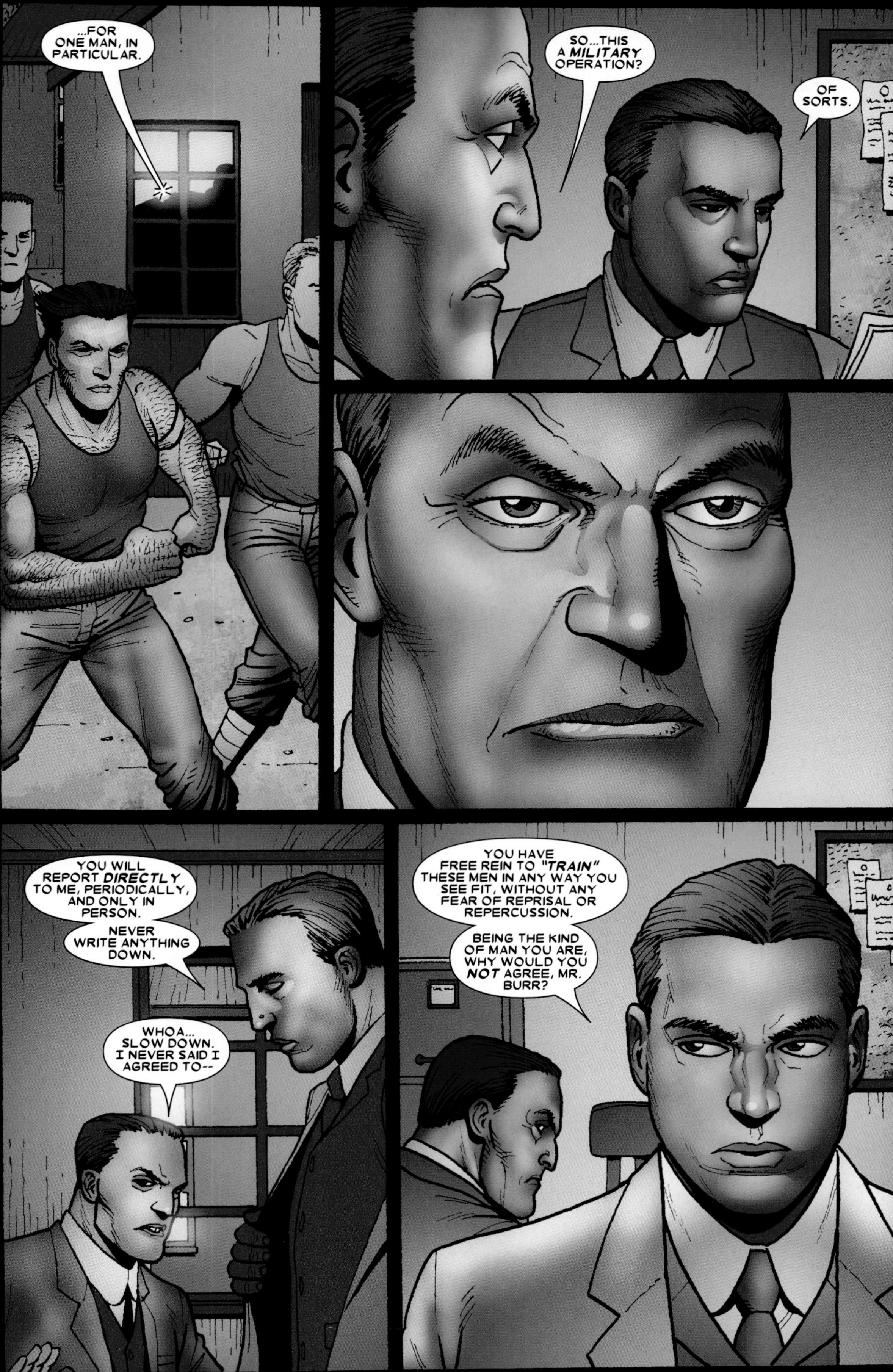
...FOR ONE MAN, IN PARTICULAR.
SO...THIS A *MILITARY* OPERATION?
OF SORTS.
YOU WILL REPORT *DIRECTLY* TO ME, PERIODICALLY, AND ONLY IN PERSON.
NEVER WRITE ANYTHING DOWN.
WHOA... SLOW DOWN. I NEVER SAID I AGREED TO--
YOU HAVE FREE REIN TO *"TRAIN"* THESE MEN IN ANY WAY YOU SEE FIT, WITHOUT ANY FEAR OF REPRISAL OR REPERCUSSION.
BEING THE KIND OF MAN YOU ARE, WHY WOULD YOU *NOT* AGREE, MR. BURR?

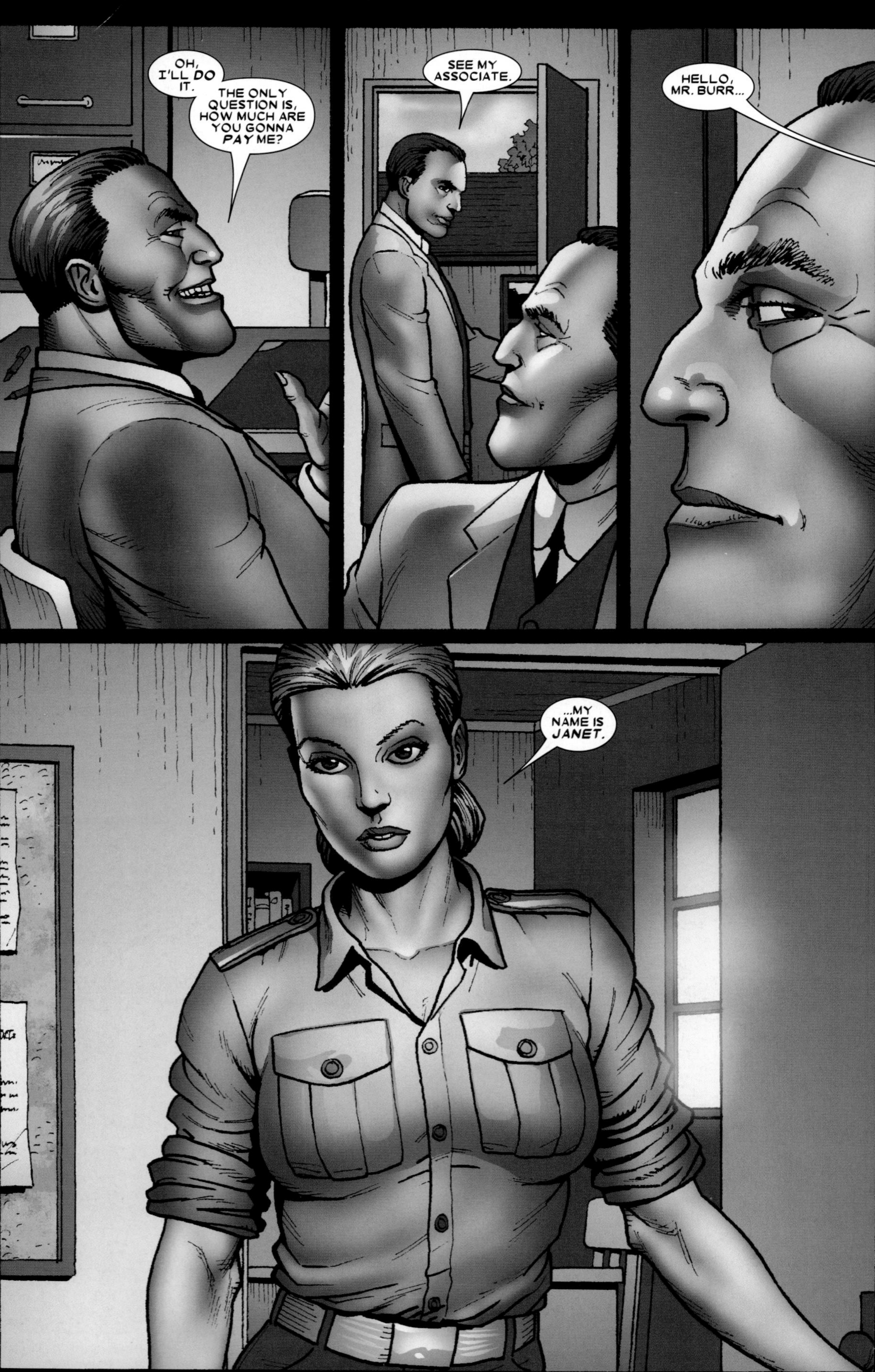
OH, I'LL DO IT.
THE ONLY QUESTION IS, HOW MUCH ARE YOU GONNA PAY ME?
SEE MY ASSOCIATE.
HELLO, MR. BURR...
...MY NAME IS JANET.

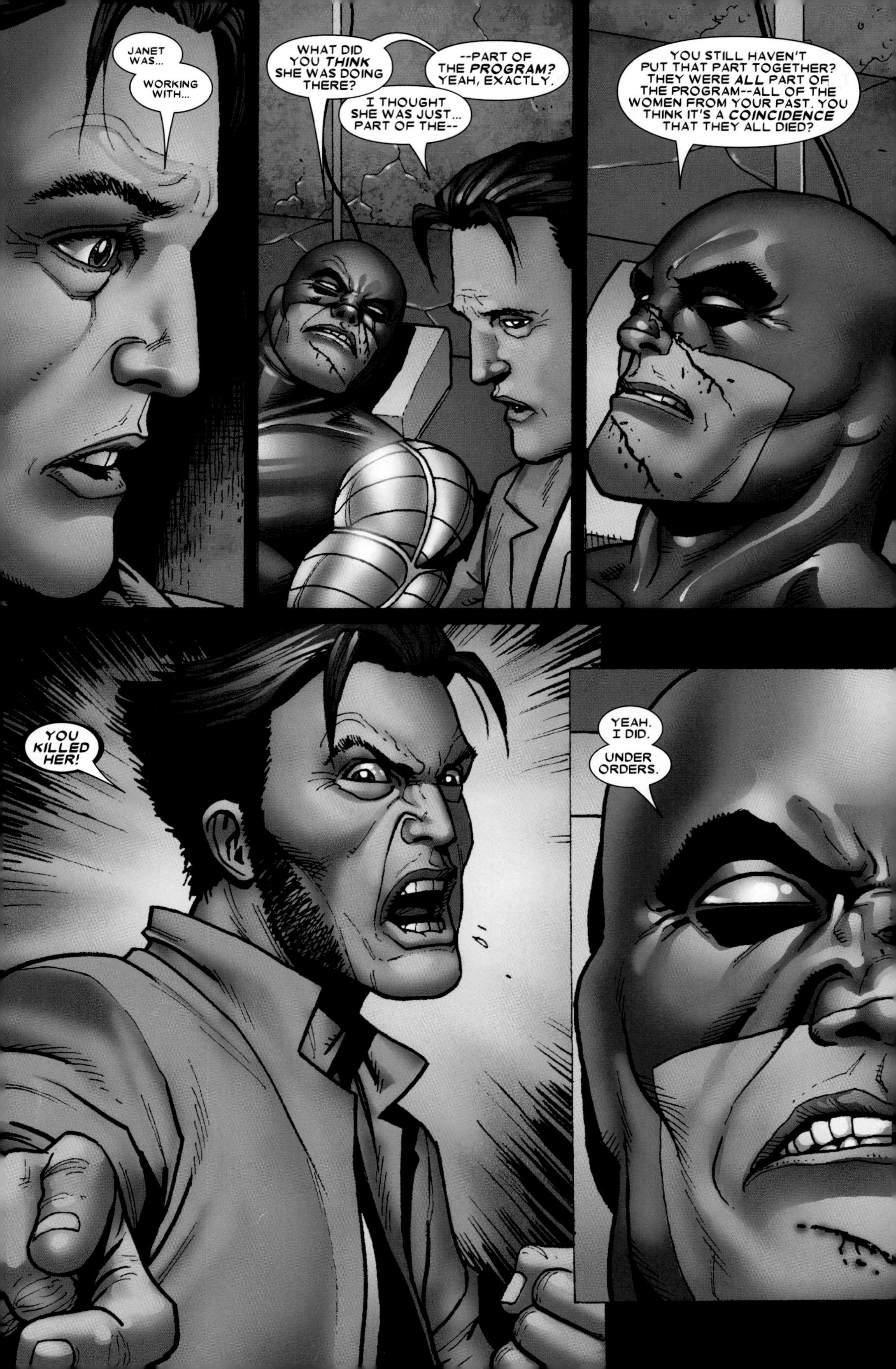
JANET WAS...
WORKING WITH...
WHAT DID YOU *THINK* SHE WAS DOING THERE?
I THOUGHT SHE WAS JUST... PART OF THE--
--PART OF THE *PROGRAM?* YEAH, EXACTLY.
YOU STILL HAVEN'T PUT THAT PART TOGETHER? THEY WERE *ALL* PART OF THE PROGRAM--ALL OF THE WOMEN FROM YOUR PAST. YOU THINK IT'S A *COINCIDENCE* THAT THEY ALL DIED?
YOU *KILLED HER!*
YEAH. I DID.
UNDER ORDERS.

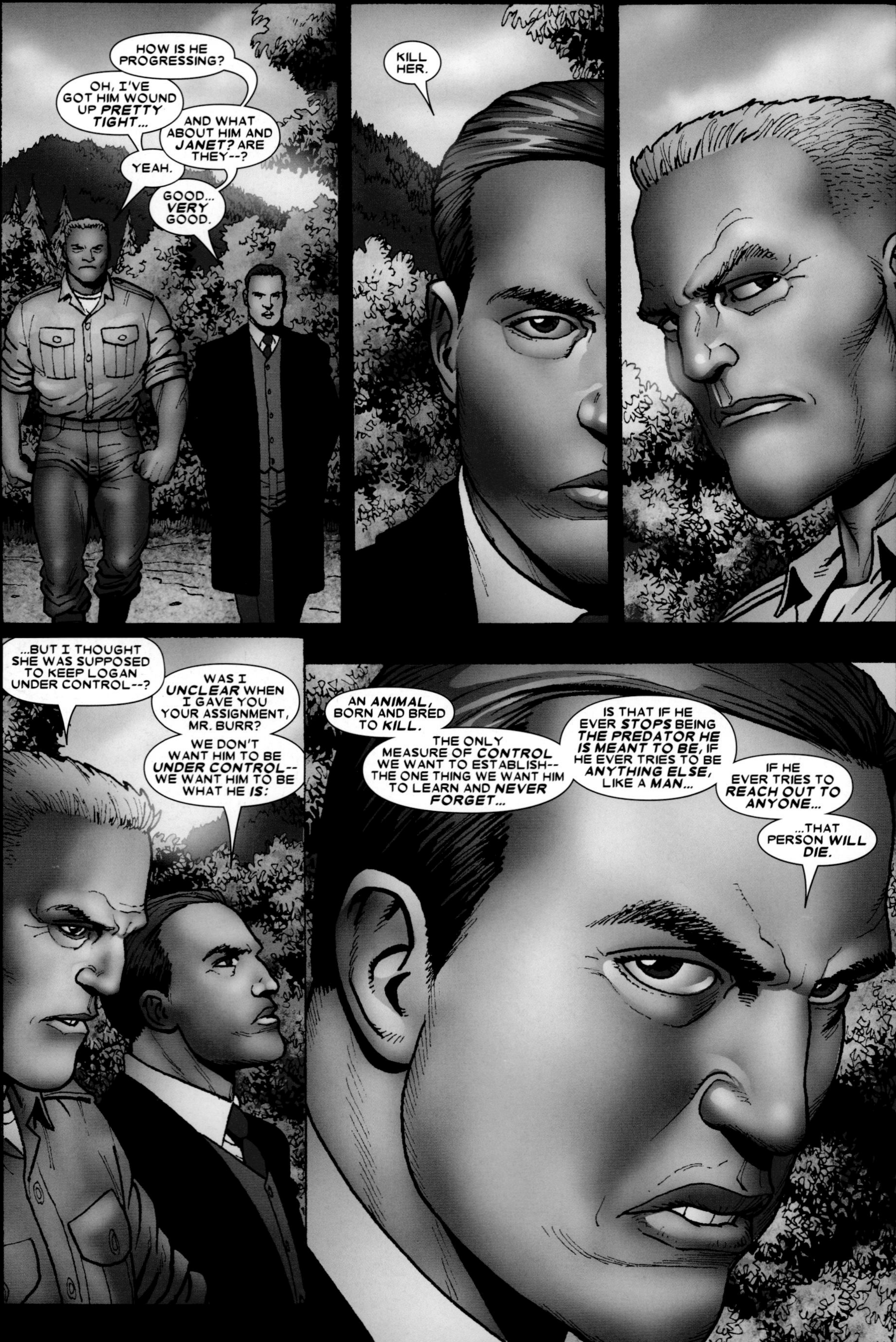
HOW IS HE PROGRESSING?
OH, I'VE GOT HIM WOUND UP PRETTY TIGHT...
AND WHAT ABOUT HIM AND JANET? ARE THEY--?
YEAH.
GOOD... VERY GOOD.
KILL HER.
...BUT I THOUGHT SHE WAS SUPPOSED TO KEEP LOGAN UNDER CONTROL--?
WAS I UNCLEAR WHEN I GAVE YOU YOUR ASSIGNMENT, MR. BURR?
WE DON'T WANT HIM TO BE UNDER CONTROL-- WE WANT HIM TO BE WHAT HE IS:
AN ANIMAL, BORN AND BRED TO KILL.
THE ONLY MEASURE OF CONTROL WE WANT TO ESTABLISH-- THE ONE THING WE WANT HIM TO LEARN AND NEVER FORGET...
IS THAT IF HE EVER STOPS BEING THE PREDATOR HE IS MEANT TO BE, IF HE EVER TRIES TO BE ANYTHING ELSE, LIKE A MAN...
IF HE EVER TRIES TO REACH OUT TO ANYONE...
...THAT PERSON WILL DIE.

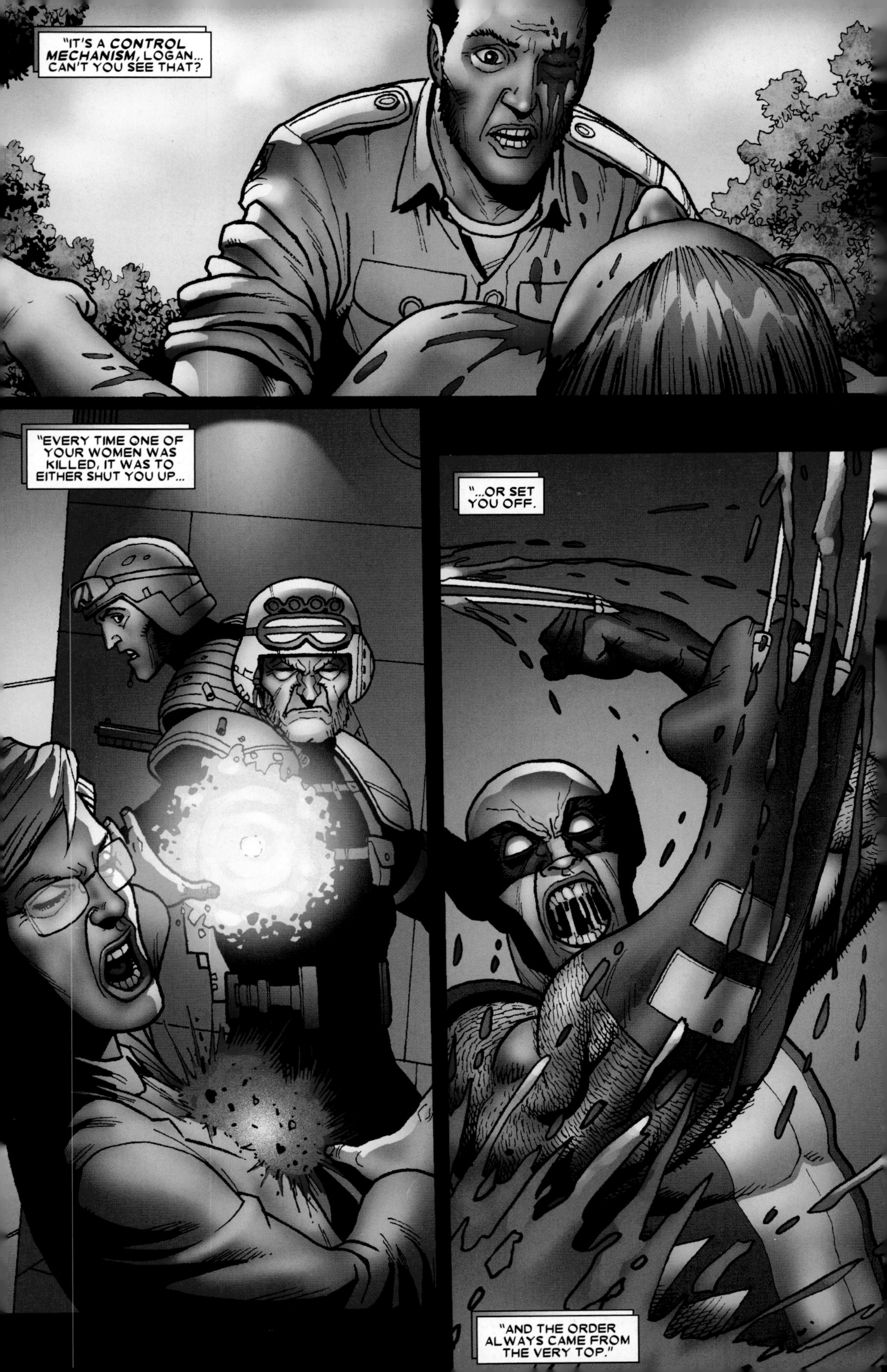
"IT'S A CONTROL MECHANISM, LOGAN... CAN'T YOU SEE THAT?
"EVERY TIME ONE OF YOUR WOMEN WAS KILLED, IT WAS TO EITHER SHUT YOU UP...
"...OR SET YOU OFF.
"AND THE ORDER ALWAYS CAME FROM THE VERY TOP."

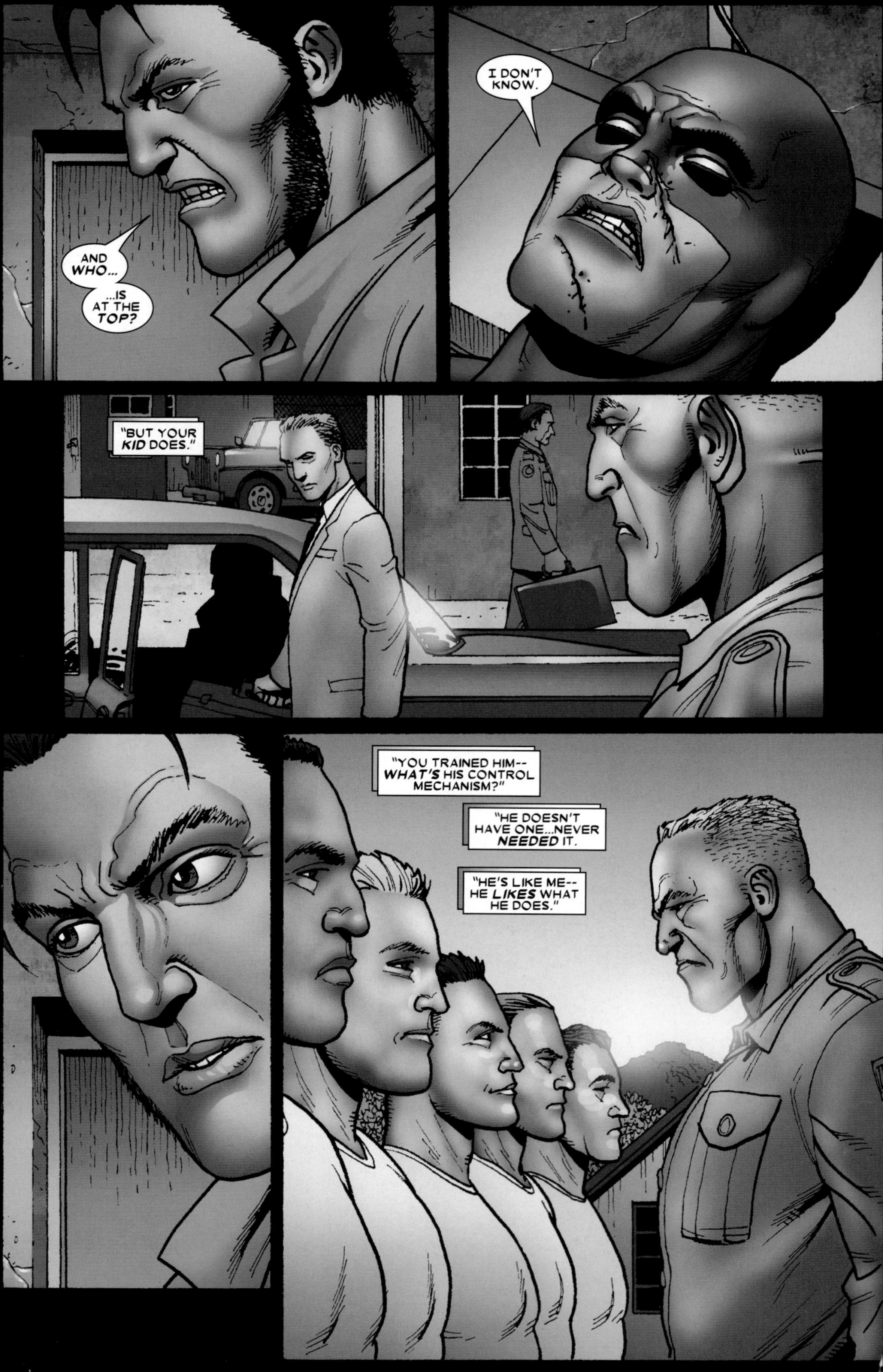
AND WHO...
...IS AT THE TOP?
I DON'T KNOW.
"BUT YOUR KID DOES."
"YOU TRAINED HIM-- WHAT'S HIS CONTROL MECHANISM?"
"HE DOESN'T HAVE ONE...NEVER NEEDED IT.
"HE'S LIKE ME-- HE LIKES WHAT HE DOES."

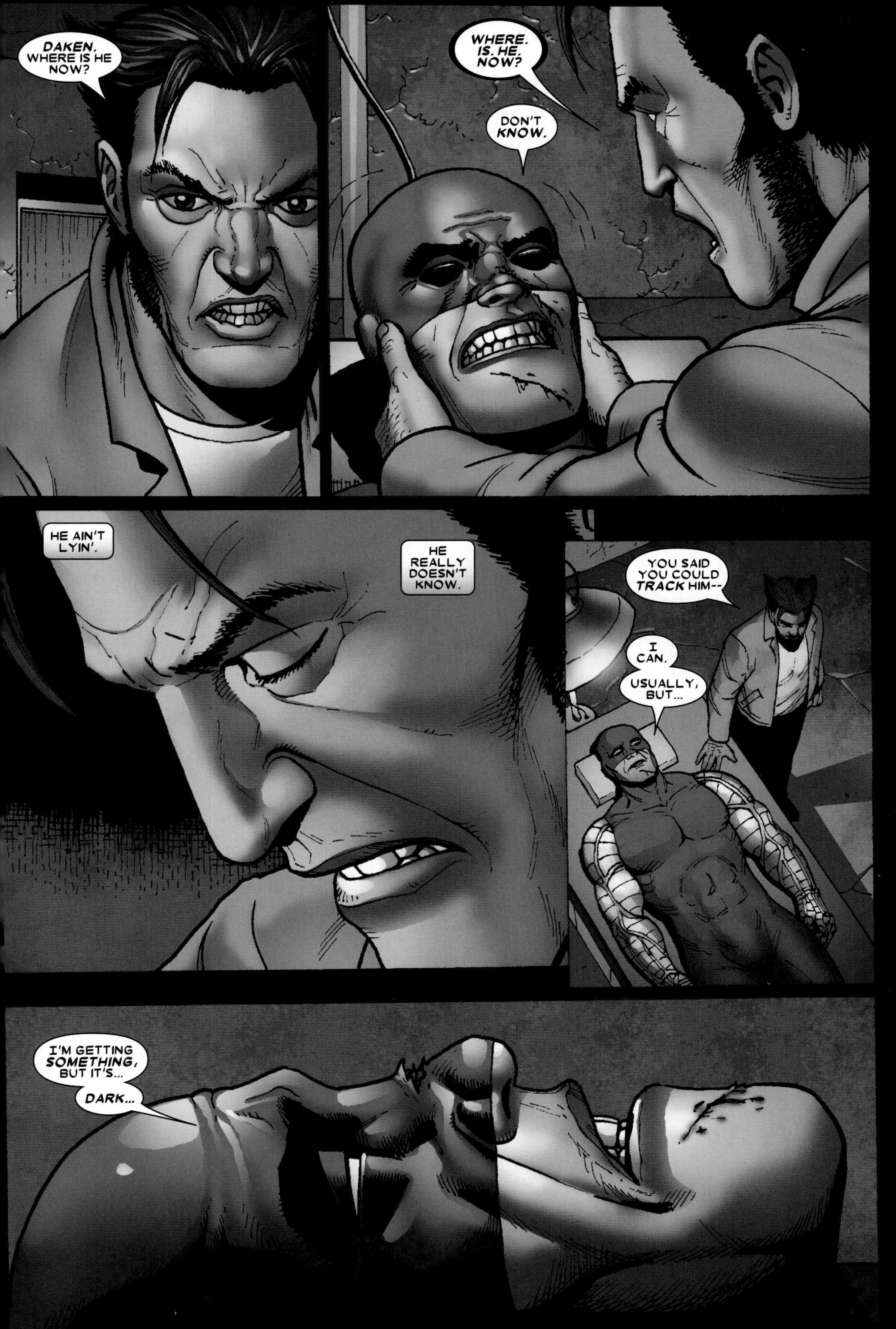
DAKEN. WHERE IS HE NOW?
WHERE. IS. HE. NOW?
DON'T KNOW.
HE AIN'T LYIN'.
HE REALLY DOESN'T KNOW.
YOU SAID YOU COULD TRACK HIM--
I CAN.
USUALLY, BUT...
I'M GETTING SOMETHING, BUT IT'S...
DARK...

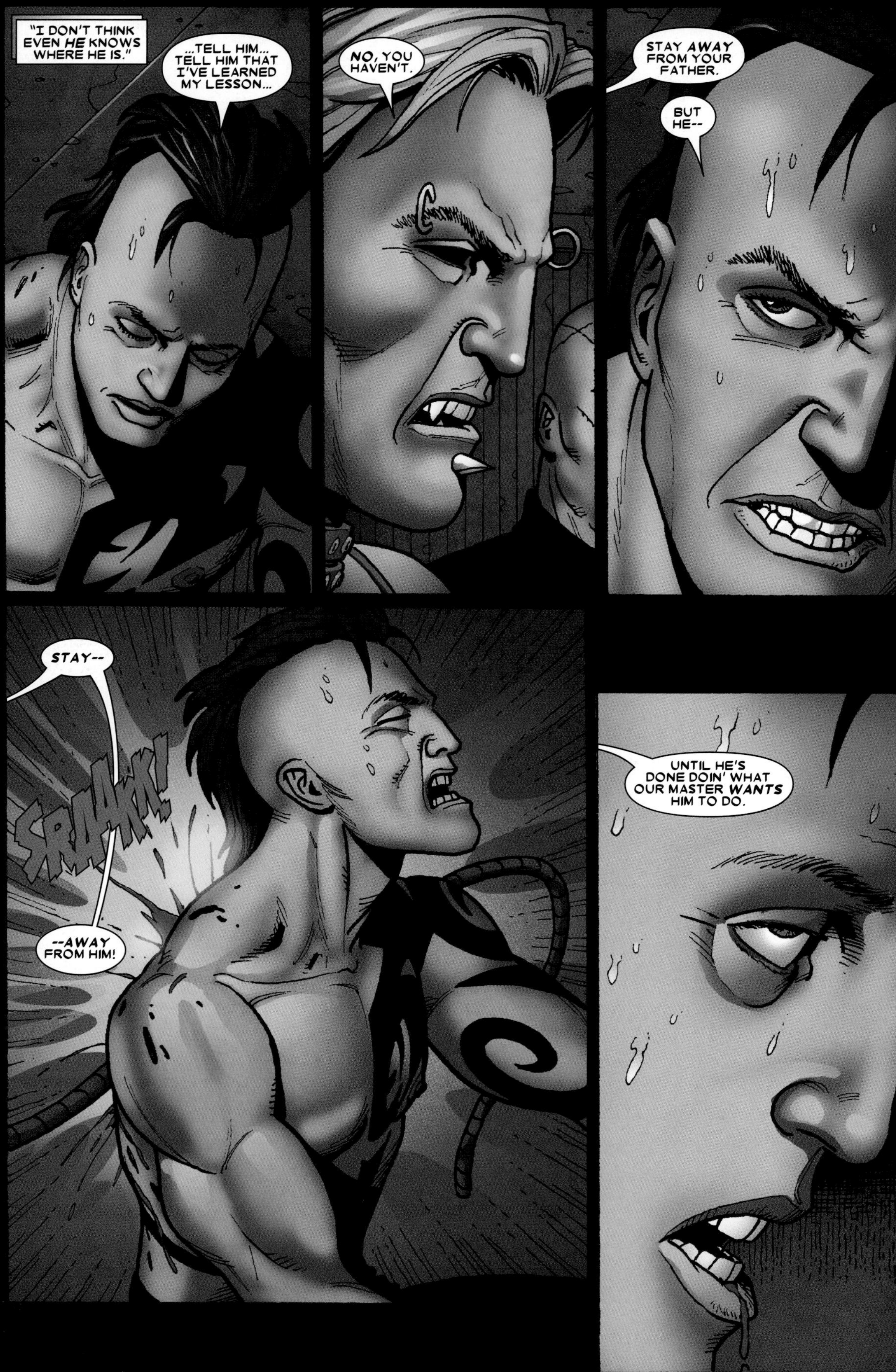
"I DON'T THINK EVEN HE KNOWS WHERE HE IS."
...TELL HIM... TELL HIM THAT I'VE LEARNED MY LESSON...
NO, YOU HAVEN'T.
STAY AWAY FROM YOUR FATHER.
BUT HE--
STAY--
SRAAKK!
--AWAY FROM HIM!
UNTIL HE'S DONE DOIN' WHAT OUR MASTER WANTS HIM TO DO.

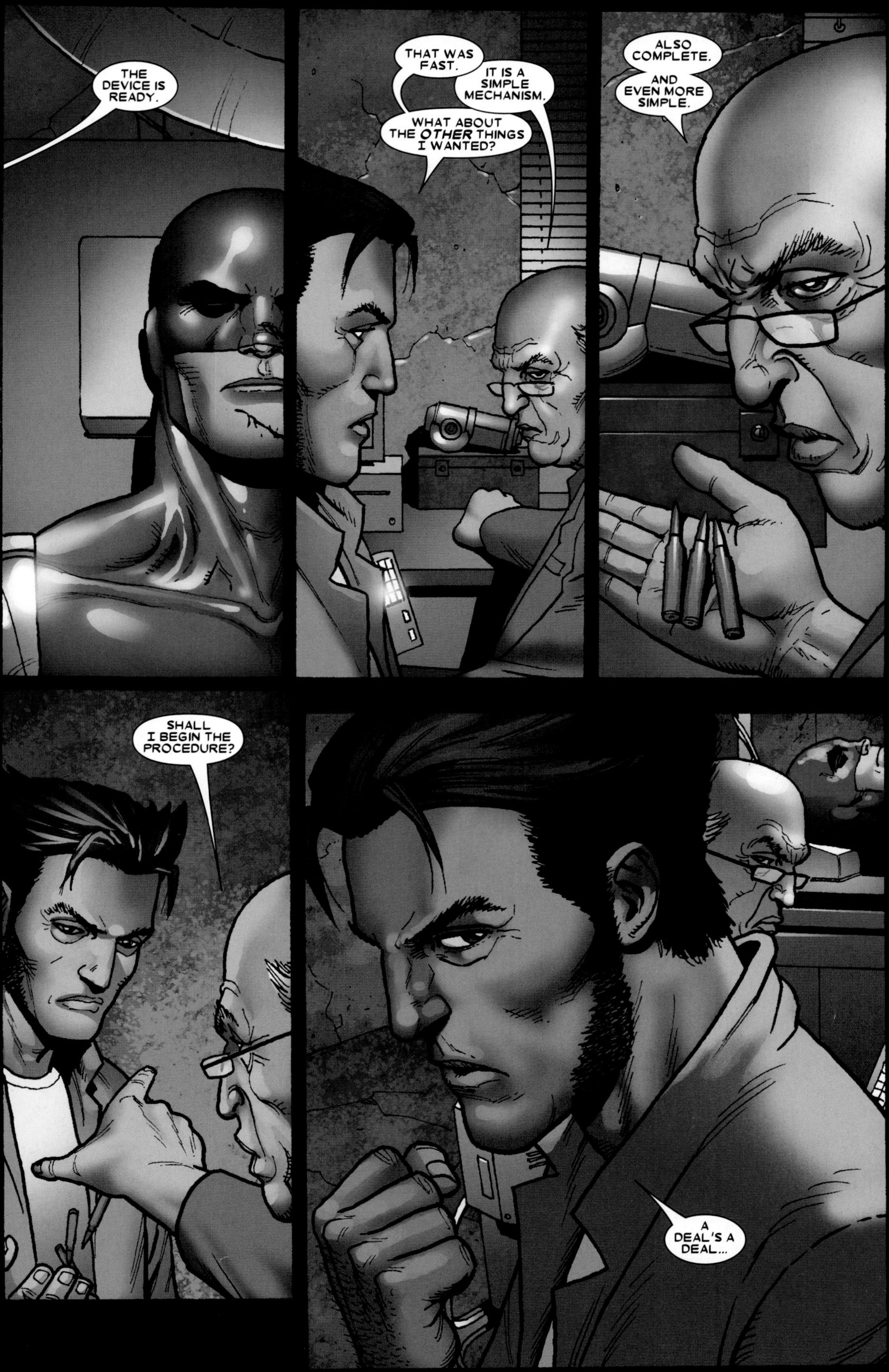
THE DEVICE IS READY.
THAT WAS FAST.
IT IS A SIMPLE MECHANISM.
WHAT ABOUT THE OTHER THINGS I WANTED?
ALSO COMPLETE.
AND EVEN MORE SIMPLE.
SHALL I BEGIN THE PROCEDURE?
A DEAL'S A DEAL...

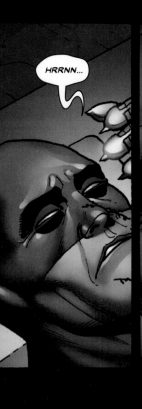

HRRNN...

WHAT...?

WHAT THE HELL IS *THIS*?

ESSENTIALLY? A *PACEMAKER.*

OBVIOUSLY, DUE TO THE FACT THAT YOUR BODY IS ENCASED IN ADAMANTIUM, THERE WAS NO POSSIBILITY OF *IMPLANTING* THE DEVICE.

WHY DIDN'T YOU PAINT A *BULL'S-EYE* ON IT?

I BEG YOUR--?

ANYBODY LOOKING TO TAKE ME OUT ISN'T GOING TO HAVE TO DO MUCH THINKING BEFORE THEY REALIZE THAT ALL THEY HAVE TO DO IS HIT THIS!

HMM...

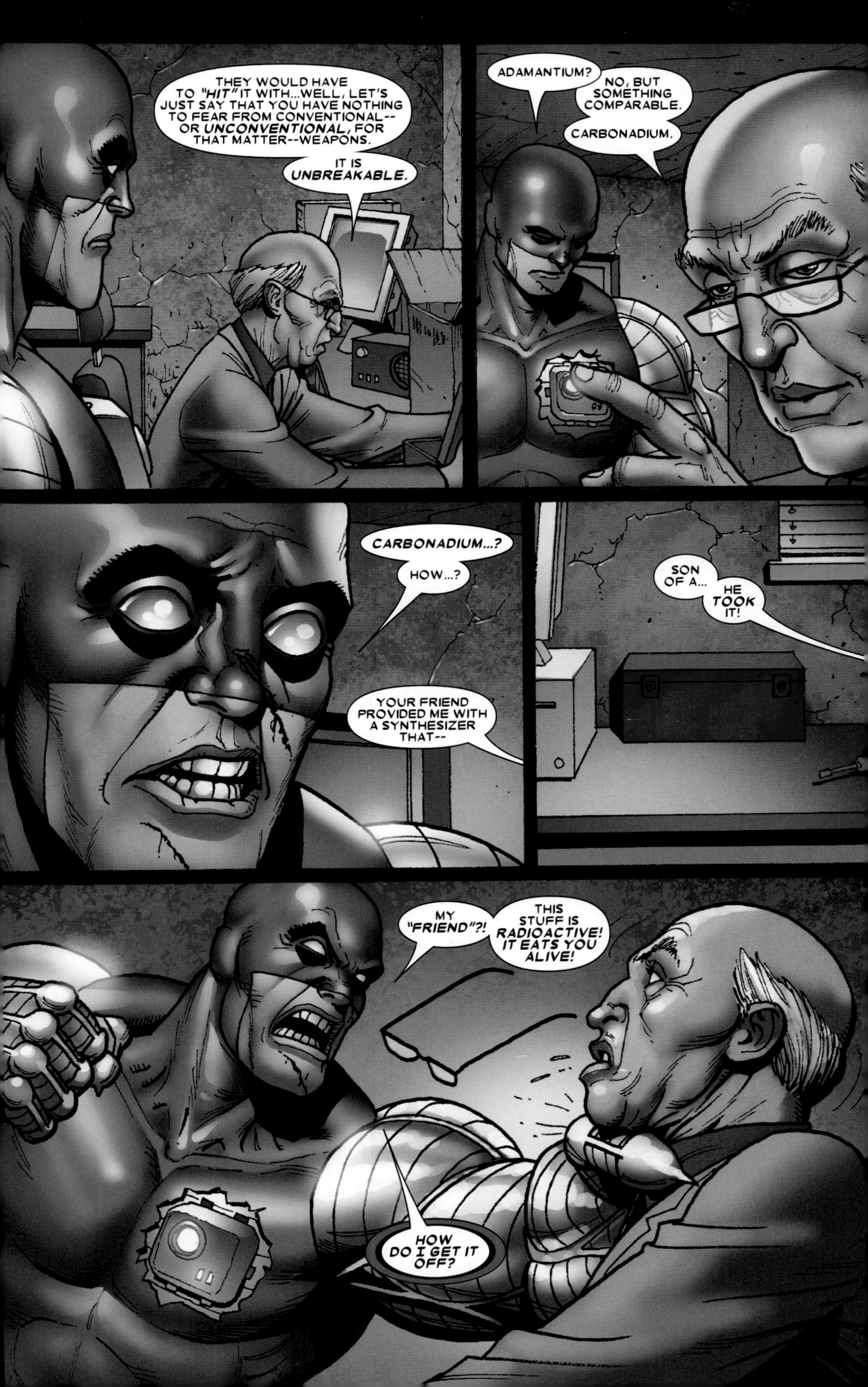
THEY WOULD HAVE TO "HIT" IT WITH...WELL, LET'S JUST SAY THAT YOU HAVE NOTHING TO FEAR FROM CONVENTIONAL-- OR UNCONVENTIONAL, FOR THAT MATTER--WEAPONS.
IT IS UNBREAKABLE.
ADAMANTIUM?
NO, BUT SOMETHING COMPARABLE.
CARBONADIUM.
CARBONADIUM...?
HOW...?
YOUR FRIEND PROVIDED ME WITH A SYNTHESIZER THAT--
SON OF A...
HE TOOK IT!
MY "FRIEND"?!
THIS STUFF IS RADIOACTIVE! IT EATS YOU ALIVE!
HOW DO I GET IT OFF?

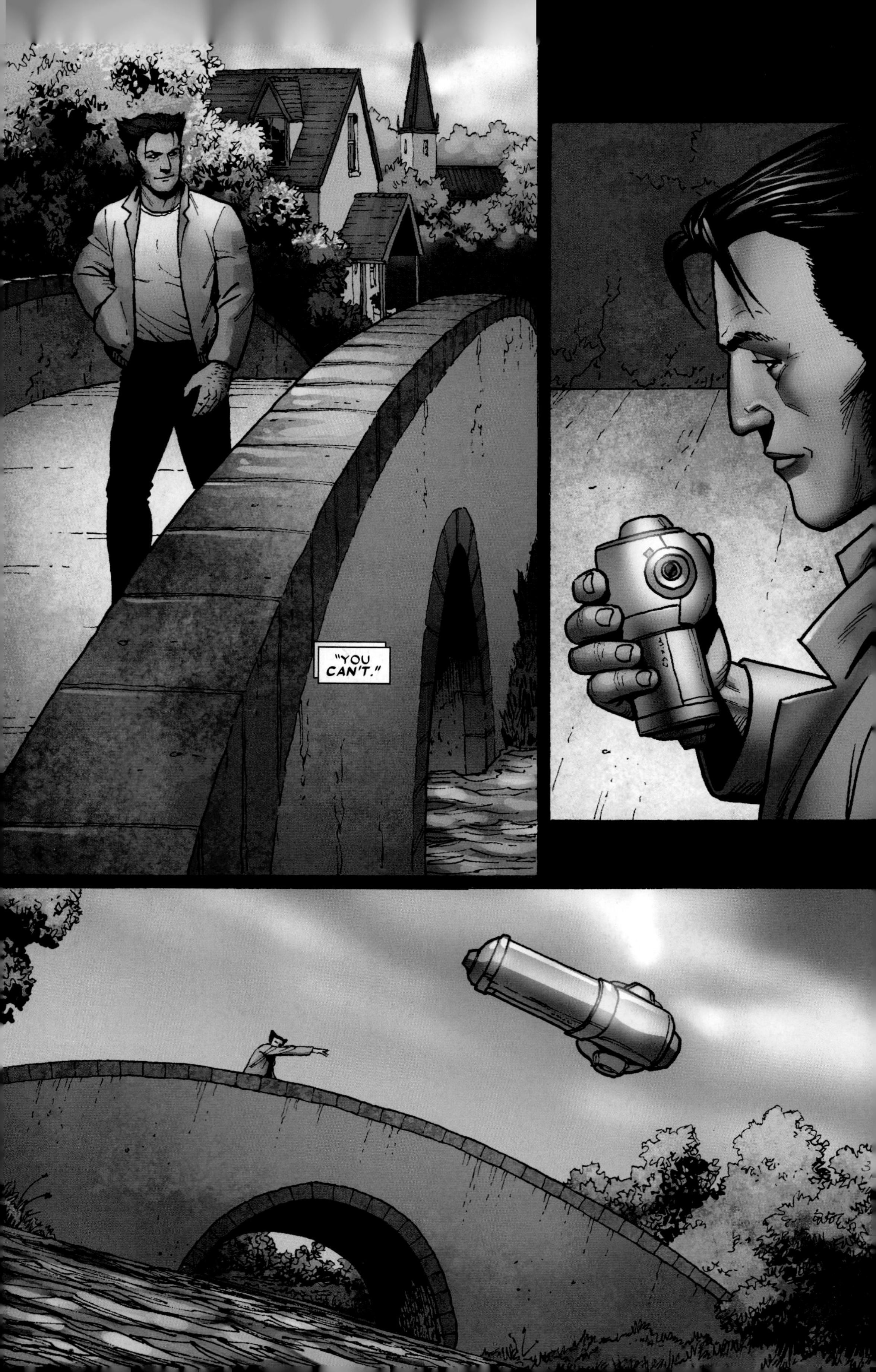
"YOU CAN'T."

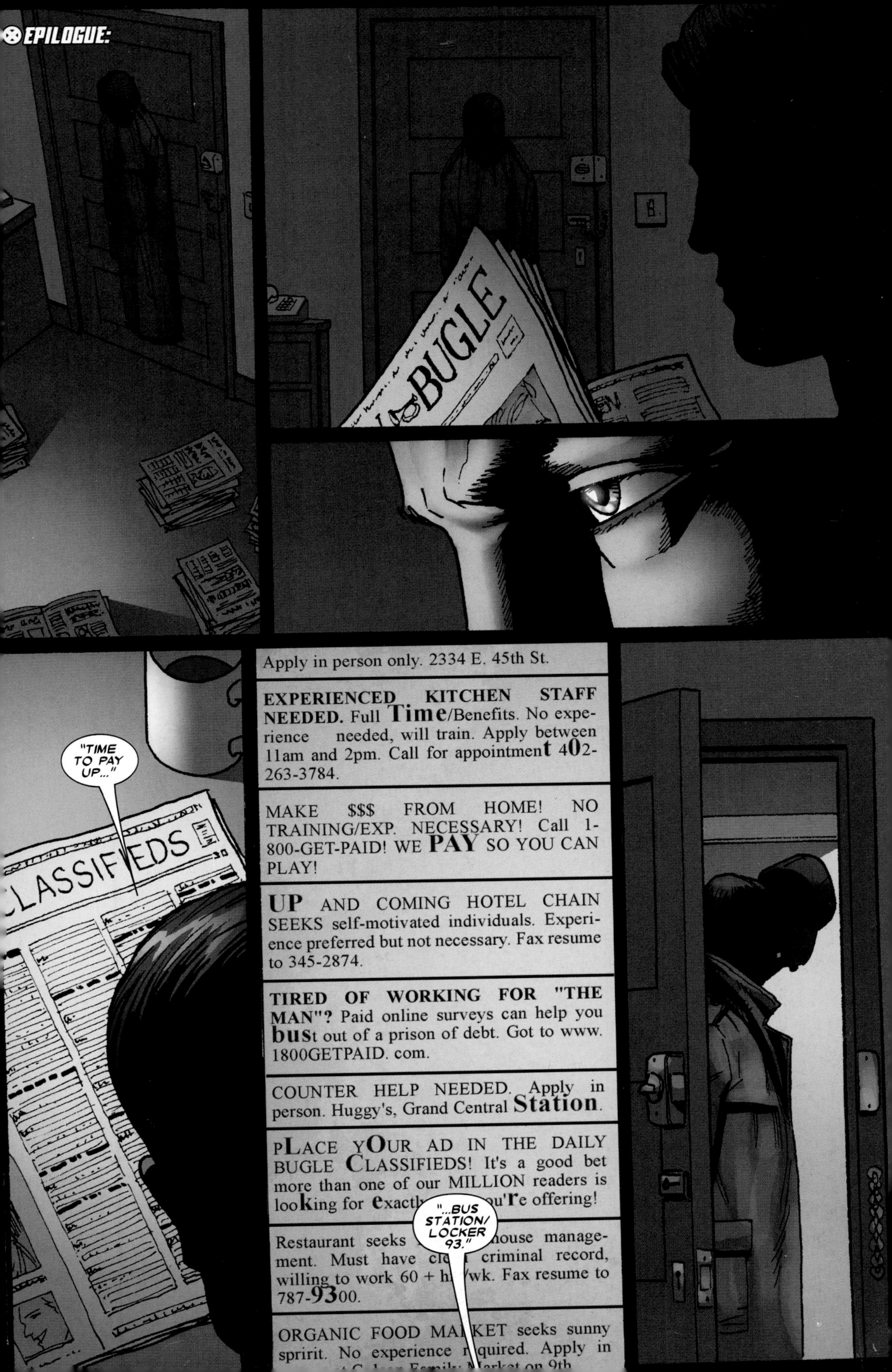
EPILOGUE:
BUGLE
CLASSIFIEDS
"TIME TO PAY UP..."
Apply in person only. 2334 E. 45th St.
EXPERIENCED KITCHEN STAFF NEEDED. Full Time/Benefits. No experience needed, will train. Apply between 11am and 2pm. Call for appointment 402-263-3784.
MAKE $$$ FROM HOME! NO TRAINING/EXP. NECESSARY! Call 1-800-GET-PAID! WE PAY SO YOU CAN PLAY!
UP AND COMING HOTEL CHAIN SEEKS self-motivated individuals. Experience preferred but not necessary. Fax resume to 345-2874.
TIRED OF WORKING FOR "THE MAN"? Paid online surveys can help you bust out of a prison of debt. Got to www. 1800GETPAID. com.
COUNTER HELP NEEDED. Apply in person. Huggy's, Grand Central Station.
PLACE YOUR AD IN THE DAILY BUGLE CLASSIFIEDS! It's a good bet more than one of our MILLION readers is looking for exactl ou're offering!
"...BUS STATION/ LOCKER 93."
Restaurant seeks house management. Must have cle criminal record, willing to work 60 + h /wk. Fax resume to 787-9300.
ORGANIC FOOD MA KET seeks sunny spririt. No experience quired. Apply in

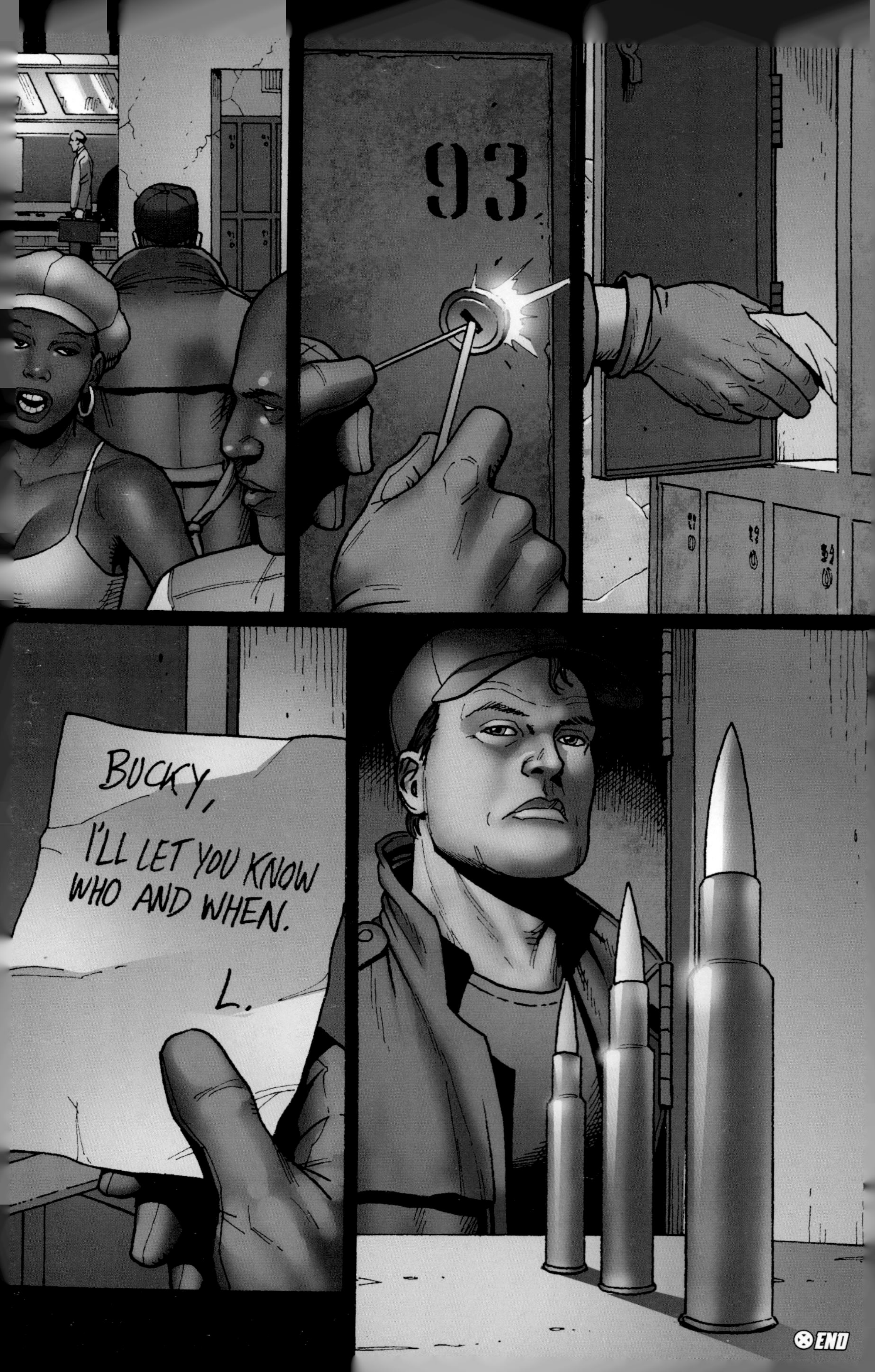
93
BUCKY,
I'LL LET YOU KNOW WHO AND WHEN.
L.
END